STRAW VOTES

PREPARED UNDER THE AUSPICES OF THE
COLUMBIA UNIVERSITY COUNCIL FOR RESEARCH
IN THE SOCIAL SCIENCES

STRAW VOTES

A STUDY OF POLITICAL PREDICTION

BY

CLAUDE E. ROBINSON

SOMETIME GILDER FELLOW IN SOCIOLOGY
COLUMBIA UNIVERSITY

WITH A FOREWORD BY

ROBERT E. CHADDOCK

PROFESSOR OF STATISTICS
COLUMBIA UNIVERSITY

NEW YORK   M·CM·XXXII

COLUMBIA UNIVERSITY PRESS

Copyright 1932
Columbia University Press

Published September, 1932

PRINTED IN THE UNITED STATES OF AMERICA
BY FRANCIS EMORY FITCH, INC.

TO
E. M. R.

FOREWORD

This research, interestingly enough, had its beginnings in a class in Vital Statistics. The lecture for the day—it was in October, 1928, when the Hoover-Smith campaign for the presidency was at its height—was on the use of sampling in the study of the prevalence of morbidity, and the discussion quite naturally veered to the somewhat spectacular attempt then being made by the *Literary Digest* to sample the presidential preferences of the people on a nation-wide scale. Would the results of this straw-vote sample be corroborated by the official election returns, and would the technique of sampling find general use in the political field as it had in the field of public health? The curiosity of one of the participants in that discussion was aroused to the point of making further inquiry. He secured the final straw-vote returns and compared them with the official election figures. In some states the proportionate division of the straw vote between candidates was found to be quite similar to the division recorded in the official balloting, but in other states the similarity was less pronounced. What caused this variation in the predictive reliability of the straw poll? Was the answer to be found in the sampling technique employed? In the size of the return? In change of voting intention after the straw ballots had been marked? Here, indeed, were intriguing problems.

The inquiry inevitably broadened. The *Literary Digest* had conducted straw polls in earlier presidential campaigns where candidates and issues were different. What was the predictive reliability of these previous canvasses, and how did it compare with that of the poll of 1928? Moreover the *Literary Digest* had employed the straw vote to sound out the wishes of the people on governmental questions, particularly on prohibition. Could this sampling technique be employed for general referendum purposes as well as for measuring the voting intentions of the people on candidates standing for public office?

Was experience with straw votes limited to the polls of the *Literary Digest*, or had other organizations conducted such tests? If so what were the methods employed by these sponsors and what were the results achieved? Search yielded an astonishing number of polls of all descriptions taken in various types of campaigns as far back as 1904. These data furnished a wide foundation of experience upon which to base conclusions about straw votes.

At an early stage of the inquiry it became apparent that sponsors of straw polls were not the only persons who were interested in measuring preëlection preferences, nor was the straw-vote technique the sole means for achieving this end. The politician, for example, is eminently concerned with how the people intend to vote, because his bread and butter depend upon it. Continually throughout a campaign, he takes soundings of popular favor and in the light of this information maps out his electioneering strategy. While the politician's purpose in gauging voting sentiment is not primarily one of political prediction, his measurements have a forecasting connotation which he himself freely recognizes and exploits. What methods of appraisal does the politician use and how do his results compare with those obtained from straw polls?

The newspaperman is interested in the problem for the same bread-and-butter reasons as the politician. The business of the journalist is to gather and print the news, and the way people intend to vote is news of the first importance, not alone to the general public whose attention is captivated by the struggle of the rival candidates, but also to thousands of specialized interests whose fortunes are in one way or another bound up with the election outcome. In major political campaigns, therefore, newspapers and news-gathering organizations make a great effort to ascertain and report the status of voting intention. Apart from the straw poll—American dailies have been the chief sponsors of these tests—what methods does the newspaperman use in gauging preëlection sentiment and how accurate are his appraisals?

Where other states transact their principal election business on the first Tuesday after the first Monday in November, Maine elects her state officers and representatives to Congress on the second Monday in September. The returns from this early election are believed to provide a forecast of the division of the vote in the nation in November, the traditional saying "As goes Maine, so goes the nation" receiving wide credence from politicians, newspapermen, and the general public alike. What is the story of the Maine election barometer and how dependable are its predictions of the country-wide political weather?

Finally, one cannot long deal with election statistics before similarities in the party division of the vote from one election to another become noticeable. Can the data of past elections be used to advantage in gauging the current voting intention of the people and, if so, what form should this analysis take?

Thus from a single question on the validity of straw polls has developed this comprehensive study of political prediction, comprising a survey of the techniques used in measuring voting sentiment on candidates standing for public office and upon governmental issues. The results of this three-year search are given in this book.

In presenting his findings, the author has chosen to order his subject matter in a somewhat different sequence than that characterizing the growth of the work. In Chapter I he discusses the politician as predictor. In Chapter II attention is centered on the forecasting activities of the newspaperman. Chapter III is devoted to a consideration of the Maine September election as a national political barometer. Chapters IV and V deal with straw votes on candidates, and Chapter VI treats of straw polls on issues. The work is concluded in Chapter VII, with a discussion of the use of past-election data in political prediction.

The data used in this study were drawn almost entirely from original sources. The author scanned scores of newspapers and periodicals published in all parts of the country, consulted official documents bearing on the subject, and interviewed personally or through correspondence a large number of political leaders and newspapermen. In the course of his field work he traveled extensively through the states along the Middle and North Atlantic seaboard and throughout the Middle West.

For the chapters on straw polls the author secured, not alone the published reports of the organizations conducting these tests, but wherever possible sought additional information through interview with the sponsors. The executives of the *Literary Digest*, for example, with great generosity, furnished him with all available information on their straw canvasses, and before destroying the ballot cards gathered in the presidential poll of 1928 allowed him to make statistical experiments designed to throw light upon the limitations and the validity of straw-vote procedures. The officials of the *Hearst Newspapers* likewise contributed material at their disposal, as did the officers of the *Columbus Dispatch, Cincinnati Enquirer, Chicago Tribune, Chicago Journal,* the *Pathfinder* and others. Some polls undoubtedly escaped notice, but the search was wide and thorough, and it is safe to say that the most significant experience with straw votes has come within the author's purview. His efforts to secure pertinent data for other sections of the work were similarly exacting.

It has been my privilege as Chairman of the Committee on Supervision for this study, appointed by the Council for Research in the Social Sciences of Columbia University, to have participated in the counsels of this research, and to have observed its development from simple beginnings to its present status. The author, I am sure, does not presume that he has said the final word on the measurement of voting intention and its use in political prediction; rather he presents his findings as a pioneering report, hoping that subsequent researches will expand knowledge in this field and that the conclusions here presented will be corroborated or rejected as future evidence may warrant. It is my belief that this book will prove of utmost interest to both practical and scientific workers in the field of politics.

ROBERT E. CHADDOCK

COLUMBIA UNIVERSITY
June, 1932

PREFACE

The Foreword for this work has been generously prepared by Dr. Robert E. Chaddock. Here it is only necessary to make clear the meaning of terms used in the volume and to thank those who have given assistance during the course of the study.

Political prediction is concerned with forecasting the outcome of elections. Elections are decided by votes and votes are cast by people; hence, if there is any way of knowing in advance of the polling day how people will vote, it must be through knowing how they intend to vote. Political prediction, therefore, is a problem of measuring or appraising voting intention.

There are two ways to learn how people intend to vote. The first or direct way is to ask them, to ask every qualified voter, or at least as many as possible, or to ask only a limited number and assume that this sample stands for the whole electorate. The inclusive precinct canvasses conducted by party organizations fall under the former heading, and, under the latter, the maxim, "As goes Maine, so goes the nation"—the Maine September returns being regarded as a sample of the voting intention prevalent in the nation—and, more particularly, straw votes. The second, or indirect way, is through analysis of current election factors in the light of past alignments of the voters. All appraisals of voting intention partake of one or both of these forms. If but one appraisal of voting intention is made, the forecaster projects his figures forward to the day of the election on the assumption that the voters will not materially alter their preferences. If several appraisals are undertaken at intervals before the election, usually the latest measurement is projected forward on the assumption of no change, though the forecast might take the form of a projection of the trend or "swing" in voting intention revealed by successive measurements. In this case the predictor would assume stability of trend. It follows that an appraisal of voting intention may be valid at the time it is made, but because of subsequent change in the preferences of the voters, invalid as an election forecast. It also follows that the gauging techniques employed in election forecasting may have other than predictive uses. These are freely discussed in the course of the work.

It has been found convenient in the pages that follow to use the word "sentiment," along with the words "intention" and "preference," to indicate the disposition of a voter, or the summated dispositions of the voters, to favor one candidate or one side of an issue, over another. Some may prefer to employ the terms "attitude" or "opinion" for this purpose, but the sense in which the terms are here used is clear, and there will be no confusion on this point.

The findings in Chapter III, on Maine as a political barometer, have appeared in the *Political Science Quarterly*. Also some of the material in Chapter VI, on the 1932 *Literary-Digest* prohibition poll, was drawn upon for an article in the *New Republic*. With these exceptions, none of the data here presented have been previously published.

Many persons have coöperated with me to make possible the writing of this volume. I desire to thank warmly all those who rendered assistance. In particular I wish to express appreciation to the Council for Research in the Social Sciences, Columbia University, for the research grant; to Mr. and Mrs. Leonard Elmhirst and to the Honorable Ruth Pratt, who helped to finance the study; to the supervisory committee of the Council, Dr. Robert E. Chaddock, Chairman, Dr. Arthur W. Macmahon, and Dr. Frank A. Ross, for their critical advice and encouragement; to the executives of the *Literary Digest* for their generous coöperation in placing their straw-vote records at my disposal for the research; to the managers of the *Hearst Newspapers*, the *Columbus Dispatch*, the *Cincinnati Enquirer*, the *Chicago Journal*, the *Chicago Tribune*, the *Pathfinder*, and more generally to those editors, political leaders and librarians in various parts of the country who furnished materials and interviews; to Major John Buckley, the Honorable Henry E. Dunnack, Dr. Fabian Franklin, Dr. Robert S. Lynd, Dr. Samuel McCune Lindsay, Dr. Robert M. MacIver, the Honorable William R. Pattangall, Mr. Stephen S. Slaughter, Dr. Alvan A. Tenney, and Mr. Stanley Went, for reading and criticizing various portions of the manuscript; to Mr. Richard Hull, Miss Jessica Miller, and Miss Helen Schuldenfrei for competent research assistance in the early part of the study; to Mrs. Victoria K. McGarrett for her efficiency in computation and painstaking labor on many problems presented in the research; to Mrs. Jean R. Calef and Mr. R. F. Robinson for special assistance in collecting election data in the city of Portland, Oregon, and finally to my wife, Elizabeth M.

Robinson, for her never-failing encouragement and constant aid in all phases of the work.

NEW YORK CITY
June, 1932

CLAUDE E. ROBINSON

CONTENTS

FOREWORD BY ROBERT E. CHADDOCK........................ VII

PREFACE.. XI

I. THE POLITICIAN AS PREDICTOR......................... 1
How political leaders gauge preëlection sentiment—Accuracy of predictions by political leaders—The elation complex—Recapitulation

II. THE NEWSPAPERMAN AS PREDICTOR..................... 14
Plurality predictions—Electoral-college forecasts—Conclusion

III. MAINE—POLITICAL BAROMETER......................... 25
How it all began—Barometer politics, national—Barometer politics, local—Testing the barometer—The literal formula—The formula of the Republican norm—The formula of identical fluctuation—Conclusion

IV. STRAW POLLS ON CANDIDATES......................... 46
The straw poll and the principle of sampling—American experience with straw polls on candidates—Why newspapers and magazines sponsor straw polls—How straw ballots are gathered—Straw poll accuracy, definition—Straw-poll accuracy, experience—Predictive record of straw polls, politicians and newspapermen compared—Causes of straw-poll error—Manipulation of returns by sponsors—Stuffing the ballot box—Geographical bias

V. STRAW POLLS ON CANDIDATES (*Continued*).............. 90
Class bias—Bias of selection in coöperation—Bias of participation, nonparticipation—Size of sample, Adequacy—Change of sentiment over time—Interpretation by weighting—Interpretation on theory of recurrent bias—Interpretation in light of indicated past preferences—Interpretation, general considerations—The sponsor and sound sampling practice—The utility of the straw poll—The possible harm of straw polls

VI. STRAW POLLS ON ISSUES.............................. 145
Polls on public questions—The LITERARY-DIGEST prohibition polls—Reliability of 1930 and 1932 LITERARY-DIGEST polls—Other appraisals of prohibition sentiment—Reliability of 1930 and 1932 LITERARY-DIGEST polls recapitulated—Reliability of 1922 LITERARY-DIGEST poll—Interpretive correction of the LITERARY-DIGEST polls—Growth of sentiment for repeal—Reliability of straw referenda in general

CONTENTS

VII. PAST ELECTIONS AND PREDICTION.................... 172
   Party continuity and the stability of the partisan vote—Charting the past party vote—Use of charts in prediction—Need for qualitative data—A twofold approach to political prediction

APPENDIX A... 187
   Electoral college predictions used in Chapter II to test forecasting ability of newspapermen

APPENDIX B... 190
   State prohibition referenda, 1919-1930

INDEX.. 195

DIAGRAMS

I. SCATTER DIAGRAM SHOWING THE RELATION BETWEEN GUBERNATORIAL PLURALITIES IN MAINE AND PRESIDENTIAL PLURALITIES IN THE NATION (HORIZONTAL AND VERTICAL SCALES SHOW PLURALITIES PER 100 VOTES CAST).. 41

II. RECENT APPRAISALS OF SENTIMENT FOR REPEAL COMPARED. LITERARY-DIGEST POLLS, 1930 AND 1932; OFFICIAL REFERENDA IN TEN STATES, 1926-1930; ESTIMATES BY EDITORS OF DAILY NEWSPAPERS, 1931; BECK-LINTHICUM VOTE, 1932. STATES RANKED BY WETNESS ON BASIS OF 1932 LITERARY-DIGEST RETURNS.......... 161

III. REPEAL VOTE, LITERARY-DIGEST POLL, 1922, AND OFFICIAL REFERENDA IN TEN STATES, 1919-1924, COMPARED. STATES RANKED BY WETNESS ON BASIS OF 1922 LITERARY-DIGEST RETURNS............................ 166

IV. GROWTH OF ANTI-PROHIBITION SENTIMENT AS REFLECTED BY A COMPARISON OF THE VOTE CAST FOR REPEAL IN THE LITERARY-DIGEST POLLS OF 1932, 1930, AND 1922. STATES RANKED BY WETNESS ON BASIS OF 1932 LITERARY-DIGEST RETURNS...................................... 169

V. STABILITY OF PARTY ALIGNMENTS. DISTRIBUTIONS OF VARIATIONS BY STATE OF THE REPUBLICAN PERCENTAGE OF THE TOTAL VOTE CAST FOR PRESIDENT IN SUCCESSIVE REGULAR ELECTIONS FOR THE PERIODS 1872-1900 AND 1900-1928.. 175

VI. VOTE FOR PRESIDENTIAL ELECTORS BY PARTIES IN NEW JERSEY, 1888-1928.................................... 178

TABLES

1. Plurality Error of State Estimates by Politicians in the 1928 Presidential Campaign.................... 9
2. Plurality Error of Forecasts by Political Leaders.. 12
3. Plurality Error of Forecasts by Newspapermen..... 17
4. Nonresident Speakers in Maine September Campaigns, 1910-1928...................................... 28
5. Plurality per 100 Votes Cast for Governor in Maine and for President in the United States.............. 40
6. Turnout Predictions for the Nation on the Basis of the Maine Barometer and Simple Rule............. 45
7. Hypothetical Returns (Expressed in Percentages) for Two Straw Polls and the Official Election..... 60
8. Plurality Error by State for Nine Nation-wide Presidential Straw Polls........................... 67
9. Plurality Error of Straw Polls of Four Middle-western Newspapers over Period of Twenty-Five Years—Also Plurality Error by State, Literary-Digest Polls, 1916 and 1920........................ 68
10. Plurality Error of Straw Polls under Miscellaneous Sponsorship................................... 69
11. Average Plurality Error by State for Nation-wide Straw Polls...................................... 70
12. Plurality Error of 1928 State Presidential Predictions by Political Leaders, Newspapermen, and Straw Polls..................................... 76
13. Plurality Error of 1928 Presidential Predictions for Ohio by Political Leaders, Newspapermen, and Straw Polls..................................... 76
14. Weighted and Unweighted Literary-Digest Presidential Poll Prediction for Six States, 1928........ 88

TABLES

15. PARTY COMPLEXION OF THE 1928 LITERARY-DIGEST MAILING LIST AND REGISTERED ELECTORATE IN MULTNOMAH COUNTY, OREGON, IN PERCENTAGES.................... 94

16. SIZE OF SAMPLE AND PLURALITY ERROR FOR STRAW POLLS OF CHICAGO JOURNAL AND CHICAGO TRIBUNE IN THREE CAMPAIGNS... 105

17. SIZE OF SAMPLE AND PLURALITY ERROR FOR ONE DAY'S RETURNS AND COMPLETE RETURNS FOR SEVEN STATES IN 1928 LITERARY-DIGEST PRESIDENTIAL POLL............. 106

18. TWO REPORTS FROM THE 1928 WISCONSIN-NEWS POLL... 109

19. COMBINED DAILY RETURN OF BALLOTS FROM SEVEN STATES IN 1928 LITERARY-DIGEST PRESIDENTIAL POLL... 111

20. HYPOTHETICAL RETURNS FROM THE GAZETTE STRAW POLL. 114

21. STRAW-VOTE PREDICTION FROM PAST PREFERENCES COMPUTED BY METHOD OF NET SHIFT...................... 119

22. STRAW-VOTE PREDICTION FROM IMPERFECT SAMPLE COMPUTED BY NET-SHIFT METHOD........................ 119

23. STRAW-VOTE PREDICTION FROM PAST PREFERENCES COMPUTED BY METHOD OF PARTY-TO-PARTY SHIFT........... 120

24. STRAW AND OFFICIAL ELECTION RETURNS WHICH SHOW A 30-PERCENT ALIENATION OF X VOTERS TO THE Y PARTY. 121

25. STRAW-VOTE PREDICTION FROM IMPERFECT SAMPLE COMPUTED BY NET-SHIFT AND PARTY-TO-PARTY METHODS... 122

26. PRESENT STRAW-VOTE PREFERENCES CORRECTED BY PARTY BIAS OF PAST STRAW PREFERENCES............. 123

27. ERROR IN PREDICTING THE PROPORTION OF THE TOTAL VOTE RECEIVED BY THE WINNING CANDIDATE BY FOUR METHODS OF COMPUTATION............................ 125

28. COÖPERATION BY GROUPS OF TWELVE STATES, RANKED ACCORDING TO WETNESS, FOR THE 1928 PRESIDENTIAL AND 1930 AND 1932 PROHIBITION POLLS OF THE LITERARY-DIGEST... 152

29. COMPARISON OF REPEAL SENTIMENT IN TEN STATES, AS SHOWN BY OFFICIAL REFERENDA, 1926-1930, AND THE LITERARY-DIGEST POLLS OF 1930 AND 1932.............. 155

30. REPEAL SENTIMENT BY STATES AS REPORTED BY THE LITERARY-DIGEST STRAW POLLS OF 1922, 1930, AND 1932 AND BY OPINION ESTIMATES OF THE EDITORS OF DAILY NEWSPAPERS... 159

31. COÖPERATION BY GROUPS OF TWELVE STATES, RANKED ACCORDING TO WETNESS, FOR THE 1924 PRESIDENTIAL AND 1922 PROHIBITION POLLS OF THE LITERARY DIGEST.. 164

32. COMPARISON OF REPEAL SENTIMENT IN TEN STATES AS SHOWN BY OFFICIAL REFERENDA, 1919-1924, AND THE LITERARY-DIGEST POLL OF 1922..................... 165

33. PRESIDENTIAL ELECTION RETURNS (IN TERMS OF PERCENTAGE OF THE TOTAL VOTE CAST) FOR THE STATE OF NEW JERSEY, 1888 TO 1928................................ 179

Chapter I
THE POLITICIAN AS PREDICTOR

The predictions of the politicians with which the public is most familiar are undoubtedly the most inaccurate that the politicians make. These are the predictions of sweeping victory issued in advance of the election by the candidates themselves, by their headquarters staff and by local political offices. Such predictions are of course part of the current coin of electioneering. It is no good admitting in advance that your candidate has but a poor chance of being elected; to do so is to throw up the sponge without waiting for the decision of the referee. For purely practical purposes it is thought necessary to strain every effort to create a victorious psychology, not only to keep the campaign workers on their toes, but to attract the so-called "bandwagon" vote which prefers to back the winning side. In the present study predictions of this type will be wholly ignored, and attention will be paid only to those preëlection estimates which the politicians formulate for the guidance of their campaigns.

How Political Leaders Gauge Preëlection Sentiment

Political leaders effect liason with the voting public chiefly through their party organization. Like a great business corporation that promotes national distribution of its products, a political party endeavors to maintain agents in every "sales" territory in the country to attend to its election interests. These territories are called precincts, into which the electorate is organized for convenience in voting. A precinct may include but a single block, as in a big city, or it may cover a township, as in the more sparsely settled districts. In some cases it contains only a handful of voting inhabitants; in others, several hundred. In 1928 the number of persons of voting age averaged about 600 to a precinct.[1] The party representatives in these districts are called precinct chairmen and chairwomen.

On registration and election days, eligible citizens go to their

---

[1] The Associated Press estimated that there were 115,527 precincts in the United States in 1928 (*Chicago Daily News*, Nov. 8, 1928 as quoted from Merriam and Gosnell, *The American Party System*, revised ed., p. 70.) The adult population for that year numbered roughly 69,000,000. (Interpolated figure—1920 and 1930 censuses.)

precinct polling place, and there qualify to vote or cast their ballots. The precinct leader of each party shepherds these little political communities in the exercise of their voting rights. He attends to the details of the polling place. He makes sure that the citizens of his political faith qualify as electors and, later, that they come to the polls to cast their ballots. He is a dispenser of minor political favors, nominating people to election board jobs, securing a street light for the neighbors on a given corner, seeing the judge for a constituent who has parked his car too long in a traffic lane, and, in general, acting as go-between for the voter and his governing officials in numerous details of small import.

A good precinct leader knows every voter in the neighborhood, knows each citizen's customary political affiliation, his pet grievances and enthusiasms, where he works, who are his friends, what are his wife's ambitions, and the names of his children. As a participating member of the community, the local leader belongs to the church and the lodge, he appears at dances and social functions, and he assists in public enterprises. He is often a seasoned veteran in the political arts and through long experience in campaigning he has developed a political sense that enables him to go quickly to the heart of a situation and calculate the probable results in terms of votes. If the party organization is good, the precinct leader is on the job 365 days out of the year, mending political fences, and holding party membership intact. It is principally through these precinct field men that the party chieftains keep in touch with the voting masses.

During a political campaign, the call comes from the authority above: How many votes can you deliver on the day of the election? The neighborhood leader takes stock of the probabilities. Green is angry with the party's stand on the tariff and will vote with the opposition. Jones is dyed-in-the-wool and can be counted on. The Smith twins come of age this year and will vote as the old folks do. Black favors the party but he can never be drawn to the polls. Ideally, the leader should be in a position to forecast every vote that will be cast. Practically, however, the very intimacy of his contacts in the neighborhood may at times serve to defeat his ends. Neighbors on good terms with the precinct captain will not reveal their intention to bolt the party ticket, for to do so would be to invite the accusation of disloyalty with possible reprisal in the form of tax discrimination or refusal of political accommodation when sought for. Thus the local leader, in returning Brown or Gray as "regular" when they are really intending to bolt the ticket, is unwittingly introducing error into his preëlection estimate. Naturally, too, all precinct captains are not of the ideal type here described. The human equation enters in, and the lazy worker anywhere down the line, who substitutes guesswork for the hard monotony of "pounding pavements" and "pushing doorbells," makes the business of prediction that much more uncertain.[2]

When the precinct captain has completed his estimate, he gives it to the ward or county leader, who compiles the figures for all the districts under his control. This leader, in making up his tabulation, shades the neighborhood reports according to his experience in past elections and his knowledge of the forces at work in the present campaign. The captain in the eighth precinct, he reasons, is known to be a perennial pessimist, always delivering at the polls a larger vote than he anticipates. His estimate, therefore, must be marked up twenty-five votes. Word has come from independent sources that there is acute disaffection in the fifteenth district. The leader there is not fully aware of that condition. He thinks he can deliver 160 votes, but he will be doing well if he can get 120. His forecast must be scaled down by one quarter.

With the appraisals of the precinct captains, together with information derived from independent sources, all seasoned by his own insight or "feel" for the situation, the ward or county leader makes up his estimate of the voting intentions of the citizens for whom he is responsible. This information forms the basis for the conduct of the campaign in his own territory. He may shower an ailing neighborhood with posters, hold a rally on one street corner in preference to another, see important people, make promises of jobs or political favors, stimulate "the boys" (the precinct leaders) with an extra ten dollars apiece for "campaign expenses," marshal rolling stock for transportation purposes on election day, or draw from his bag any one of the innumerable campaign tricks that long experience in politics has taught.

When the call comes from state headquarters for preëlection

---

[2] Political parties, moreover, are not able to maintain local representatives in every territory. In many southern states, for example, Republican organization is hardly more than a name, and in G O. P. strongholds of the North, like Pennsylvania, Michigan and Vermont, Democratic organization exists more in theory than in substance. Within states, too, where party structure is on the whole strong, local areas may remain unorganized for lack of votes or effective leadership. These gaps in party organization naturally lower the efficiency of the politicians' predictive machinery.

estimates, the county leader hands over his figures to the state leader, who then draws up a tabulation sheet for purposes of the wider strategy. Like the captains below him, the state generalissimo scales the figures up or down according to known penchants of the reporting subordinates and in the light of information from independent sources, all tinted with his own knowledge of the situation and his political sagacity. This tabulation is used in the conduct of the state campaign. Eventually it is passed on to regional and national party headquarters, where it is reworked, in the light of independent reports and special political considerations, to serve party chieftains in the direction of the national campaign.

While most of the systematic preëlection check-ups undertaken by party organizations are like that described, consisting of opinion estimates based on close contact with the voting public and seasoned with political shrewdness, many party check-ups, especially where the contest is close, take the form of what may be called an "inclusive canvass." In these canvasses special endeavor is made to "get a line" on every voter in the territory. The precinct leader, or party workers whom he hires, are supposed to go from door to door in their bailiwick, engaging each householder in conversation, giving him the "campaign arguments," and attempting to take a census of how he intends to vote. This type of canvass is intended to be very thorough, and the estimates resulting from it are looked upon as exceedingly trustworthy.

In the systematic check-up that is dependent largely on opinion, estimates are rendered in the form of expected pluralities. With the inclusive canvass, however, voting intention is generally tabulated in three categories: favorable, unfavorable, and doubtful, or, what amounts to the same thing, Republican, Democrat and doubtful. The smaller the number of people classed as doubtful, the more certain are the politicians of their position. In the lore of politics, the doubtful class is called the "silent vote" and generally gives the politicians great concern, particularly if its numbers are large enough to constitute a balance of power between the two major candidates.

The number of systematic check-ups undertaken by party organizations during a political campaign depends upon the closeness of the contest, upon special circumstances arising during the course of the struggle, and upon the character of party leadership. When the major candidates are about evenly matched and small *blocs* of votes may determine the winner, check-ups are likely to be frequent.

Developments during the campaign may cause disaffection, and require an extra recount of the probabilities to determine its extent. Or, again, one party chairman may trust his own judgment more than that of local subordinates and ask for fewer estimates from organization sources than another chairman. Some leaders ask for reports every two weeks; some content themselves with one preelection survey; a few call for no estimates at all, preferring to depend on casual information and their own observation for their knowledge of voting intention. The practice most frequently followed is to conduct three systematic check-ups during the course of a campaign, at ninety-, sixty-, and thirty-day intervals before the date of the election.

In addition to the regular preëlection surveys, conducted through organization channels, political leaders fortify themselves with information from other sources. Every leader of importance has a wide circle of friends, from whom he constantly seeks information on political conditions. Usually state and national headquarters employ trained scouts who go through the country interviewing men familiar with local sentiment, discussing politics with the man in the street, and generally trying to size up political conditions. Sometimes special canvasses are made of occupational or racial groups, to determine their state of mind. Automobile tags and posters in windows are counted, and campaign orators are questioned concerning the applause that greeted their remarks. Most politicians find that the auditory sensibilities of their speech makers are stimulated with great ease, and as a consequence the discount rate on this type of information is invariably high.

Accuracy of Predictions by Political Leaders

With an understanding of the technique by which politicians gauge preëlection sentiment, we are in a position to inquire as to the accuracy of their predictions. Edward M. Sait in his *American Parties and Elections*, declares that "The astute politicians are rarely misled."[3] On the other hand, Frank Kent, the provocative observer of politics for the *Baltimore Sun*, thinks that the preëlection estimates of the politicians are reliable only when the apathy of the electorate allows the course of events to run along customary channels. When new factors enter the situation, such as a big registration of voters, the politicians, says this authority, can only guess as to the outcome.[4]

[3] Page 501. [4] *Baltimore Sun*, Oct. 27, 1928.

Most political leaders, no doubt, rate their predictive ability highly; some flatly state that campaign estimates can never be made with a high degree of certainty.

The question is difficult to answer objectively because the necessary data are extremely elusive. Predictive reports that cross the desks of party leaders are largely confidential in nature and are difficult to obtain during the heat of the campaign. Following the election, versions of what happened in a predictive way are often unreliable, because the forces of rationalization have been set to work to smooth over the mistakes. A large number of good estimates are then available, but bad forecasts are difficult to find. Similarly, as pointed out at the beginning of the chapter, the published claims of political leaders are of no value in solving the present problem because these forecasts are nearly always propagandistic.

Notwithstanding these difficulties, however, the author has been able to collect some trustworthy data which give insight into the prognosticative skill of the men who make a business of politics. This material, all of which comes from the presidential campaign of 1928, is of two types. The first type consists of plurality estimates collected by Republican headquarters in three states, and generously given to the author by the men who assembled and used the data during the course of the campaign. In evaluating the accuracy of these forecasts, the difference between the estimated and actual (official) pluralities will be computed and this difference, or "plurality error," will be expressed as a percentage of the total vote cast so that one prediction may be freely compared with another. This will be the meaning of the term "plurality error" as used throughout this volume.

The first example of plurality estimates for counties comes from a West North Central state. The party chairman in this commonwealth called upon his county leaders for an estimate of probable Hoover pluralities three weeks in advance of the election day. The local leaders replied with plurality predictions made up, as described earlier in this chapter, from precinct and ward reports, from opinions of leading men in the several communities, and from their own seasoned knowledge of political conditions in their counties. These estimates, supplemented by independent advices, comprised the data by which the state chairman was enabled to visualize in advance of the election his party's position in terms of votes. The most accurate county predictor in this state said he would deliver a plurality of

300 for Hoover, whereas he actually returned a margin of 296 votes in a turnout of 3,500. This was a plurality error of only 4 votes, or one-tenth of one percent of the total vote cast. The least accurate county predictor showed a plurality error of 41 percent. He prognosticated a Hoover margin of 1,500 votes in his county, whereas the Republican presidential candidate actually received 5,600 in a total of 9,900 votes cast. The average plurality error for the upward of seventy-five county estimates was 13 percent. When all the county predictions were added for the state, the combined forecast undershot the true plurality mark by 8 percent, or 8 votes in every 100 cast. It is to be expected that the error in the state forecast would be smaller than the average error by counties, because in the combined estimate the overpredictions by some local leaders compensate for the underpredictions of others.

The second example comes from an industrial state on the Atlantic seaboard and, like the first case, consists of estimates given to the state chairman by the county leaders about one month before the date of the election. The best county forecaster in this state declared that Hoover would receive a plurality of 40,000 in his county. Actually the party candidate received a plurality of 38,700 in a total of 140,000 votes cast. This is a plurality error of nine-tenths of one percent. The worst predictor said that 1,300 would be Hoover's margin. Actually it was 9,300 in a total vote cast of 15,400. This is a plurality error of 52 percent, or one vote for every two cast. The average error in plurality prediction by counties was 14 percent. The error for the state taken as a whole was 9 percent.

The third example comes from an East North Central state and illustrates the predictive reliability of an inclusive house-to-house canvass. This survey was made during the first week in October, practically one month before the election, and represents a vast effort on the part of the party organization, the workers having been paid to trudge from door to door and interview every householder of the state on the current status of his political convictions. Unlike the two previous examples of state estimates, which show expected pluralities only, this poll gives a tabulation of the number of people interviewed who intended to vote for Hoover or for Smith, and of the number who refused to divulge their voting intentions or who declared that they had not yet made up their minds. Assuming that the citizens classed as "doubtful" intended to vote for the two major candidates in the same proportion as the people who revealed their intentions,[5] it was found that the best county appraisal was in error by one-half of one percent. A 9,700 Hoover plurality was predicted, whereas the Republican candidate actually led by 10,000 in a total vote of 64,000. The worst forecast conceded Smith a plurality of 750 votes, which turned out to be less than 50 in a total of 2,000 votes cast, an error of 35 percent. The average plurality error by counties was 13 percent. The plurality error of the combined county estimates for the state was 6 percent. So much for this type of predictive experience.

The second type of data which throws light on the predictive ability of the politicians consists of estimates by states—as distinguished from estimates by counties—which were made by the political leaders who were responsible for the conduct of the presidential campaign in those states. The figures for this test were gathered by means of correspondence and conversation with party leaders who had participated in the making of the appraisals, and with newspapermen who had had good opportunity to learn of the pluralities actually expected by those in charge of the campaigns. For each forecast, corroboration from independent sources was sought, and only those predictions that satisfied the author on the score of trustworthiness were preserved. No attempt will be made here to document the source of this information, both for the reason that space is not available and, more particularly, because many of the men interviewed by the author are intimately connected with politics, and desire that their names be not revealed.

The predictions for the several states for which figures were obtained are given in Table 1. In some cases the estimates made by both parties are shown and in other instances those of but one party. The estimated and actual pluralities are displayed, and also the error in prediction, expressed first in the number of votes by which the forecast missed its mark, and next as a percentage of the total vote cast. Where the prediction was made by the party leaders in terms of a maximum and a minimum estimate, the two figures were averaged and the result was accepted as the forecast. Where party leadership was divided between two factions,

[5] Of the total number of people interviewed, 13 percent were classed as doubtful. Some political observers believe that the "silent vote" is a class apart, and that its political stand is different from that of the run of citizens who are willing to reveal their voting intentions. The author, however, is of the opinion that much unnecessary mystery has been attributed to this doubtful class of voters and that the division between the two major parties in the known columns probably holds within reasonable limits for the doubtful classification as well.

and where predictions from both factions were available, an average of the two statements was taken.

TABLE 1

Plurality Error of State Estimates by Politicians in the 1928 Presidential Campaign

1	2	3	4	5	6	7	8	9
			Democratic estimates			Republican estimates		
State	Total vote cast	Actual Hoover plurality	Estimated plurality	Plur. error (Diff. col. 3 and col. 4)	Percent plurality error (col. 5 ÷ col. 2)	Estimated plurality	Plur. error (Diff. col. 3 and col. 7)	Percent plurality error (col. 8 ÷ col. 2)
Ill....	3,106,489	454,324	S. 200,000	654,324	21	H. 450,000	4,324	0
Ind....	1,421,314	285 599	......	......	..	H. 125,000	160,599	11
Iowa...	1,009,360	244,882	......	......	..	H. 100,000	144,882	14
Ky....	940,596	176,994	S. 40,000	216,994	23	H. 50,000	126,994	13
Md....	528,348	77,853	S. 10,000	87,853	17	H. 37,000	40,853	8
Minn...	970,976	164,526	......	......	..	H. 93,000	71,526	7
Mo....	1,500,235	172,004	S. 60,000	232 004	15	H. 97,500	74,504	5
Neb....	547,344	147,786	H. 62,000	85,786	16	H. 62,000	85,786	16
Nev....	32,417	4,237	......	......	..	H. 3,800	437	1
N. Y...	4,405,626	103,481	H. 15,000	88,481	2	H. 150,000	46,519	1
Ohio...	2,508,346	763,336	H. 150,000	613,336	24	H. 400,000	363,336	14
Ore. ..	319,942	96,118	......	......	..	H. 128,000	31,882	10
Pa.....	3,150,610	987,796	H. 350,000	637,796	20	H. 750,000	237,796	7
S. D...	261,489	54,763	......	......	..	H. 40,000	14,763	6
Texas..	708,999	26,004	......	......	..	H. 37,500	11,496	2
Wyo....	82,835	23,449	......	......	..	H. 18,000	5,449	7
				Median av. 18			Median av. 7	

The table shows some very good predictions and some very bad ones. The average plurality error for the eight Democratic prognostications was 18 percent. This means that for every 100 votes cast, the difference between the predicted and actual plurality was 18 votes. The average Republican error was considerably lower, 7 percent, suggesting that the Republicans were better predictors than the Democrats in 1928. Part of this predictive superiority of the G. O. P. was due, no doubt, to more efficient organization, the minority party having been badly demoralized by the defeats of

1920 and 1924; but a more likely explanation, the author believes, is that in 1928 the Democrats were the victims of sort of self-hypnosis leading to a feeling of elation with regard to their election prospects. This is a state of mind not uncommon to members of the party which proves the loser in a political campaign, and, since it probably constitutes the chief weakness in the predictive technique of the politicians, it will be worth while to digress for a moment to consider the phenomenon.

The Elation Complex

Most candidates for public office and political managers working for the same end believe mightily in the prospects of their success at the polls. To do so is to have heart for their labors, to inspire their followers and to win votes. The men who believe they are whipped are almost sure to be beaten, but the men who never say die sometimes turn the tide in their own favor. But this will to do, however necessary it may be to buoy up the spirit of political campaigners, inhibits cerebration on the true status of the candidate and his party with the citizens who cast the votes. It opens the door to delusions of grandeur and power, and causes otherwise normal men to see great and sweeping victories where fate holds crushing defeat in store.

In the 1920 campaign for the presidency, for example, the betting odds, straw votes, opinions of newspapermen, and other indices of the prevailing current set down Governor Cox, the Democratic candidate, as a beaten man, but no one was more sure of winning than he. Eight days before the election Mr. Cox passed through Washington, D. C. on a speaking tour, and was interviewed by George Rothwell Brown, an able newspaperman connected with the *Washington Post*. According to this reporter, Mr. Cox was fanatically convinced that he was in tune with the soul of America, and that he was riding on the crest of a wave of popular feeling that had risen but a few days before and which was destined to carry him into the White House.

> This change which I have sensed in the minds and hearts of the people [Governor Cox is quoted as saying] has had a tremendous effect upon me. It is coming from deep down in the pent-up souls of the people. There is no mistaking its powerful sweep. That force is resistless and it is growing stronger every hour. I know it, not because anybody has told me so, but because I feel it. . . . Everywhere the people are rising up like a torrent.[6]

[6]Quoted by Mark Sullivan, *Utica Daily Press* (New York), Nov. 3, 1928.

Cox was one of the worst defeated candidates in the history of the country.

In 1928 Al Smith was similarly confident that he would be the next president of the United States. Everywhere he went, in Chicago, Milwaukee, Boston, Baltimore, he received tumultuous welcome. Streets were filled with enthusiastic humanity shouting for "Al," and people jammed his speaking halls and cheered themselves hoarse for this leader from the sidewalks of New York. After a final speaking tour that had been marked by one great ovation after another, reporters asked Mr. Smith what this mass enthusiasm meant. The Governor replied with perfect sincerity and conviction. "It means victory," he said. "It is in the air.[7]" Smith won but 87 out of 531 electoral college votes, the smallest number for any Democratic candidate since the Civil War. As for the popular vote polled in the nation, only Davis in 1924, Cox in 1920 and Parker in 1904 received fewer votes proportionate to the total cast, then he.

The game of politics, of course, demands that the candidates of the lost causes be hoodwinked into believing that they will win; otherwise their spirit would be sapped and their morale broken, but the elation complex does not stop with candidates alone, but often infects party managers as well. In 1916 the Republicans thought that they would surely elect Mr. Hughes, and in 1928 the will to win was rampant in the headquarters of Mr. Smith's candidacy. Following a visit to the General Motors Building in New York where the Democratic generals were located in 1928, Arthur Sears Henning, the veteran political correspondent of the *Chicago Tribune*, reported that "elation" charged the atmosphere of the place.[8] After a similar visit, Frank Kent, of the *Baltimore Sun*, wrote:

> In one way or another practically every man and woman at work there completely believes in the success of his cause. There is no doubt about that[9].

Similar reports came from writers who had visited state headquarters of the Democratic party in other sections of the country.

The turbulence of life around party headquarters during an important campaign is well calculated to distort the judgment of even the most level-headed campaign managers. The necessity of injecting optimism into the candidates eventually leads the directing

---

[7]*New York Times*, Nov. 2, 1928.   [8]*Chicago Tribune*, Nov. 1, 1928.

[9]*Baltimore Sun*, Nov. 2, 1928.

minds into believing what they say, the noise of the mob obscures the votes of the less demonstrative, and the hordes of "yes" men who come to headquarters with rosy prospects contingent upon financial aid to their territories tend to blind the party managers to the true facts of a political situation. Under these circumstances a fleeting sense of defeat may be turned into the obsession of victory, and managers as well as candidates find it easy to believe in ground swells, undercurrents, landslide reversals, popular tides, and last-minute switches that are at least comforting if not realistic.

Given the will to win on both sides of a bipartisan political struggle, the party that does carry the day will almost invariably be shown to be the better forecasters and, by the same token, the party that loses will be revealed as the worse predictors. The author is thoroughly of the opinion that if the records of preëlection measurements were available for the campaign of 1916, when Woodrow Wilson beat Charles E. Hughes for the presidency, the Democrats would stand first in predictive accuracy and the Republicans second.

RECAPITULATION

The predictive error shown by the several examples of plurality forecasts by politicians may now be brought together in Table 2 for a quick review.

TABLE 2
PLURALITY ERROR OF FORECASTS BY POLITICAL LEADERS
(In Percentages)

	Average plurality error by counties	Plurality error by states
Democratic forecasts for 8 states, 1928..................	..	18 (av.)
Republican forecasts for 16 states, 1928................	..	7 (av.)
Republican forecasts for 3 states, 1928 (by counties and by states):*		
Opinion canvass, West North Central State..........	13	8
Opinion canvass, Atlantic Seaboard State............	14	9
Inclusive canvass, East North Central State.........	13	6

*County error expressed as average plurality error for all counties within the state. State prediction calculated by combining plurality predictions for counties.

For 1928 the average Republican plurality error for 16 state predictions is shown to have been 7 percent, or 7 votes per 100 cast. In the three states for which Republican forecasts for counties were secured, the plurality error proved to be about the same. The average plurality error by counties for these states was somewhat larger, being approximately 13 percent. The Democratic plurality error for eight states averaged 18 percent, showing that the losing politicians were the worse predictors. The forecasting error in 1928, as between winning and losing politicians, was distinctly bimodal, and this phenomenon is probably a feature of most political campaigns.

In drawing general conclusions from these figures, caution must be exercised because the predictive experience here given has been taken from a single campaign. The tabulation probably affords a satisfactory picture of the forecasting skill of the politicians in 1928, but in campaigns of other years or in contests involving offices other than that of the presidency, the results might be different. Some may hold that public sentiment in 1928 was especially difficult to gauge, because of the abnormal increase in registration, and because of the baffling factors introduced by the issues of religion and prohibition. If this is true, the plurality error of the politicians may prove to be smaller in other years.

Chapter II
THE NEWSPAPERMAN AS PREDICTOR

If anyone is able to gauge preëlection sentiment accurately, it should be the skilled newspaperman. He is a trained observer of public opinion; he is close to the politicians who are endeavoring to manipulate public beliefs; he has the opportunity to gather information from all quarters; and, in addition, he has the newspaperman's intuition, which comes through long association with political affairs. Armed with this equipment, how well does the newspaperman discharge his reportorial obligations, how accurate are his political forecasts?

In this case abundant data are available for making an objective judgment, for unlike the politicians who guard their true estimates from the public, the newspaperman gives his predictions freely to all who can read. He has no need for camouflaging the truth. On the contrary, he must tell the truth as he sees it, since his reputation for veracity and that of his newspaper are at stake. For practical purposes, therefore, a definite forecast made by a political reporter in the columns of his newspaper can be taken to represent his best forecasting efforts.[1]

Plurality Predictions

The data for a demonstration of the predictive accuracy of the newspapermen are of two kinds: first, plurality estimates for presidential and other elections; and second, predictions of the division of votes in the electoral college for a number of presidential elections. An example of the first type of forecast is the poll of newspaper editors taken by *Editor and Publisher*, the leading trade journal of the newspaper profession, in the Hoover-Smith campaign of 1928. This magazine sent a letter to editors of all daily English-language newspapers, asking each editor, on the basis of "newspaper experience,

[1] In some cases, where a newspaper is enthusiastically supporting a candidate and where the political reporter finds that the chances of election of the favored contender are nil, the resulting forecast may be shaded a bit to be more palatable to the owner. In these circumstances, printed estimates misrepresent the newspaperman's predictive skill to a certain extent. But there are distinct limits to which such shading can be safely carried and, moreover, the better type of publishers endeavor to keep their news columns free from editorial bias. Most newspapermen who write political forecasts would, no doubt, be willing to be judged by their printed estimates.

devoid of partisan feeling," to predict the presidential winner in his state and the winner's plurality. Out of 1,939 editors canvassed, 925, approximately one-half, replied with estimates. Using the procedure for stating forecasting precision described in the last chapter—i.e., plurality error is the difference between the predicted and the actual plurality, expressed as a percentage of the total vote cast—the average plurality error for the 48 state predictions was 13 percent.[2] The local editors generally credited Smith with more strength than he demonstrated at the polls, overestimating the Democratic vote in 40 of the 48 states. The southern newspapermen apparently had no thought that the Republicans would break the Solid South, for the editors in Florida, North Carolina, Texas, and Virginia predicted that their states would go for Smith, whereas Hoover actually won the electoral votes of these commonwealths. Tennessee was also given to Smith by the local editors, but was subsequently carried by Hoover. In the northern Republican strongholds of Massachusetts and Rhode Island, which were carried by Smith by very narrow margins, the local editors predicted that Hoover would win.

A second illustration of plurality forecasts in presidential elections comes from the campaign of 1912, when the *New York World* asked newspaper correspondents in each state to predict the presidential pluralities for their state.[3] The average plurality error for the 48 states (between the two leading candidates) was 9 percent. Unlike the estimates gathered by *Editor and Publisher*, in which the winning candidate was almost universally underpredicted, Woodrow Wilson's strength was underestimated in 30 states and overestimated in the remaining 18.

In 1920 the *New York World* made a similar canvass, calling upon 300 editors of the largest newspapers for a presidential forecast for their states.[4] The average plurality error for the 48 states was quite large, being 22 percent. The editors were well aware that Harding would win, but they had no adequate idea of the avalanche of postwar emotion that was to make Cox one of the worst beaten candidates in the history of presidential campaigns. Harding's pluralities were underestimated in all but 2 states. Six states that had been predicted

---

[2]This figure is calculated on the basis of the concensus of editorial opinion or the estimates of the majority, and disregards the estimates of the minority. Since the minority were more frequently wrong than the majority, the present figure must be regarded as a minimum statement of error. See *Editor and Publisher*, Oct. 13, 1928, for original data.

[3]*New York World*, Nov. 3, 1912.   [4]*New York World*, Oct. 31, 1920.

for Cox by the newspaper forecasters were subsequently carried by the Republican candidate.

The newspapermen's predictions cited in the foregoing paragraphs have been for the political units of states. The remaining examples show the accuracy of estimates for counties within states, as well as for the state units themselves. Curtis Betts, the able political correspondent for the *St. Louis Post-Dispatch*, toured the state of Missouri in 1928 and, after observing conditions first-hand, and talking with influential local leaders, made county estimates that erred 14 percent on the average. His plurality error for the state as a whole was 8 percent.[5]

The *Portland Oregonion*, in 1928, asked the editors of the county newspapers in Oregon to predict for their respective counties the number of votes that Hoover and Smith would each receive.[6] These men, as correspondence with them reveals, used a variety of data in making up their forecasts: registration figures, statistics of past votes, interviews with political leaders, conversation with citizens, influence of local elections, intuition. The average plurality error of their predictions was 9 percent per county. For the state as a whole, the plurality error was 5 percent. Though most of the editors stated that they had supported Mr. Hoover, the larger proportion of them underestimated his strength, which suggests that subconscious political bias does not necessarily operate to overpredict the vote of the editor's own candidate.

Some very remarkable predictions have been placed on record by Thomas B. Cromwell, a Kentucky newspaperman, writing for the *Cincinnati Enquirer* in 1916[7] and 1918.[8] In the memorable presidential campaign of the former year, Cromwell sent letters to capable observers in every county in Kentucky asking for a county forecast. These data he sifted out on the basis of his own experience, making what he deemed to be the correct allowance for such factors as the colored vote, the German vote, local conditions, etc. His prediction was that Woodrow Wilson would carry Kentucky by winning 52.1 percent of all the votes cast. Actually Wilson won the state by polling 52.7 percent of the total vote. This is a plurality error of a trifle more than 1 vote in 100. The average plurality error by counties was larger, of course, being 4 percent. Two years later, in the hot race for United States Senator from Kentucky, Cromwell

[5]From unpublished material furnished the author by Mr. Betts.
[6]*Portland Oregonion*, Oct. 28, 1928.   [7]Oct. 29, 1916.   [8]Nov. 3, 1918.

THE NEWSPAPERMAN 17

duplicated his feat by forecasting 51.1 votes per 100 for Stanley, the Democratic candidate, whereas Stanley's actual score was 50.8, a plurality error of less than 1 percent. The average plurality error by counties in this forecast was 5 percent.

As a final example, the *Columbus Dispatch*, in 1910, secured estimates from correspondents in 88 counties in Ohio on the race for the office of secretary of state.[9] The average plurality error of these predictions for the counties was 7 percent. For the state as a whole the plurality error was 3 percent.

The accuracy of the newspapermen in predicting plurality margins, as revealed by the several examples here given, may now be presented in a single tabulation.

TABLE 3
PLURALITY ERROR OF FORECASTS BY NEWSPAPERMEN

National predictions	Average plurality error by counties (Percent)	Plurality error by states (Percent)	No. states in which minority vote overestimated	Total number state forecasts
1912—President—*New York World* poll of newspapermen in 48 states—Average by state.................	..	9	30	48
1920—President—*New York World* poll of 300 editors of leading dailies in 48 states—Average by state.....	..	22	46	48
1928—President—*Editor-and-Publisher* poll of 925 editors of daily papers in 48 states—Average by state........	..	13	40	48
Predictions for individual states				
1910—Secretary of State—*Columbus-Dispatch* poll of correspondents in 88 counties—Estimate for Ohio.....	7	3	1	1
1916—President—Thomas B. Cromwell, *Cincinnati Enquirer*—Estimate for Kentucky....................	4	1	1	1
1918—United States Senator—Thomas B. Cromwell, *Cincinnati Enquirer*—Estimate for Kentucky...........	5	1	1	1
1928—President — *Portland-Oregonion* poll of county editors—Estimate for Oregon.......................	9	5	1	1
1928—President — Curtis Betts, *St. Louis Post Dispatch*—Estimate for Missouri........................	14	8	1	1
			121	149

[9] *Columbus Dispatch*, Nov. 4, 1906.

These examples of plurality predictions by newspapemen are not the result of special choosing on the part of the author, but are such as have come to hand during the course of newspaper scanning required in the research for the present volume. They probably give a fair picture of journalistic skill in this type of forecasting, because they include the results of three national polls of editors in which each editor ventured a presidential forecast for his own state, the political territory with which he was presumed to be the most familiar. The average state plurality error for these predictions ran as low as 9 percent and as high as 22 percent. Predictions for county units showed a larger average plurality error than forecasts for the same state on the basis of the cumulated county forecasts, because overpredictions in some counties compensated for underpredictions in others. The vote of the losing candidate, the examples show, was generally overpredicted. For the state predictions this occurred in 121 out of the 149 cases, or about four-fifths of the time. The test finally shows that states which suddenly shift, after having voted for one party for a long time, are frequently predicted incorrectly by the newspapermen.

Electoral-College Forecasts

A second and perhaps a more popular type of political forecasting with newspapermen is the attempt to place states correctly in the electoral college, and thereby predict the winner of the presidential election. In every presidential campaign, these electoral-college forecasts appear in the large metropolitan dailies, and they are also syndicated to the smaller papers throughout the nation by the leading press services. They are usually written by veteran political correspondents who have had wide experience in national campaigns, and who make it their business to follow the course of the struggle for votes in each one of the forty-eight states. Generally these men make extended tours of the nation a month or two months before the date of the election, consulting with political leaders, men of affairs and brother newspapermen, who can give them information on local political conditions. By telegraph, correspondence and interview they endeavor to keep their fingers on the national pulse until a day or so before the election, when they write a final forecast of the probable electoral college vote. These electoral college predictions furnish an excellent opportunity to check up on the predictive skill of the newspapermen.

In gathering the data for the test, approximately 65 leading metropolitan dailies were scanned for a few issues previous to election day for the seven presidential campaigns beginning with the Roosevelt-Bryan contest of 1904 and ending with the Hoover-Smith struggle of 1928. From these papers were gleaned from 10 to 21 predictions for each campaign, the number of forecasts for all seven campaigns totaling 103.[10] In every case the prediction abstracted was the last one made by each writer before the election, and it usually represents the prognosticator's opinion two or three days before the voters went to the polls.

This collection of electoral-college forecasts is wholly representative of the prognosticative skill of the journalistic world, because it reflects the best ability of the profession at work on a wide variety of predictive problems. There were, for example, the baffling factors of religious intolerance, prohibition and increased registration in 1928, the extremely close contest of 1916 and the one-sided contests of 1904 and 1908, the emotional explosion of 1920 following a period of war restraint, the party split of 1912, and the strong independent candidacy of 1924. The list of forecasters, to name only a few, includes such writers as Walker S. Buel, Raymond Clapper, Edward B. Clark, Sumner Curtis, Arthur M. Evans, Carter Field, Clinton W. Gilbert, Arthur Sears Henning, James P. Hornaday, W. M. Kiplinger, Gould Lincoln, Angus McSween, Mark Sullivan, Charles Michelson, James Morgan, Frederick William Wile, and Walter Wellman.

The form in which these writers most commonly cast their electoral-college predictions was to classify the several states in three columns. In the first and third columns, they enumerated all states which they felt sure would go Republican or Democratic.[11] In the second column, they catalogued those commonwealths where the outcome was believed to be in doubt. The titles given these columns varied, but by and large their meaning was the same with all forecasters. The "sure" columns were sometimes headed "probable," "certain," "fairly certain," or simply "Republican," or "Democrat," but whatever the symbol, the prognosticator meant that this list of states was safely in the fold of the party that was designated. The states in which the outcome was held to be uncertain were, in the majority

---

[10] The complete list of the forecasts used in this test is given in Appendix A.

[11] In 1912 and 1924, when the contest was three-sided, an extra column was added for the states predicted as "sure" for the third party.

of forecasts, placed under the simple title of "doubtful." Some writers, however, hazarded a guess as to the probabilities in these by breaking the category into "leaning Republican" and "leaning Democrat," while others employed these two categories, together with a simple category of "doubtful" to express three shadings of uncertainty. For the purposes of the present check-up, these refinements in prognostication of a few writers have been ignored, and the most commonly used categories of "sure" for one party or the other and "doubtful" have been adopted. Under this latter head have been listed all the states described with terms of uncertainty, such as "leaning Republican" or "leaning Democrat" or plain "doubtful."

In summarizing this mass of predictive data, prognostications for each of the seven campaigns were condensed into one forecast based on majority opinion, and this concensus of opinion was accepted as typifying the newspaperman's ability to predict states in the electoral college. In 1928, for example, 20 reporters said that Alabama was sure to go Democratic. Only one marked the state as doubtful. In the summary concensus of opinion, Alabama was placed in the "sure" column. With Nevada, further to illustrate the point, 9 reporters said that the state was safe for Hoover, 2 predicted that it would go for Smith and 10 said that it was doubtful. The last group being the largest, the state was characterized as doubtful in the summary tabulation.

With the data thus condensed and compared with what actually happened in the ensuing election, some highly interesting conclusions can be drawn. Altogether in the seven presidential campaigns from 1904 to 1928, the newspapermen were compelled to forecast the outcome of 331 state elections. As things came to pass, 164 of these elections were decided by overwhelming pluralities of 20 or more votes per 100, as in the case of the Solid South or in Republican strongholds like Vermont and Pennsylvania. Another 77 state elections resulted in what can be called "comfortable" or "safe" plurality margins of from 10 to 20 votes per 100 cast, as is common in such states as New Jersey and Illinois. The remaining 90 state elections for which the newspapermen were compelled to hazard predictions, were decided by narrow pluralities of fewer than 10 votes per 100 cast, as is frequently the result in such commonwealths as Kentucky, Missouri, Maryland, and Tennessee. Let us examine the newspapermen's predictions for each of these three groups and see how closely they hit the mark.

In the first group in which public sentiment leaned overwhelmingly toward one candidate (plurality margin of 20 votes or more per 100), the newspapermen placed every state correctly in the electoral college. The decisions required in these 164 state elections were made with a feeling of certainty on the part of the predictors, for in all but 7 instances the states were catalogued in the "sure" column.

In the second group of 77 state elections which were decided by comfortable or safe margins (plurality of more than 10 and fewer than 20 votes per 100 cast) the newspapermen stayed on the scent about three-fourths of the time, recognizing these states as "sure" for the correct party in 53 of the 77 instances, becoming confused and calling them doubtful in 20 cases, and losing the trail completely in 4 others by handing them over as "sure" states to the wrong party.

In the third group of 90 state elections in which voting decisions were rendered by pluralities of fewer than 10 votes per 100 cast, the political reporters recognized 32 as "doubtful," predicted 39 "sure" for the right party, and called the remaining 19 "sure" for the wrong party. Thus the newspapermen were most confused in the states in which sentiment was closely divided, being completely wrong in 20 percent of the cases, predicting the right party but misjudging the closeness of the contest in 45 percent of the instances, and recognizing the real element of uncertainty in the remaining 35 percent.[12]

Stating the conclusions of this test in a somewhat different manner, from a preëlection as distinguished from a postelection angle, we may say that the newspapermen predicted 272 of the 331 state elections as "sure" to go to a given candidate. Of these, 249 were duly carried by the contestant as forecast, and 23 went to the opposition. This means that, on the basis of predictive experience from 1904 to 1928, about 8 percent of the states placed in the electoral college as "sure" for a given candidate were carried by an opposing candidate. The remaining 59 of the 331 state predictions were classed as "doubtful." Of these 34 were actually decided by plurality

[12]It is interesting to note that in the 39 cases predicted "sure" for the right party, the actual outcome was decided by about the same pluralities as in the 32 cases predicted "doubtful." For the former, the average plurality was 5 votes per 100 cast, while for the latter it was 4 votes for every 100 cast. In a number of instances, particularly in 1916, a state which had customarily given large pluralities to the candidates of one party was placed as "sure" by the newspapermen, but, subsequently, was carried by a narrow margin. This explains the large number of correct placements in the plurality range that might ordinarily be regarded as "doubtful."

margins of 10 or more votes per 100 cast; hence in more than one-half of the states in which the newspapermen felt uncertain, the voters' decision was rendered by what has been here called a "safe" margin.

Despite the use of the doubtful category in the electoral college forecasts, which conceivably might have made the predictions of the newspapermen indeterminate, enough "sure" votes were assigned in each of the 7 presidential elections to predict a winner. In all but one election, the course of events followed the ordering of the prognosticators, the single exception being in the campaign of 1916, when the political reporters gave the defeated candidate, Charles E. Hughes, 267 "sure" electoral votes, or one more than enough to elect. In this campaign the political correspondents failed to appreciate the real hold that Woodrow Wilson had upon the voters at that time. The concensus of newspaper opinion had it that Mr. Hughes was "sure" to carry 21 states; actually the Republican candidate won but 4 of these by safe margins, carried another 10 by very narrow pluralities and lost 7 to the Democratic aspirant. It is true, of course, that the 1916 campaign was very close, being finally and dramatically decided by only 3,906 votes from the state of California, but the point is that these circumstances were interpreted by the press correspondents as a "sure" victory for Hughes. In the remaining six elections between 1904 and 1928 the newspapermen predicted the winner correctly.

Political solidarity, the test indicates, proved a stumbling block to the journalist prognosticators. In 1928 practically every writer adhered to the custom of conceding the Southern states to the Democrats, but after the election, when the ballots had been counted, it was found that Hoover had carried Florida, Texas, Virginia, and North Carolina, and had come within a very few votes of carrying Alabama as well. Tennessee affords another example. From 1872 to 1920 this state voted for Democratic presidential candidates. In 1920 the concensus of newspaper opinion held that it would again go Democratic, but Mr. Harding actually won the state. In 1924 the forecast for Tennessee was again Democratic, and the prediction was fulfilled. In 1928 this state was called "doubtful" and was subsequently carried by the Republicans. Once political solidarity had been shattered in Tennessee, the newspapermen became wary of hasty placement. In future campaigns, no doubt, placement of Florida, Texas, Virginia, and North Carolina will be made with considerable caution. By showing political solidarity to be a cause of misprediction on the part of newspapermen, the present test corroborates the evidence on plurality forecasts presented earlier in the chapter. The reader will recall that in the *Editor-and-Publisher* poll none of the southern states was conceded to Hoover, nor were the Democratic victories in the Republican strongholds of Massachusetts and Rhode Island forecast by the local editors.

Like the evidence on plurality predictions, too, the present test shows that the newspapermen almost invariably overestimated the strength of the losing candidate. In 1928, for example, Mr. Smith was given, among other states, Florida, Virginia, Texas, and North Carolina, none of which he carried. Also the Democratic contender was thought to have a chance in Arizona, Kentucky, Maryland, Missouri, Montana, Nebraska, Nevada, New Mexico, and Tennessee, all of which he lost by substantial pluralities. In 1924 La Follette was assigned North Dakota, which Mr. Coolidge won, and was said to have a good chance in Iowa, Nebraska, South Dakota, and Washington, which were all carried by the Republicans by safe margins. The political correspondents knew that Mr. Harding would win in 1920, but they did not sense the landslide proportions of the victory that he was to achieve. The Hughes overprediction of 1916 has already been described. In the campaigns of 1904 and 1908 Judge Alton B. Parker and William Jennings Bryan, the Democratic contestants, were both given states in the electoral college that they actually lost to their Republican opponents. Only in 1912 was the rule partially upset. In this campaign, the strength of Mr. Taft was overpredicted, but the vote of the second loser, Theodore Roosevelt, was underrated by the newspapermen, the leader of the Bull Moose forces being conceded 49 electoral college votes in the forecast and actually winning 88.

Observers of predictive phenomena may differ as to why newspapermen consistently inflate the prospects of the losing candidate, but two plausible reasons may be advanced. In the first place, most men tend to think of a presidential campaign as "anyman's battle." The activities of the minority party are almost as well publicized as those of the majority and, on the face of it, the struggle appears to be a matching of the strength of equals or near equals. For the period under consideration, however, the race for the presidency has been largely one-sided. The newspapermen, influenced by the idea of an even contest, tended to forecast on the side of the mean, rather than upon that of the extreme; hence they are here shown to have overpredicted the losing candidates.

A second reason is that the correspondents are misled by rival claims of the party managers. As a part of good reporting, newspapermen seek prognosticative information from the headquarters of both the major parties. The minority, as was noted in the last chapter, is often in the throes of an elation complex during the last ten days or two weeks of a campaign, and the majority deprecates the rosy outlook lest they become weak with overconfidence. The reporter cannot help but be influenced by the elation of the minority, on the one hand, and by the concern of the majority on the other. The natural result is overprediction of votes for the candidate who is fated to lose.

Conclusion

The upshot of the discussion of the predictive skill of the newspapermen may now be briefly indicated. It was found that the error of state-plurality forecasts in presidential campaigns ranged from 9 to 22 votes per 100 cast. In electoral-college forecasts, about 8 percent of the states placed as "sure" for a given candidate were won by the opposing contestant, and more than half the states declared to be doubtful were subsequently carried by pluralities in excess of 10 votes per 100 cast. In six out of the last seven presidential elections, the newspapermen correctly predicted the winner. States which suddenly shifted their allegiance, after having consistently voted for one party, proved to be stumbling blocks. The vote of the losing candidate was overpredicted about three fourths of the time. These observations should be helpful in evaluating newspapermen's prognostications in presidential campaigns to come.

Chapter III
MAINE—POLITICAL BAROMETER

In election parlance, Maine is known as an "early state." Contrary to the generally accepted custom of holding elections on the first Tuesday after the first Monday in November, this New England commonwealth chooses state officials and representatives to Congress on the second Monday in September. Every four years a second election is held in November to vote for presidential electors. As the first state to test political sentiment, Maine is widely regarded as an election barometer, the saying "As goes Maine, so goes the nation" being heard in every national campaign. Whether or not this predictive maxim is reliable is a question upon which there is great divergence of opinion. The *New York Times* would relegate the slogan to the "dictionary of superstitions."[1] The *New York Herald Tribune*, on the other hand, declares that the September election "is a barometer that seldom errs."[2] In this chapter we shall inquire into the worth of the Maine returns as a forecast of the national outcome. In making this evaluation, we need first to sketch briefly the beginnings of the "As goes Maine" slogan, then explain its implications for practical politics and, finally, conduct forecasting experiments that will determine the dependability of the slogan.

How It All Began

Maine gained her reputation for prognosticating the national election returns in the memorable "Log Cabin and Hard Cider" campaign for the presidency in 1840. In that year the Whigs, with General William Henry Harrison as their candidate, were struggling to overturn Jacksonion control of the White House by defeating Martin Van Buren, the Democratic nominee. The clash of these opposing interests raised people's emotions to fever pitch, and there occurred, as a result, one of the most boisterous and spectacular political campaigns in American history.

Maine, at that time, was regarded as a solidly Democratic[3] state. For two decades since her entry into the Union she had, with few

---
[1] Sept. 13, 1926.   [2] Quoted from the *Literary Digest*, Sept. 20, 1930, p. 8.
[3] That is, the party of Thomas Jefferson, originally called the Republican party.

exceptions, elected Democrats to the places of public trust, and now this party was considered impregnable in the state. In the gubernatorial campaign of 1840 even the Whigs themselves expected defeat as a matter of course. A great surprise, however, was in store. On election day the Whigs overturned the customary Democratic plurality and elected their candidate, Edward Kent, to the governorship by a margin of sixty-eight votes.

The nation was electrified by this political upset. The Democrats were dumfounded. The Whigs joyously hailed the result as a portent of what was to come in November. Everywhere they celebrated the Maine victory with doggerel and song, chanting the now familiar lines:

> Oh have you heard how Old Maine went?
> She went hell bent for Governor Kent,
> And Tippecanoe and Tyler, too!

In November General Harrison was elected, carrying 19 of the 26 states, and the widely heralded portent from Maine was dramatically fulfilled. From that day to the present, the September returns from Maine have been charged with prophetic authority, and the slogan "As goes Maine, so goes the nation" has been of concern to men interested in the ebb and flow of the national political tide.

It will be noted, significantly enough, that Maine's barometric reputation did not arise from scientific induction, *i.e.*, repeated observation that the nation voted in November as did Maine in September, but rather as a result of a combination of historical circumstances, the simultaneous happening of which might justly be regarded as fortuitous. Maine held an early election; the presidential campaign of 1840 aroused people's emotions and made them impressionable; the political apple cart in Maine was unexpectedly upset; the event was publicized as a forewarning of the November outcome in the nation; Harrison won and the portent from Maine came true—this is the historical stuff out of which Maine's initial prestige as a political barometer was wrought.[4]

[4]The simple fact that Maine held an early election and therefore supplied one of the first official voting tests of the campaign season would, in any event, have made the September balloting of interest to the country at large. At least this was the case with the September election in Vermont which was abolished only in 1913, and with other early states such as Pennsylvania, Indiana, Ohio, and Iowa, which held state elections in October until the 1870's and 1880's. But without the spectacular debut in 1840, the Maine prophecy probably would not have been so indelibly impressed upon the national consciousness, and would not have carried the glamour and authority that gave Maine a unique place among early states.

Barometer Politics—National

The widespread popular belief that the September election in Maine foretold the November returns in the nation made the local campaign of marked interest to the leaders of the two major parties. A victory in this early election, they believed would tend to bolster party morale throughout the country and would attract the so-called "band-wagon" voter, whose chief interest in an election is to align himself with the winning side. It was part of good political strategy, therefore, to manipulate the election pressures in Maine, so far as possible, in order that the barometer reading that would go out to the nation on election night should be "right." This tinkering with the barometer has become a part of the game of politics, and we wish to consider this aspect of the subject next, first, from the point of view of the national party leaders, and then from the standpoint of the local political chieftains.

The national leaders seek a favorable portent from Maine by reinforcing the local party workers with campaign orators and money. The extent and character of this aid has been made the subject of special investigation by the author. From 1910 to 1928, 337 speakers, it was found, had been sent to Maine by the two major parties to orate in their behalf in the September campaigns.[5] Of these nonresident speakers 215, or about two-thirds, brought the message of the G. O. P., while the remaining 122 carried the appeal of the Democracy. The list of orators is an impressive one, giving evidence that the responsibility of persuading the electorate of the barometer state to vote "right" is not placed upon the shoulders of hack workers in the party, but is largely reserved for men of the first rank. From 1910 to 1928 the political audiences of Maine heard ranking dignitaries as shown in Table 4.

A veritable bluebook of American politics and enterprise, the list contains the names of scores of outstanding leaders whose genius has helped to direct the destinies of the nation. For the Republicans, for example, there have journeyed to Maine such illustrious men as Theodore Roosevelt, Charles Evans Hughes, William E. Borah, Nicholas Longworth, Will H. Hays, Calvin Coolidge, Theodore Burton, Henry Cabot Lodge, Charles W. Fairbanks, George W.

---

[5]This figure was arrived at by scanning the pages of four leading newspapers for a period of one month in advance of the election day. It is not likely that all political addresses by nonresidents were reported in these newspapers, nor that the investigators caught every story that was published; hence this figure must be regarded as a minimum estimate.

Norris, Charles Curtis, James E. Watson, Frank B. Willis, George W. Pepper, George H. Moses, Ogden Mills, Warren G. Harding, James R. Garfield, and Simeon D. Fess. On the Democratic side, we find such luminaries as Champ Clark, William G. McAdoo, Josephus Daniels, Newton D. Baker, William C. Redfield, Franklin D. Roosevelt, J. Hamilton Lewis, Oscar Underwood, Thomas R. Marshall, Alton B. Parker, Bainbridge Colby, Samuel Untermeyer, Dudley Field Malone, Atlee Pomerene, Thomas P. Gore, Albert S. Burleson, Thomas W. Gregory, and Charles Dana Gibson.

On their appearance in Maine, many of these dignitaries spoke not once but several times. Brass bands and huge halls packed to the eaves with eager humanity are not necessary to draw the illustrious to this Down-East state, for even the biggest orators willingly mount small platforms there and speak to little clusters of people whether in Skowhegan or Caribou.[6]

TABLE 4
NONRESIDENT SPEAKERS IN MAINE SEPTEMBER CAMPAIGNS, 1910-1928

	Republicans	Democrats	Total
Former presidents and former vice presidents	3	..	3
United States senators	33	10	43
Cabinet officers	4	9	13
Congressmen	98	40	138
Governors	16	6	22
Mayors and state legislators	3	5	8
Other officials	10	10	20
Professional and business men and others	48	42	90
Total	215	122	337

It is not as easy to check upon the monetary as upon the oratorical aid sent to Maine by the national party headquarters, since the data are less available, but, by piecing together several scraps of material, a satisfactory approximation of the extent of this assistance can be secured. The author is informed by at least three substantial local

[6] A comparative study of nonresident orators appearing from 1910 to 1928 in the November campaigns in New Hampshire, where there was no barometric factor present, reveals the participation of 153 outside speakers. The comparable figure for Maine was 337. New Hampshire, of course, is worth only four votes in the electoral college to six for Maine, but it is geographically as accessible to speakers and is perhaps a little more in need of oratorical talent, since the customary pluralities separating the two major parties are not as large as those in Maine. If, for the sake of the argument, it be allowed that between the two states all comparative factors that might influence the appearance of nonresident speakers, save worth in the electoral college, cancel one another, then it is observed that the parties send over twice as many platform men to Maine as to New Hampshire, though the former state is worth but one-third more in the electoral college than the latter.

leaders that in recent presidential years the Republican National Committee has customarily contributed from $20,000 to $50,000 for use in the September campaigns. The Democratic figure, according to these men, varies widely, and ranges from nothing to $50,000, with sums of more than $10,000 the exception rather than the rule. From other sources of information, specific amounts can be cited. In 1912 the local Republican leaders drew $20,000 from national headquarters. This was more than one-half of the total cost of the state campaign.[7] In 1916, the grant was $40,000[8], in 1924, $19,000, of which $6,000 was returned;[9] and in 1928, $38,000.[8] The Democratic National Committee made up a $50,000[8] war chest for the exciting September campaign of 1916, contributed nothing in 1920[8] and 1924,[8] and sent $7,000[8] in 1928.

In both oratorical and monetary assistance, it will be observed, the Republican National Committee has made heavier contributions to the September campaign in Maine than the Democratic National Committee. This is largely a reflection of the political advantage to be derived, for, generally speaking, the party that is locally dominant can make the greatest use of the barometer reading for purposes of national advertising. Having been in power in Maine practically without a break since 1856, the Republican party reaps this tactical advantage. In most campaigns, the Republican exchequer has been amply filled, and the party leaders have not hesitated to concentrate men and money on the September fight. To do so is clearly shrewd political business, for the news of Republican victory in Maine is carried to the nation with booming headlines, and the party spokesmen are enabled to hail the returns as evidence of popular approval of the party's stand on national issues and as a portent of November victory.

For the Democrats, on the other hand, the sending of reinforcements to the September battle ground is something of a tactical luxury. The Republican point of view is so strongly entrenched in the minds of the local voters, that, the only reward which the Democrats could expect from such an effort at best, would be to reduce the customary G. O. P. pluralities. This might be proclaimed

[7]*Portland Daily Press*, Oct. 3, 1912.

[8]Information supplied to the author by Miss Louise Overacker, of Wellesley College, who has made special studies of campaign expenditures.

[9]Orren Chalmer Hormell, *Cost of Primaries and Elections in Maine.* Bowdoin College Bulletin, No. 157, Municipal Research Series, No. 6.

throughout the country as a moral victory, but it would not carry much popular conviction since the newspaper headlines would still read, "Republicans Win Maine." Never too well supplied with campaign funds and not wishing to make a decided stand on a field where they are sure to be publicly whipped, the Democrats have usually been content to expend their electioneering energies in other directions. Conceptions of political advantage, of course, rule Democratic as well as Republican strategy. In 1916, for example, when the election of Woodrow Wilson depended upon the number of Progressives who could be kept from returning to the Republican ranks, the Democrats hurled their best oratorical shock troops and $50,000 into the Maine contest, in an effort to secure a barometer reading that would show this disposition of the Progressive vote. Similarly, the interest of the national Democratic chieftains in future Maine elections will, no doubt, be governed by tactical considerations.

BAROMETER POLITICS—LOCAL

From the point of view of the local political leaders in Maine, the prophetic prestige of the September state election represents an opportunity to be capitalized. A favorable omen in the first test of the political season, they know, is worth something to the strategy of a national campaign; hence they do not hesitate to press their claims for assistance upon the national party directorate. The aid thus obtained helps the local leaders to elect their men to the state offices. The assignment of distinguished orators makes it possible to stage political rallies with an all-star cast; the monetary appropriation hires workers, buys ink and paper and otherwise furnishes the sinews of political war.

But more than oratorical and monetary assistance from national headquarters, the barometric renown of the September election provides for the dominant party, at least, an effective electioneering theme. As pointed out previously, because the Republican party has been in the majority in Maine almost consistently since 1856, this party has made principal use of the theme. As urged upon the voters in every September campaign, the argument is that the whole nation is looking to the Maine returns, particularly to the vote for governor, for a prophecy of the outcome of the national election in November. The local faithful, therefore, must make sure that the Republican gubernatorial candidate receives a large plurality, for this will draw to the party's presidential nominee the floating vote that desires to be on the winning side, and will inspirit the party workers in other states to renewed labor. Should the Republican voters fail in their duty and allow the Democrats to cut down the usual G. O. P. majorities, the chances of the party in the nation will be severely injured. In the face of this larger responsibility to the nation, local prejudice should be set aside. The real issue at stake in September is not so much the governor and local questions, but it is the word that shall go out from the barometer state on election night.

By means of slogans, speeches from the public platforms, and editorials in newspapers, this barometer-duty appeal is skillfully hammered into the consciousness of the voters. The slogans employed are designed to link the gubernatorial vote with that for the presidency. In the campaign of 1908, the motto was "A vote for Fernald is a vote for Taft." The cry in 1916 was "Vote for Milliken and vote for Hughes." In 1920 the appeal was "Parkhurst by 25,000," it being thought that a plurality of that size would be regarded abroad as a tremendous Republican triumph and an omen of a Harding landslide. As a matter of fact, Parkhurst won the governership by a plurality of 65,346 votes, which made the Maine victory seem impressive, indeed.

From the public platform, national issues are continually discussed during a September campaign and the importance of the Maine vote to the psychology of the national effort is unceasingly emphasized. In 1920, to give but a single example of the numberless ones that might be cited, a Republican rally was held at Lake Cobbossecontee, near Augusta, at which Mr. Frederick H. Parkhurst, the party candidate for governor, and Mr. Will H. Hays, Chairman of the Republican National Committee, were the principal speakers. Mr. Parkhurst called attention to the momentous issues then facing the American people, particularly that of the League of Nations, and declared that Maine's "paramount obligation" was to blaze the political trail.

> Our September election [said the gubernatorial nominee] will exercise a vital if not a controlling influence over the November election. . . . The issues of the campaign are pregnant with importance, and upon their determination depends the destiny of our country, perhaps the civilized world."

Mr. Hays then followed Mr. Parkhurst to the rostrum and, in

[10] *Kennebec Journal*, Aug. 23, 1920.

the course of a stirring speech against the Democratic stand on the League of Nations, made an eloquent appeal to the citizens of Maine to do their duty.

> You hold the post of honor [Mr. Hays told his audience]. You must point the way. So before you go to the polls, let your eyes rest for a moment upon the twenty-third star of the forty-eight which gleams from the background of Blue. That is your star, the star of Maine, the North Star of the Union, unblemished from the time, more than a century ago, when it was added to the galaxy of our national emblem. Let it not be tarnished now. Illumine it afresh by sending forth the message that Maine continues inflexibly American and rejoices in the privilege of being the first to voice to her sister states the spirit of complete victory which surely in November will crown Warren G. Harding and Calvin Coolidge—now leaders of the party, then leaders of the Republic.[11]

The editors of Maine newspapers likewise do their part in tutoring the Republican voters on the national significance of their September ballot, drawing word pictures of a nation turning anxious eyes on the Maine vote and then profoundly influenced by the results. Back in 1856, when North and South were aflame over the question of extending slavery in the newly-settled territories of Kansas and Nebraska, the *Bangor Whig and Courier* editorially declared that the Maine September election could be justly regarded as a "turning point in the cause of freedom." Should the Democrats carry Maine, said the editor, the Republicans might lose the national election and thus give a permanent victory to the slave powers, "fixing the policy of slavery upon the American Union so long as it shall exist."[12]

In 1930, with the country in the throes of industrial depression and with the administration party confronted with a possible loss of the House of Representatives, an opportunity for service, scarcely less great than that of 1856, was seen by the *Portland Press-Herald*.

> A substantial Republican victory in Maine next Monday [said the *Herald*] may have an excellent effect upon the rest of the country. It may be what is required to turn the tide, to provide the impetus which is necessary to stimulate business and to pull the country out of the slough of inertia which it now seems to be in.[13]

The use of the barometer theme for local electioneering purposes is seldom of advantage to the Democrats, because this party is in the minority. To win the governorship of Maine, the Democrats must poll many votes that ordinarily go to the Republican candidates. The Republican voters are educated to the belief that their

[11]*Ibid.*   [12]Sept. 2, 1856.   [13]Sept. 3, 1930.

vote on state officers affects the national outcome; hence, should the Democratic leaders urge the people to do their barometer duty, they would gain no more support from their own followers, and would certainly lose many votes from Republicans who might be willing to scratch their state ticket if they could be assured that such action would not damage the chances of their party in the nation. Only in a few instances have the Democrats been able to make political capital out of the September election. In 1852, for example, when Democratic ascendancy in the state was being threatened by rebellion in the ranks over prohibition and slavery, the regulars urged people to stand by the caucus nominee lest the Democratic candidacy of Franklin Pierce for the White House be hurt.[14] In 1884, again, the Democratic leaders told their followers that the best way to beat James G. Blaine for the presidency was to reduce the customary Republican plurality in his home state.[15] In 1912, when national victory loomed for the party as a result of the Republican-Progressive split, Democratic orators urged the desirability of electing a governor of their political faith so that it "will point the way to an overwhelming victory [in the nation] in November."[16]

On the whole, however, the early election, with its barometer implications, is a political liability to the local Democrats. They receive little aid from their national headquarters, and they seldom have an opportunity to use the barometer-duty appeal in electioneering. It is not strange, therefore, to find that the Democrats have made repeated efforts in the state legislature to initiate a change in the voting date from September to November, thereby to eliminate the barometer factor from state politics. To change the voting date in Maine requires a constitutional amendment, which necessitates the authorization of a popular referendum by a two-thirds vote of both houses of the legislature, and then approval of the amendment by the people at the polls. Since one or both branches of the legislature have been consistently dominated by the Republicans, or at least controlled to the extent of blocking a two-thirds vote, all attempts to alter the state-election calendar have failed. The usual procedure has been to kill the bill in committee or to send the proposal to the floor with an unfavorable report, which is

[14] L. C. Hatch, *Maine, A History*, Vol. II, p. 360.

[15] Editorial, *Portland Argus*, Sept. 8, 1884.

[16] From a speech by Champ Clark at Ellsworth, Maine, as reported in the *Lewiston Journal*, Aug. 31, 1912.

speedily adopted by a straight party vote. From 1909 to 1929 every legislature except those of 1921, 1927, and 1929 has gone through this motion, and the legislative journal shows that similar occurrences took place in the sessions of 1889, 1887, and 1883, and in those of 1876 and 1875.[17]

Although the whole contest over the change of the voting date in Maine is essentially one of political advantage, the debates on the proposal in the House and Senate, as revealed by the legislative journal, are largely carried on in other terms. If there is a slight variation in the tenor of the remarks between the party spokesmen, it is perhaps the lot of the Democrats to touch the real issue somewhat more directly, since they are cast by the force of circumstances in the role of the dissatisfied minority. The Democratic legislators protest that the September voting date tends to make the state election a football for national politics and that, in the scramble for large and impressive pluralities, the proper consideration of local issues is precluded. They argue further that the September voting date involves a needless waste of money, since in presidential years a second election must be held in November to choose presidential electors. Finally, the Democrats contend, many farmers and fishermen, who cannot spare the time from their harvests to vote in September, would be able to go to the polls if the state election were held in November.

In opposing the change in the state-election calendar, the Republican legislators argue that the September date is best fitted to Maine's climatic and industrial needs, that this date has traditionally been accepted for a long period of time, and that the people are wholly satisfied with the present arrangement. Maine, they point out, is a northerly state where the winter climate is severe. In September the weather and the condition of the roads permit people to attend political rallies to hear discussions of the issues involved in the campaign, and later to go to the polling places to deposit their ballots. In November, on the other hand, the county roads have become mired and frozen, and travel to and from the polling places would be uncomfortable to the point of hardship, thus

[17]Only once (1923), so far as the author is aware, has a bill for the change of Maine's voting date been introduced by a Republican. Curiously enough, one Republican Governor, Bert M. Fernald, recommended the change, in his inaugural address of 1909, on the ground that it was "a waste of time and money to hold two elections [in presidential years] where one can do as well," but no contemporary observer conversant with state politics of two decades ago, with whom the author has talked, has been able to offer an explanation of this unusual act.

tending to disfranchise the farmers, the aged and decrepit, and the women. The men who go "up the river" in the fall to work in the lumber camps or to hunt and guide would also be disfranchised by the November voting date, say the spokesmen for the *status quo.*

That the September election involves extra expense, the Republicans readily agree, but they contend that the money is well spent, since the early voting date enables many people, who would otherwise be disfranchised, to exercise their voting rights. In presidential years the marked decline in turnout in the November election as compared with that in September, two months previous, is evidence, the majority leaders say, that the early election makes greater participation possible.[18]

While many of these arguments have been urged with conviction, and contain of themselves a certain measure of plausibility, the correct interpretive key to this legislative combat is that of political advantage. No one can read the record of the debates and fail to detect the twinkle in the eyes of many legislators as they spoke for the purpose of the public record. More than in impassable roads or in the disfranchisement of the various types of voters, the Republicans are interested in retaining the September voting date for the help it brings from the National Committee and for the electioneering value of the barometer appeal. More than with the fishermen bobbing off the coast in September while others vote, or with the cost of a second election every four years, the Democrats are concerned with the handicap that Maine's early election compels them to work under. The Republicans are "in" and their knowledge of politics bids them yield no advantage that will make it easier for them to be put "out." The Democrats are "out," and if they could remove the barometer handicap, it would be easier to get "in." This is the substance of the issue in a nutshell.

It becomes clear from the above discussion that the Maine early election, which gained its initial renown as a result of a "historical accident," has proved of tactical advantage to the party leaders and has been skillfully exploited by them. However much of truth there may be in the saying "As goes Maine, so goes the nation," at least part of the unique authority which the maxim has exercised

[18]This latter argument, of course, neglects the fact that the chief electioneering effort is made in September. It is then that the state officers are elected, and it is then that the political fireworks—parades, rallies, speeches, placarding, house-to-house canvasses, etc.—are touched off. Practically no campaigning is done by either party for the November presidential election.

in the field of political prediction can be ascribed to the publicity given to it as a result of its propagandistic value.

Testing the Barometer

We can now proceed to an experimental analysis of the "As goes Maine" rule to determine how much truth there is in this predictive maxim. Certainly a great may people have believed in the reliability of the formula. Hardheaded politicians, apart from their use of the slogan for electioneering purposes, have been known to set their courses in the light of the September returns; newspaper editors have sworn by the saying, and thousands of voters and lesser party workers have believed in its authenticity. Are these people placing their faith in superstition or in fact? How sound is the logic of the concept? How accurate are the political predictions from Maine?

The customary approach for a critical examination of the Maine barometer has been to test the premises upon which the predictive formula is based. Are the Maine voters typical of those in the nation at large, and are the factors that enter into the state election in September comparable to those at work in the presidential election in November? Here a great deal of data might be introduced to show the character of the state and national population and the purport of the issues fought out in the local and national elections. But this approach will be avoided in the present discussion, because no analytical headway can be made from this angle of attack. After similarities and dissimilarities of population and political issues were noted between Maine and the nation, it would still be necessary to consider actual predictive performance, for that is the only item that really counts. If the barometer is reliable, the outcome of national elections can be experimentally forecast from the Maine returns; if the device is unreliable, test prognostications will show themselves wide of the mark. Let us, therefore, examine the Maine slogan in the concrete terms of election figures.

The first question must be: What specifically is the barometer formula? In meteorological work, technicians read their instruments according to set rules, and these readings they fit into prescribed formulas to arrive at weather predictions. Before we can proceed with our analysis, we must find analogous rules for reading the Maine barometer, and definite formulas to follow in making our test predictions of the country-wide political weather. The search through the Maine literature for such procedure reveals a surprising amount of vagueness, generality, and difference of opinion, but at least three interpretations can be distinguished which are definite enough to give direction to our check-up experiments.

THE LITERAL FORMULA

Probably the most widely held and the least critical interpretation of the Maine barometer is the literal one: "As goes Maine, so goes the nation." If the Pine Tree State elects a Republican governor, the nation will elect a Republican president. It was this interpretation that Alfred E. Smith was endeavoring to refute when, upon receiving the news of a Republican victory in Maine in 1928, he said:

> There used to be an old saying that "As goes Maine, so goes the nation"—except when a Democratic President is elected. I never was optimistic enough to think Maine would be anything other than Republican.[19]

The literal formula has a very plausible ring that makes a rational appeal to even the most hardheaded men. The author asked an editor in Maine if he believed it to be true that the nation goes politically in November as his state goes in September, and the editor's answer was: "Isn't it a fact that the election of a Republican governor in Maine is most often followed by the election of a Republican president?" And, indeed, this is true. The skeptic who is familiar with the succession of governors in Augusta and of presidents in Washington can name exceptions—1916, 1912, 1892, etc.—but the editor is right, for the literal rule succeeds in prediction more often than it fails. If we go back to 1840, when Maine first came into the limelight as a political barometer, we find that in 16 of the 23 elections from that date to the present, the party that seated the governor of Maine also elected the president of the United States. Sixteen successes out of 23 trials is not a bad record; at least anyone with gaming proclivities, who depended upon the literal formula for inside information, would not think it so. But this high percentage of successes does not prove that the Maine September election is a good instrument of prediction; rather it is but a reflection of the fact that both Maine and the United States have been predominantly Republican since 1856. Eighteen of the 19 Maine governors elected in presidential years, and 14 of the 19 presidents elevated to the White House during this period have belonged to the Republican party. None of the 5 Democratic presidential victories, from the

[19] *New York Times*, Sept. 12, 1928.

election of James Buchanan to the second election of Woodrow Wilson, have been preceded by the seating of a Democratic governor in the September election. Since 1856, therefore, the prophecy from Maine, under the literal interpretation, has been reliable only when a Republican has been elected president. Before 1856 when the Democrats were in power in Maine, the right signal was given in 1840, 1844, and 1852, but in 1848 a Democrat was chosen to head the state government, whereas the Whig, Zachary Taylor, won the presidency.

If for the predictive maxim, "As goes Maine, so goes the nation," we should substitute the comparatively simple slogan "Whig and Republican presidents forever," we should achieve the same number of predictive successes, for in 16 out of the 23 elections since 1840, a Whig or Republican has won the first office of the land. The latter rule, in fact, is a shade the better, because it is simpler and is less troublesome to apply. The political prognosticator who follows its tenets is not compelled to wait breathlessly for the September returns before giving out his forecasts, but can sit back in his easy chair and predict a Republican president for 1932 with the assurance of past experience that his prophecy has just as much chance of being correct as any based on the Maine election under the literal formula. This being true, it must be apparent that this interpretation of the Maine returns offers no practical predictive aid that the use of a simpler technique would not give.

The Formula of the Republican Norm

The next interpretation of the barometer is a more complex one, advanced by the majority of political experts and journalists who speak or write on the subject. These men take the position that, because Maine is customarily Republican, the significance of the early election does not turn on party victory, but upon the size of Republican plurality. According to this version, the following sequences are operative:

Maine September Election		National November Election
Normal Republican victory	*indicates*	Normal Republican victory
Republican landslide	*indicates*	Republican landslide
Subnormal Republican or Democratic lead	*indicates*	Democratic victory

Under this formula, Republican pluralities are generally computed in terms of the vote for governor. The figure that constitutes a "normal" G. O. P. victory is customarily determined by the experience of the preceding few elections. After the Civil War, many Republican gubernatorial candidates won office by margins of 15,000 to 20,000 votes, and this range was widely accepted by commentators as the "normal" plurality for this party. Any return falling within these limits, it was believed, gave reasonable assurance of Republican ascendancy in the nation in November; a lead of more than 20,000 foreshadowed a landslide for the party and one of less than 15,000 signified probable defeat. With the coming of woman suffrage, many observers raised this norm to 40,000; but it is difficult to find unanimity of opinion on this question, since the plurality figures for 1920, 1924, and 1928 vary widely and since electioneering motives often obscure unbiased judgments. The propagandists with majority-party sympathies are prone to define the norm in low numbers in order to make the actual pluralities appear more impressive by contrast, while those of the minority party set the norm high so that the significance of the impending majority victory may be discounted.

Let us test this second formula in the light of actual election figures. In Table 5, for the period from 1856, when the Republican party first contested the presidency, to 1928, are given the popular pluralities per 100 votes cast for the Maine governor and for the president of the United States. No plurality figures, it will be observed, are shown for the elections of 1856, 1860, 1880, 1912, and 1924. This is because the gubernatorial race in Maine and the presidential contest in the nation were not fought out along the same major party lines. Any use of the Maine election for predictive purposes assumes that the party categories, at least the major ones, are the same for both the state and the nation. When this is not true, a comparison of the two campaigns has doubtful meaning.

The plurality per 100 votes cast is given for each election, rather than the actual number of votes separating the two leading candidates, in order to make the figures of the several elections comparable with one another. In political circles, it is customary to compare pluralities from one election to another without reducing these margins to percentages. If the total vote cast in each election is the same, such comparisons are valid, but if the turnout varies, the practice may obviously lead to faulty reasoning. A plurality of 480 votes in a turnout of 8,000, $\left\{\frac{480}{8,000} \times 100 = 6 \text{ percent}\right\}$ for example, is a better showing than a plurality of 1,000 in a turnout of 25,000, $\left\{\dfrac{1,000}{25,000} \times 100 = 4 \text{ percent}\right\}$ though the former appears to be the smaller when judged in terms of actual votes. By expressing pluralities as percentages of the total vote cast, this difficulty is avoided, the plurality for any election so expressed being comparable with that of any other election stated in similar terms.

TABLE 5

PLURALITY PER 100 VOTES CAST FOR GOVERNOR IN MAINE AND FOR PRESIDENT IN THE UNITED STATES

Year	Governor		President
1856	Rep.—Dem.—Whig	noncomparable	Rep.—Dem.—American
1860	Rep.—Dem.	noncomparable	Rep.—Two Dems.—Const. Union
1864	R 17		R 10
1868	R 15		R 5
1872	R 13		R 12
1876	R 11		D 3
1880	Rep.—Fusion Dem. and Greenback	noncomparable	Rep.—Dem.—Greenback
1884	R 14		D 1
1888	R 12		D 1
1892	R 10		D 3
1896	R 39		R 4
1900	R 28		R 6
1904	R 20		R 19
1908	R 5		R 9
1912	Rep.—Dem.	noncomparable	Rep.—Dem.—Prog.
1916	R 9		D 3
1920	R 32		R 26
1924	Rep.—Dem.	noncomparable	Rep.—Dem.—Prog.
1928	R 39		R 17

To aid in visualizing the relationship between the popular pluralities of the Maine governor, on the one hand, and those of the President of the United States, on the other, the plurality indices given above are plotted by pairs in Diagram I. On the horizontal scale are laid out the Maine gubernatorial figures, and on the vertical scale the presidential indices for the nation. In September, 1864, for example, the Republican party elected the governor of Maine with a margin of 17 votes for every 100 cast. In November this party's candidate, Abraham Lincoln, won the presidency by a popular plurality of 10 votes per 100 cast. To plot these figures, we count 17 on the Republican half of the Maine scale and 10 on the

AS GOES MAINE

Republican half of the national scale and mark the point as in the diagram. Other election pairs are plotted in similar manner.

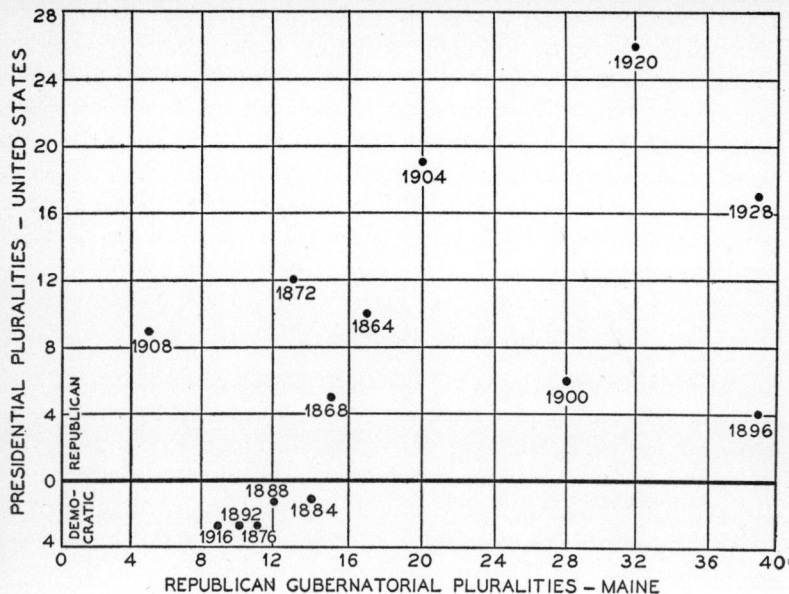

DIAGRAM I

Scatter Diagram Showing the Relation between Gubernatorial Pluralities in Maine and Presidential Pluralities in the Nation
(Horizontal and vertical scales show pluralities per 100 votes cast.)

Now if the broad currents of political sentiment in the nation are truly reflected by the Maine September returns, the plotted points on the chart should show an orderly pattern. As the Maine gubernatorial pluralities grow smaller, or approach zero on the diagram, the national pluralities should likewise be drawn toward this point. As the Maine pluralities grow larger, the national pluralities should show the same tendency. The reader will observe that the diagram demonstrates no such prognosticative sensitivity, the plotted points being scattered over the chart with little rhyme or reason. In 1872, for example, a Republican gubernatorial margin of 13 percent (13 votes per 100 cast) in Maine foreshadowed a 12 percent presidential plurality for this party in the nation, but in 1884, with virtually the same barometer reading, 14 percent, the Democrats won the presidency by a popular plurality of 1 percent. Again, in the elections of 1868, 1896, and 1900, the Republican presidential plurality in the nation was practically the same, 5, 4, and 6 percent, but the readings from Maine varied widely, 15 percent in 1868, 39 percent in 1896, and 28 percent in 1900. In other words, the record shows that the barometer is not consistent, sometimes promising sun when there were clouds and clouds when there was sun. The reader can multiply these illustrations from the data given on the chart. Because of this demonstrated lack of sensitivity between the size of Maine gubernatorial margins and presidential pluralities in the nation, we are forced to the conclusion that the September returns under this second interpretation are of no value for practical forecasting purposes.[20]

The Formula of Identical Fluctuation

A third interpretation of the Maine prophecy is one which appears frequently in newspaper discussions and which finds such an able exponent as Mark Sullivan, the noted Washington political correspondent and author of the widely-read contemporary history, *Our Times*. This formula, briefly stated, is that party strength in the forty-seven states, as expressed in terms of the popular vote for presidential electors, fluctuates in the same direction and to the same degree as that of the party nominee for governor in Maine. To illustrate, the G. O. P. gubernatorial candidate polled approximately 70 percent of the total vote cast in Maine in 1928. Suppose he polls but 60 percent in 1932. This would mean that the 1932 Republican strength in Maine is $\frac{6}{7}$ of what it was in 1928. According to Mr. Sullivan, it would then be predicted that the Republican

[20]Measured mathematically by means of Pearsonion correlation, the sensitivity of the relationship betwen Maine gubernatorial and national presidential pluralities is $r=.53$. The nonstatistical reader can follow the argument by knowing that if $r=1$ (unity), the Maine barometer would perfectly predict the presidential pluralities in the nation. Any value of r less than unity gives progressively less accuracy in prediction. It is true, of course, that the electoral, not the popular, vote determines the winner of the presidential election, but if there were any predictive validity in the Maine returns, we should expect to find it in the popular vote, since the electoral vote often fluctuates erratically as a result of small shifts in the popular vote. The relation between Maine gubernatorial and electoral college pluralities is $r=.41$.

A similar test applied to the vote for Congressmen in Maine and the nation yields a correlation coefficient of $r=.58$. Between the proportion of the total vote polled by Republican candidates for Congress in Maine and the proportion of the total seats in the House won by the Republicans the relation is $r=.48$. Correlation of Maine election returns with those of individual states shows varying degrees of sensitivity, but none of these relationships is close enough to give practical predictive aid.

proportion of the total popular vote for presidential electors in each of the 47 states would be $\frac{6}{7}$ of what it was in 1928.[21]

The author has taken the pains to test this interpretation with actual election figures and has found that the resultant predictions are as erroneous as those based on other formulas. The reader will not be burdened with the details of the somewhat involved experiments necessary to prove the point. Suffice it to say that the major premise upon which the formula is based is, in good part, inconsistent with the facts. According to the rule, party strength in "all" states fluctuates in the same direction as in Maine. Actual tests show that, barring the influence of third-party irregularities, this proposition holds true in but 64 percent of the cases. With the political trend in one third of the states moving in the opposite direction from that in Maine, it is apparent that the predictive formula set forth by Mr. Sullivan cannot be productive of reliable forecasts.

A second interpretation advanced by Mr. Sullivan is that the September canvass forecasts the number of people who will attend the November polls. "This," he says, "is probably the most reasonable of all the inferences to be made from the Maine vote."[22] In 1920, to use Mr. Sullivan's illustration, 205,615 ballots were cast in the September election in Maine. Four years later the local turnout was 251,836. This was a gain of 23 percent, or, in other words, the 1924 attendance at the September polls was 123 percent of what it was in 1920. From this it could be predicted that the number of people who would go to the polls in November in each state would be 123 percent of the total who voted in that state in 1920.

In his illustration Mr. Sullivan makes no allowance for varying rates of population growth between Maine and other states. For the past five decades, at least, the natural increase of the electorate has been much more rapid in the nation than in Maine; hence, under the system of computation used in the illustration, the barom-

---

[21]If the drift were reversed, *i. e.*, if the Republican candidate for governor polled 60 percent in 1928 and 70 percent in 1932, the shift, in order to avoid absurd results, would be expressed as a fraction of the greatest possible movement toward 100 percent. In this case the rise would be $\frac{70-60}{100-60}$ or $\frac{1}{4}$ of the greatest possible gain. This figure could then be appropriately applied to other states.

[22]*New York Tribune*, Sept. 11, 1924.

eter might perfectly foreshadow country-wide interest in voting, yet erroneously predict actual turnout. Since the Maine election is supposed to reflect political conditions alone, not population changes, the latter factor must be eliminated from the predictive formula. This can be done by expressing turnout as a percentage of the population 21 years and over $\frac{\text{Total attending polls}}{\text{Pop. 21 years and over}} \times 100$ instead of the actual number of votes cast. Satisfactory approximations of the adult population on the date of any given election can be made by adjusting the latest census figures in the light of annual population growth.[23] Turnout forecasts can then be computed according to the principle set forth in the discussion of the first interpretation of the Maine barometer by Mr. Sullivan, as given on page 42.

With this necessary modification, let us put Mr. Sullivan's turnout formula to the pragmatic test. The period between 1884 and the present is selected for the experiment because the needed census figures on the population 21 years and over are available only for these years. Using the forecasting rule set forth above, the proportion of the people of voting age who would attend the November polls in the nation was predicted from the September turnout in Maine for the twelve presidential elections held during this period. The average error of these predictions, as shown in Column 6 of Table 6 was 4 persons for every 100 in the adult population. In order to set up a standard for comparison, a ridiculously simple forecasting maxim was then concocted, namely, that the same proportion of the adult population in the nation will vote in the current presidential election as voted in the election of four years previous. Under this rule the average turnout error was 4 persons per 100 in the adult population (see Col. 7 of Table 6) which is exactly the same margin of inaccuracy as that sustained by the Maine formula. This final interpretation of the barometer, therefore, must be rejected, since it offers no predictive aid that cannot be had by the use of simpler techniques.

Conclusion

This discussion of the Maine barometer as an instrument of political prediction may now be summarized in three propositions. These are:

[23]For the period antedating the latest census, this can be done by arithmetically interpolating figures between census dates. For the post-census period, figures may be arithmetically extrapolated on the basis of the actual growth for the preceding ten years.

(1) The September election in Maine initially gained barometric authority as a result of a fortuitous combination of historical circumstances, and not through scientific observation that the nation voted as did Maine.

(2) For tactical advantage, political leaders have consistently publicized and affirmed (often with real conviction) the "As goes Maine, so goes the nation" slogan, and this propagandistic usage has done much to conserve the popularity of the maxim.

(3) The Maine early election is not a sensitive indicator of political trends in the nation and offers no practical forecasting help that cannot be had by the use of simpler techniques.

In the light of these findings, the September returns from Maine cannot be seriously regarded as an omen of the national election outcome.

TABLE 6

Turnout Predictions for the Nation on the Basis of the Maine Barometer and Simple Rule

	Percentage of adults 21 years* and over				Error in predicting national turnout	
(1)	(2)	(3)	(4)	(5)	(6)	(7)
Year	Actually voted in Maine in Sept.	Actually voted in nation in Nov.	Would vote in nation in Nov. on basis Maine barometer	Would vote in nation in Nov. on basis of simple rule	Maine barometer (Diff. col. 3 and col. 4)	Simple rule (Diff. col. 3 and col. 5)
1880....	79	72				
1884....	74	70	68	72	2	2
1888....	73	71	69	70	2	1
1892....	64	68	62	71	6	3
1896....	59	72	63	68	9	4
1900....	54	67	66	72	1	5
1904....	58	58	69	67	11	9
1908....	61	58	61	58	3	0
1912....	60	54	56	58	2	4
1916....	63	63	58	54	5	9
1920....	43	44	43	63	1	19†
1924....	53	45	53	44	8	1
1928....	44	54	37	45	17	9
Median average error..........................					4	4

*Male to 1916 inclusive; male and female from 1920 on.
†Advent of woman suffrage. Large error due to small percentage of female adults who attended polls.

Chapter IV
STRAW POLLS ON CANDIDATES
The Straw Poll and the Principle of Sampling

When a manufacturer desires to learn the quality of his run, he withdraws a finished piece at stated intervals and submits the product to a suitable test. A highway commissioner makes short-time studies of crossroad vehicular traffic in order to regulate the operation of his signal lights. In their work the manufacturer and the highway commissioner, are making use of the principle of statistical sampling. By testing a small sample, they have gained knowledge about a larger whole. The straw vote applies this principle to the measurement of political sentiment. In a preëlection poll, the voting intentions of a few citizens are ascertained in order that it may be known how the great mass of people are likely to vote.

However commonplace the idea of sampling is in industry or social studies, it is more difficult for people to accept the validity of its application to straw polls because of the analogy of an election. In a democracy the collective wishes of the people are ascertained by legal polls in which practically every adult has the right to engage. While only a little more than half the people 21 years of age and over in the nation actually do exercise their franchise in general elections, the number of ballots cast is sufficiently large to give the impression of universal participation.[1] With a straw vote, on the other hand, the right to participate is denied to all but the specially selected few, the number of ballots collected being very small compared to the official election totals. How such a small portion of the citizenry can speak with authority for the great body of voters is difficult for many people to understand.[2]

Theoretically, there is no reason why the technique of sampling should not be as trustworthy when applied to the measurement of preëlection sentiment as when it is employed in other fields of social

---
[1] See pp. 101-2.

[2] Some of the general distrust of straw vote returns is also due, no doubt, to demonstrated unreliability. Many polls have been taken in a very loose and unscientific manner with resultant error in the returns. Because of lack of understanding of sampling procedure, interpreters have charged these errors against straw polls in general, whereas they should be debited to straw polls in particular.

observation. The reliability of a sample, here, as elsewhere, is a matter of how the few cases are selected for test purposes. A dependable sample must first be representative of the voting population from which it is taken. This quality is sought by choosing cases by random methods, or, in other words, by arranging the selective process so that every unit in the population has a fair chance of being chosen in the sample. Secondly, a sample, to be reliable, must be adequate in size, enough units being chosen to effect stability of return. If these requirements are met, and if the character of the voting population remains in its original form—in this case, if people do not change their voting intentions—all samples, including those of preëlection sentiment, can be relied upon as representing the truth within prescribed limits.

In the present chapter and the next, interest will be centered on straw polls taken for the purpose of measuring voting preferences on candidates standing for public office. In the chapter following, attention will be given to polls designed to reflect mass sentiment on public questions.

American Experience with Straw Polls on Candidates

Although public interest in straw votes has only become widespread in the past ten years, as a result, largely, of the publicity attendant upon the nation-wide enterprises of the *Literary Digest*, preëlection polls on candidates have been taken since the turn of the century. To indicate the extent of this experience, the chief institutions that have sponsored straw votes will be named, and attention will be directed to their principal undertakings.

An early pioneer in the field of political prediction, and in the use of the straw vote as a measuring device, was the *New York Herald*. This paper made forecasts in local, state, and national elections, and, in some presidential campaigns, devoted a whole section of the Sunday paper to the subject. Before 1900, in the campaigns for the presidency, the *Herald* gathered preëlection reports and estimates from all over the nation, and, on the basis of these data, forecast the probable placement of states in the electoral college. This type of predictive activity was gradually expanded into systematic straw polls.

In the presidential campaign of 1904, the *Herald* maintained a number of scouts in up-state New York to make county estimates, and also took a poll of 30,000 registered voters in New York City.

Four years later this newspaper collaborated with the *Cincinnati Enquirer,* the *Chicago Record-Herald,* and the *St. Louis Republic,* making an electoral college forecast based on the street-corner polls of these middle-western papers, and on those taken by the *Herald* in eastern cities, together with reports received from special scouts and correspondents. In the presidential campaign of 1912, the *Herald* again collaborated with these three newspapers and also with the *Boston Globe,* the *Denver Republican,* and the *Los Angeles Times* in a nationwide poll of 37 states. In 1916 this group of newspapers conducted a poll in 36 states.

The *Cincinnati Enquirer,* one of the principal straw vote collaborators of the *New York Herald,* commenced its polling activities in the presidential campaign of 1908 by conducting a canvass in its home state of Ohio, and in the neighboring states of Indiana, Kentucky, and West Virginia. Since that time the *Enquirer* has conducted a straw poll in every biennial election in Ohio except in 1926, and in presidential years, with the exception of 1928, has polled Indiana, Kentucky, and West Virginia as well.

The *Columbus Dispatch,* another leading Ohio newspaper, sponsored its first straw vote in 1906. In that year it conducted a poll in the city of Columbus to determine the probable division of votes in the race for secretary of state and representative in Congress from the local district. Two years later, in the gubernatorial and presidential race, the *Dispatch* canvassed the city of Columbus again, announcing this poll as "the most accurate and the most comprehensive ever attempted by a newspaper."[3] In 1916, when the state of Ohio astounded political observers by breaking away from its customary Republican allegiance and voting for Woodrow Wilson, the *Dispatch* extended its straw vote to cover the state. From that time on, with the exception of 1918, this newspaper has conducted a poll in every gubernatorial and presidential campaign. The polling experience of these two Ohio newspapers, the *Cincinnati Enquirer* and *Columbus Dispatch,* provides some exceptionally good material for the study of straw votes.

Chicago has long been a center of straw-poll activity. In 1905 the *Chicago American* and the *Chicago Journal* conducted polls in the mayoralty contest of that year. During the years that followed, the *Journal* sponsored a dozen straw-vote undertakings in presidential, senatorial, gubernatorial, and mayoralty contests. The

[3] *Columbus Dispatch,* Oct. 13, 1908.

Chicago Examiner held local polls as early as 1915, and, later, as the *Herald and Examiner*, polled the city in the mayoralty contests of 1919 and 1927. The *Chicago Tribune* conducted a straw vote in the local mayoralty campaign in 1915, and, on numerous occasions since that time, has gathered straw ballots in Cook county and down-state Illinois, and in neighboring commonwealths.

The Hearst chain of newspapers has sponsored three presidential polls of national scope. In 1916 the coöperation of several independent daily papers was obtained and figures for a few localities, widely scattered, were gathered. Straw ballots were collected in 43 states in 1924, largely in metropolitan areas. In 1928 the Hearst chain conducted a systematic and thorough poll of 46 states, and made a very remarkable forecast of the election outcome.

The Rexall drug stores took a nation-wide poll in the presidential campaign of 1920, its extensive and widely-flung chain of merchandising stores serving as collecting points for the ballots.

The *Farm Journal*, a national periodical circulating among agricultural people, began gathering straw ballots in 1912, and has continued the enterprise in each presidential election since. Until the poll of 1928, however, the *Farm Journal* returns were lumped for the nation, and were very small in number. They scarcely deserve serious attention. In the 1928 undertaking, figures were gathered more or less systematically for 36 states.

Another farm periodical, the *Pathfinder*, with a circulation of about a million copies weekly, conducted a straw poll among its readers during the Hoover-Smith campaign. This publication has also canvassed the views of its subscribers on a number of controversial subjects, including prohibition.

The *Literary Digest*, whose name is almost synonymous with straw polls, commenced its forecasting activities in 1916. In that year it requested its readers to act as reporters and send information to the magazine on the sentiment in their communities for Charles Evans Hughes and Woodrow Wilson, the two principal aspirants for the office of president. The *Digest* also sought from leaders of labor opinions on how labor would vote, and conducted a postal card poll among its subscribers in the states of Illinois, Indiana, New Jersey, New York, and Ohio.

In 1920 the *Literary Digest* mailed 11,000,000 ballot cards, principally to owners of telephones, to test out public sentiment in the nation with regard to the men who were then being mentioned as possible nominees for the presidency. The ballot card specified several leading men from each major party, and asked the recipient to express a preference. The poll, therefore, was something of an unofficial presidential primary. In the subsequent presidential campaign, a post-card poll was conducted in California, Illinois, Indiana, New Jersey, New York, and Ohio.

In 1922 the *Literary Digest* conducted a postal-card poll on prohibition, and, in the same undertaking, asked for a categorical expression of opinion on the question of a bonus for World-War veterans, which was then agitating the country. Other nation-wide polls on prohibition were conducted by this magazine in 1930 and 1932.

In February, 1924, the *Literary Digest* mailed out 15,000,000 ballots to owners of telephones and automobiles scattered over the nation, asking if they favored or opposed the Mellon plan for tax reduction. In the fall of this year a nation-wide presidential poll, involving the mailing of 16,500,000 ballots, was held. Another poll of the nation was made in 1928 to test the division of popular sentiment between Herbert Hoover and Alfred E. Smith, the Republican and Democratic candidates for the presidency. In this undertaking 18,000,000 ballot cards were distributed. The voting record of the *Literary Digest* thus includes undertakings in a half dozen states in 1916 and 1920, and six nation-wide polls, three on the question of prohibition, one in the nature of a presidential primary, and two in general presidential elections.

Through correspondence with practically every editor of a daily newspaper in the United States, and through independent search, the author found that approximately 85 straw polls were held during the presidential campaign of 1928. Seventy-five of these undertakings were local in character, being confined to a city, county, or restricted trade area. Four of the enterprises, those of the *Columbus Dispatch, Cincinnati Enquirer, Chicago Tribune*, and *New York Daily News*, extended to the boundaries of the home state or included this state and neighboring commonwealths. Six of the polls were of nation-wide character. These were sponsored by the *Literary Digest*, the *Hearst Newspapers*, the *Farm Journal*, the *Pathfinder*, the *Nation*, and *College Humor*. In the polls of the last two periodicals small numbers of ballots were gathered from special classes widely scattered over the nation. They are of little significance and are not further mentioned in this study. The polls of the *Pathfinder* and the *Farm Journal* were largely participated in by the farming population. Of the six nation-wide straw votes in the campaign of 1928, the polls of the *Literary Digest* and the *Hearst Newspapers* must be regarded as the most systematic and thorough.

Why Newspapers and Magazines Sponsor Straw Polls

Practically all the experience in straw polls with which this study deals has come from newspapers and magazines. Great effort and no little expense has been incurred by these sponsoring bodies in the management of their straw votes, and there must be some special interest to prompt this expenditure of energy on the part of publishing houses. What is this interest? Why do newspapers and magazines conduct straw polls?

The first reason is that information on the voting intention of the electorate has news value. So great is the interest in a *Literary-Digest* poll, for example, that the American press uses literally thousands of column inches in reporting the straw returns.

The second and less obvious, but probably more important, reason for newspaper and periodical sponsorship of straw polls is their promotional value. As an advertising and circulation-getting device, they are extraordinarily effective. In marking a straw ballot, a person has his interest whetted in the sponsoring publication, and he is stimulated to buy that publication at the news stand in order to read about the poll in which he has participated. With the *Literary-Digest* polls, a special subscription offer is always mailed to each prospective straw voter, the order blank for the magazine forming one half of the straw ballot. The new readers obtained by this method are apparently large, for, as a result of the 1930 post-card poll on prohibition, which was mailed to 20,000,000 people throughout the nation, the *Literary Digest*, in an advertisement to prospective commercial users of magazine space, was able to say, "Almost overnight we have advanced circulation tremendously."[4]

The relative importance of the promotional and news aspects of straw-poll sponsorship varies with different publishing houses. Some managements are so absorbed in commercialism that the efficiency of their polls is destroyed, as when ballot forms are printed in a paper and people are encouraged to buy additional copies so that they may send in packets of ballots, as in a popularity contest. The more responsible directors who employ the straw vote as a

[4] *Literary Digest*, March 22, 1930, p. 3.

promotive device, however, are not so shortsighted; they realize that it is good business to produce accurate straw-vote returns, and they do not wittingly sacrifice the precision of their forecasts to near-term profits. Other publishing houses are interested less in the business and more in the news features of straw polls, sending their agents far beyond their immediate trade territories to gather voting preferences. With sponsors of long standing like the *Cincinnati Enquirer* and the *Columbus Dispatch*, preëlection polls have become a customary newspaper feature, catering to a definite reader interest. Such newspapers take a justifiable pride in their predictive records, and have a high order of responsibility to live up to. Direct promotion of circulation is here largely lost sight of, the sponsors being satisfied to pay their straw-poll costs as they would pay for the reporting of a national convention or any other important political event. The *Columbus Dispatch* expressed this attitude when it said of its 1920 straw vote: "The interest with which it has been followed by its army of readers amply repays this newspaper for the painstaking effort and expense attaching to an undertaking of this scope."[5]

How Straw Ballots Are Gathered

Straw poll reliability, as we shall see in this chapter and the two following, depends largely on the way the ballots are gathered. It is important, therefore, that we inquire next into this aspect of the subject. Three principal polling techniques can be distinguished. The first may be termed "ballot-in-the-paper," the second, "personal canvass," and the third, "mail." Each of these methods will be dealt with in turn.

The newspaper or magazine conducting a straw poll by the ballot-in-the-paper method prints a straw ballot in the publication for a certain period of time before an election. The reader is requested to cut out the ballot, mark it, and mail or carry it to the sponsoring organization. In polls of this type it is generally assumed that the readers of the sponsoring paper constitute a typical cross section of the electorate, and that large numbers of returned ballots will give a satisfactory indication of the voting intentions of the people. Many of the Hearst papers used this technique in the straw poll conducted by that chain in 1924. It is the standard practice of the *Pathfinder* and has also been employed by such

[5]*Columbus Dispatch*, Oct. 31, 1920.

papers as the *Erie Dispatch-Herald* (Pennsylvania), the *Omaha World-Herald* (Nebraska), and the *Buffalo Evening Times* (New York). Of the three principal straw-poll techniques, it is the least expensive in point of both time and money necessary to its management.

The second method has been termed the "personal canvass." This is the most common polling technique, and has been employed by such newspapers as the *Chicago Tribune*, the *Columbus Dispatch*, the *Cincinnati Enquirer*, the *New York Daily News*, and others. With this method, solicitors are employed to go around the community with straw ballots and ballot boxes, collecting votes in offices, factories, theaters, clubs, hotels, residences, trolley cars, depots, on street corners, or wherever people can be found. The solicitor accosts a prospective straw voter and makes a brief and courteous request, handing the person a blank ballot and pencil. The straw voter marks the ballot, folds it perhaps, and places it anonymously in the box held by the canvasser, who then turns to the next person and repeats the process.[6] Sometimes the canvasser maintains a booth in a public place, such as the lobby of a building or the state fair grounds. On occasion, voting machines are impressed into service, being stationed in one spot for a day or two, or hauled around a given territory on a truck. Some papers vary the method by leaving ballots and ballot boxes in stores, restaurants, and small shops. At the end of the day representatives of the newspaper call and collect the ballots. In a few instances, voting preferences have been gathered by means of telephone calls to the homes of citizens. In the Chicago mayoralty campaign of 1923, the *Chicago Tribune* employed a corps of telephone girls and collected several thousand straw votes by this method.

Although many papers send their agents out to seek ballots in a hit-or-miss fashion, trusting that by gathering straw votes in quantities they will cover all types of voting sentiment, expert users of the personal-canvass system map out definite routes and polling spots which they quite rigidly adhere to. The polls of the *Columbus Dispatch* afford a good example of this procedure. This paper commences its canvass for the November election about the first

[6] A novel and ingenious variation in this method is the personal canvass with buttons. The straw-vote taker displays a box containing campaign buttons of all presidential aspirants. He walks up to the pedestrian and offers him gratis the button of his choice. The pedestrian normally takes a button of the man he is supporting, thus revealing his voting intention. This system, though clever, is not widely employed.

week in September. Certain trained men from its regular staff are transferred from their customary tasks to the responsibility of organizing and directing soliciting crews. Each crew is assigned to specific territory from week to week, and is held strictly responsible for coverage of that area. No announcement is made to the public in advance of the appearance of these men. They enter an office or a factory without general warning, gather their ballots, and leave. In determining specific points at which the canvass is to be taken, the management thinks in terms of basic categories, such as geographical divisions, adherence to party, sex, nationality, religion, and economic calling. From long experience with straw polls and Ohio politics, the directors work out quotas, ordering a certain number of votes from the white-collar classes to be taken in specified buildings and a certain number of laboring votes from the XYZ steel mills, etc. To cover the relatively inaccessible farm vote, the personal canvass is supplemented by a post-card poll addressed to R. F. D. box numbers.[7] If the issues of the campaign appear especially to affect one economic class, leading the management to expect considerable shifting from normal party affiliation in this group, extraordinary canvassing effort is centered on this section of the electorate to make sure that whatever ferment is present is properly accounted for in the straw returns. Throughout the undertaking, a close check upon the results is maintained, and if the figures appear to exceed the bounds of reasonableness, repolls and special check-ups are ordered to give assurance of trustworthiness. The poll, considerably guided and checked by the newspapermen's "sixth sense," thus combines objectivity with intuition, which is thought to achieve the most accurate results.

Each paper that employs the personal-canvass technique for its straw polls gives the method an individual twist. The *Chicago Tribune* gathers a great many of its Chicago ballots in theaters. In polling down-state Illinois and surrounding states, it sends its canvassing crews to small towns with general instructions to get as representative a sample of the electorate as possible. Often it maintains a booth at a state fair to collect ballots from the farm groups.

In 1928 the *New York Daily News* organized a motor truck caravan that toured New York state during the presidential cam-

---

[7] The postal laws permit the addressing of mail matter to box holders without specification of name. This saves the *Dispatch* the expense of compiling a complicated mailing list.

POLLS ON CANDIDATES

paign. Each truck carried several canvassers with ballots and ballot boxes. The straw-vote truck would draw up in the main street in a small town or at a factory gate at closing time, sufficient demonstration was made to let the people know what was taking place, and then the solicitors circulated among the assembled crowd to collect the straw ballots.

The third method for conducting a straw poll is by the use of the United States mails. With this technique, stamped return post-card ballots are sent to a specified list of people. The recipient is requested to mark the post-card ballot and return it to the sponsoring agency. The mailing lists may be derived from numerous sources. Telephone directories, automobile registrations, city directories, assessment or income-tax lists, registries of qualified voters, all, or each, may supply names for the straw poll taken through the mails. Some poll sponsors buy their lists from commercial addressograph companies, allowing these companies to handle the details of mailing; other sponsors compile their own lists and contract for the detail of mailing or perform the task without outside aid.

Depending on the purpose of the straw-poll sponsor, inclusive or exclusive selections are made from these lists of names. If the undertaking is primarily for promotion, a ballot card is mailed to everyone on the list, since the business gain is proportional to the number of cards mailed. If the purpose of the poll is primarily one of news gathering, the expense is pared to the minimum, and a selection of perhaps every tenth or every twentieth name is made. In the Hearst nation-wide presidential poll of 1928, the mail method was largely employed by members of the chain. The *Literary Digest* uses this method exclusively.

Since a considerable part of the present discussion on straw polls will center upon the *Literary-Digest* undertakings, special attention to the mailing details of this publication must be given. The *Literary Digest* has long marketed its products by means of mail campaigns. As far back as 1895, it began to collect names of prospective purchasers of its books and magazines, and to keep these names on file. When published matter was announced, circulars describing the publication were sent to these people and orders were taken by mail. As first compiled, this list was made up largely of the names of professional people, lawyers, architects, physicians, engineers, club members, and so on. In 1895, it numbered 350,000 names. By 1900, the mailing list had grown to 685,000. At the present time the circularization list of the *Literary Digest* includes the enormous number of 20,000,000 names.

Since 1924 the *Literary Digest* has compiled its mailing list chiefly from telephone directories and automobile registration files, these names being more available than any other, and comprising a market in which published matter can be most readily sold. To secure the telephone names, the magazine gathers telephone directories from all over the nation. The automobile names are supplied by a commercial company that sends representatives to each of the forty-eight state capitols to transcribe the names and addresses of people who are there on record as owners of automobiles. Throughout the year the *Literary Digest* maintains a large staff of clerks whose sole duty is to keep its circularization list up to date. When the telephone directories are received at the magazine office they are handed over to this department for editing. Names of business firms are scratched out, residence addresses alone being desired. Whenever two telephones are listed for the same person, one is eliminated. By means of a large reference library containing city directories and yearbooks of all descriptions, mailing addresses are checked and verified. When the automobile list is received, the clerks, with infinite patience for details, check each name with those on the telephone list, discarding all names that already appear in the telephone directories. In this way duplication is reduced to the barest minimum consistent with the size of the editing task.

When the *Literary Digest* takes a nation-wide poll, it engages hundreds of persons, many of whom are home workers interested in earning pin money, to address the several million envelopes required to reach all the people on the magazine's circularization list. A corps of girls is then set to work in the *Digest* mailing rooms inserting in each envelope a straw ballot, a subscription offer, and such other advertising material as the magazine wishes to send to the public. These envelopes are then sealed and carried to a battery of post-office machines set up on the premises, which affix a printed stamp and cancel at the same time. Twenty or thirty postal employees take the mail as it comes from the stamping machines and arrange it by states, cities, towns and, in certain localities, even by streets, for carrier distribution. Once in the proper mail sacks, the letters containing straw ballots are carted to the mail trains in five- and ten-ton trucks, a thousand bags at a time.

To manage this mountain of detail, the *Literary Digest* is amply prepared from the point of view both of plant equipment and of past experience, for between 1915 and 1924 the magazine mailed the stupendous number of 162,000,000 circulars to prospective readers of *Literary-Digest* publications. A conservative estimate reaching to 1932 would place this figure at about 350,000,000. The efficiency with which this task is dispatched is attested to by the fact that only 1.3 percent of the mail matter sent out from the offices of the magazine is found to be undeliverable by the post office.[8]

Straw Poll Accuracy—Definition

A good deal of confusion exists as to the reliability of straw-poll returns. Many political leaders and newspapermen have told the author that they "have never seen an accurate straw poll." On the other hand, sponsors of these unofficial referenda almost universally proclaim the merits of their preëlection tests. How accurate are straw polls? In order to give the results of experience on this point, a definition of terms must first be made. This will be gone into at some length, for a great deal of dispute has arisen on the point of straw-vote accuracy, and the merits of this debate must be carefully weighed before a clear-cut and serviceable definition can be agreed upon.

First of all, straw-poll accuracy can be judged only by comparing the returns of the unofficial enterprise with those of the official election. From a logical angle, this definition presents a distinct flaw, but practically it is the only point of view that can be accepted. A straw poll taken October 1 may perfectly represent voting sentiment on that date, but if many minds are changed between then and election day early in November, the unofficial poll may prove to be quite unrepresentative. In these circumstances, the straw poll must be adjudged inaccurate even though it would have been a precise measurement of sentiment had the election been held a month earlier. As it is used here, then, the term "accuracy" means degree of coincidence between straw votes and official election returns, and the term "inaccuracy" means divergence of the straw figures from the official ones. In later pages we shall be especially interested in causes of divergence, and there inaccuracy will be referred to as "error in prediction."

The definition of accuracy in terms of coincidence and divergence

[8]The substance of this account is taken from the *Literary-Digest* booklet entitled "The Lord of Telephone Manor," eds. of 1925 and 1927.

between straw and official returns has been accepted by all straw-vote observers, but the exact form that this expression should take has been the subject of much confusion of thought and of the inevitable debate that follows. The matter can best be made clear by following the discussion between the *Literary Digest* and its critics on the precision of its nation-wide polls.

In claiming accuracy for its straw votes, the *Literary Digest* pointed out that in the 1924 presidential campaign it had predicted the winning presidential candidate correctly in all states but Kentucky and Oklahoma; and that in the contest of 1928 it had correctly placed all states in the electoral college except Massachusetts, Rhode Island, Alabama, and Arkansas.[9] In the popular mind, this demonstration gave striking proof of inerrancy, and wherever the question arose, this argument was cited in defense of the reliability of the polls. But this way of stating straw-vote accuracy, as was first pointed out by Dr. Fabian Franklin, a severe critic of the reputed precision of *Literary-Digest* polls, involves faulty reasoning.[10] Dr. Franklin's contention was substantially this: A straw poll is accurate or not according to the degree to which it correctly foreshadows the proportion of the total vote received by each candidate in the official election. The test of correct placement of states in the electoral college is a misleading criterion, since a poll may grossly overpredict the proportion of the popular vote received by the winner, yet place states correctly in the electoral college, provided the official election returns are one-sided. Only when the election is close will the electoral-college predictions of such a poll be upset and the error in forecasting the proportion of the total vote received by each candidate be revealed. In both the 1924 and the 1928 presidential campaigns, the *Literary Digest* overpredicted the popular vote of the winner, and the subsequent official returns proved to be one-sided; hence few states were mispredicted in the electoral college. Had these two contests been close, however, the *Literary-Digest* error in predicting the division of the popular vote would have caused it to assign many electoral votes to one presidential aspirant that would have been officially cast for the opposing candidate.

[9] This is on the basis of returns alone, without interpretation. The *Literary Digest* (March 24, 1928, p. 13) declared that it was fair to strike Alabama and Arkansas from the list of mispredictions because, in presenting the final straw-vote returns, it had called attention to the narrow Hoover pluralities in these two states and had suggested that they be credited to Smith on the ground that they are normally Democratic.

[10] See the *New York Times*, Oct. 15 and 20, and Nov. 26, 1928. Also the *New York World*, Nov. 29 and 30, 1928.

A concrete illustration will make this point clear. In Kansas, in 1928, the straw-poll returns of the *Literary Digest* showed that Herbert Hoover would receive 78 percent of all the votes cast in the official election. Actually Mr. Hoover secured 72 percent of the total vote cast. The *Digest*, therefore, predicted for Hoover 6 votes more per 100 cast than he actually received. But this overprediction of the Republican candidate made no difference in the placement of the state in the electoral college, because Mr. Hoover won Kansas by an overwhelming plurality. The straw vote could have forecast that he would receive 100 percent of all the ballots cast, which would have involved an error in predicting the division of the popular vote of 28 ballots per 100 (100—72 = 28), or five times that actually made, and still Kansas would have been correctly predicted for Mr. Hoover with no error in electoral-college placement. But suppose for the sake of the argument that the 1928 Republican overprediction be transferred back to the campaign of 1916. If the *Literary Digest* had taken a poll of Kansas in that year and if it had over predicted Charles Evans Hughes by 6 votes per 100 cast, as it did Herbert Hoover in 1928, underpredicting Woodrow Wilson by a like amount, and forecasting perfectly the proportion of the total vote won by the minor parties, then the magazine would have predicted a Hughes plurality of 6 votes per 100 cast, whereas Wilson actually won the state by a plurality of this size.[11]

If the *Literary Digest* had held a nation-wide poll in 1916 and made the same error in predicting Hughes' proportion of the total vote cast as it did in forecasting Hoover's strength, the magazine's forecast would have incorrectly placed nine states in the electoral college and would have given Hughes the presidency with an electoral vote of 342 to 189 for Wilson. This would have been a very grave forecasting blunder, for Wilson actually won the election with 277 electoral votes to 254 for Hughes. With identical error in predicting

[11] The figures illustrating this computation may be given here. Column 1 represents the proportion of votes received by each presidential candidate in Kansas in 1916. Column 2 gives the number of votes per 100 cast by which Hoover was overpredicted and Smith was underpredicted in Kansas by the *Literary Digest* in 1928. Column 3 represents the 1916 theoretical *Digest* prediction for the state, based on 1928 error. It is computed by adding columns 1 and 2.

Votes per 100 cast

	Col. 1	Col. 2	Col. 3
Hughes	44	+6 (Hoover error)	50 (Predicted winner)
Wilson	50	—6 (Smith error)	44 (Actual winner)
Minor	6		6
	100		100

proportion of votes received by the several candidates, therefore, the *Literary-Digest* straw vote, by the canon of state placement in the electoral college, is shown to be very accurate under the one-sided circumstances of 1928 and gravely inaccurate in a contest where the principal candidates displayed about equal strength. Obviously such a basis for reasoning on straw-vote accuracy is unsound and, as Dr. Franklin has rightly contended, must be rejected in favor of the more realistic maxim that straw votes approach accuracy only as they foreshadow the proportion of the total vote received by the several candidates in the official election.

A second essential element in the definition of straw-poll accuracy is thus established. Straw polls are accurate, not as they predict the winner of any given election, but as they forecast the proportion of the total vote received by the several candidates. The full implications of this statement will at first be difficult to accept, since it means that in many instances a straw poll that predicts victory for the wrong man must be adjudged more accurate than one that forecasts the winner correctly. The logic of the matter, however, is clear and permits of no other view. Take an example where two newspapers conduct straw polls in the same city for the same election, with results as given in Table 7.

TABLE 7
Hypothetical Returns (Expressed in Percentages) for Two Straw Polls and the Official Election

Candidates	Official	Gazette Forecast	Error	Sentinel Forecast	Error
A	51	49	—2	56	+5
B	49	51	+2	44	—5
	100	100		100	

Which newspaper made the more accurate prognostication? The answer is that the *Gazette* returns, though they forecasted B's election, whereas A actually won, were more accurate than those of the *Sentinel* that correctly predicted a victory for A, because the *Gazette* foreshadowed more closely than the *Sentinel* the proportion of the total vote that each candidate officially received.

There is no predictive virtue in a straw vote that is on the right side of an election outcome, if the range of variation due to crudeness of the measuring technique is large enough to have thrown the victory to an opposing candidate. Correct prediction of the winner under

POLLS ON CANDIDATES

these circumstances is wholly fortuitous. In preëlection interpretations of straw votes, allowance for the crudeness of the measurements must be made in the light of past experience. If the straw returns show A receiving 52 percent of the votes, and a fair approximation of measuring crudeness is 3 votes, then A's predicted proportion of the official vote may be represented by any figure from 49 percent to 55 percent. In this situation, the proportion of ballots to be received by each candidate will be known within a range of 6 votes, but, though the chances of victory for A are probably superior to those of B, the outcome must be looked upon as in doubt.

The third and final element in the definition of straw vote accuracy concerns the question of how to express error in predicting the proportionate division of the popular vote. The *Literary Digest*, using a second criterion in addition to that of state placement in the electoral college, described the accuracy of its straw vote in terms of the error in predicting the Hoover proportion of the total vote cast for all candidates. The straw returns, the magazine pointed out, showed that Mr. Hoover would receive 63.2 percent of all the votes cast in the nation, whereas, actually, the Republican candidate polled 58.8 percent of the total vote. The *Literary-Digest* poll, therefore, it was contended, was in error 4.4 votes per 100 cast.[12] The soundness of this characterization of the inaccuracy of the straw poll in terms of Hoover error against a background of the total vote cast will be discussed here in establishing the third element for a definition of straw-vote accuracy. Before dealing with this problem, however, we must give attention for a moment to an additional twist which the magazine gave to its report on the precision of its straw poll.

The *Literary Digest* argued as follows: If the *Digest* returns had shown that Mr. Hoover would receive 58.8 percent of the total official vote cast in the nation, as he actually did, this would have constituted a 100 percent perfect forecast. As a matter of fact, the magazine predicted that the Republican candidate would receive 63.2 percent of the total official vote, which involved an error of 4.4 votes per 100 cast. The *Literary-Digest* forecast, therefore, fell short of complete accuracy by only 4.4 votes, or, in other words, the 1928 *Digest* poll was 95.6 percent perfect (100—4.4=95.6).

Everyone would agree, of course, that so large a degree of pre-

[12]*Literary Digest*, Nov. 24, 1928, p. 13. The computation is based on semiofficial returns available, Nov. 14, 1928, which varied but little from the final official figures.

cision would justify all the praise the *Literary Digest* received for the reliability of its forecast. But there is a flaw in this reasoning which must be pointed out, in order that our evaluation of the *Digest* poll may rest on firm logical ground. The fallacy lies in the choice of a standard of performance, and can be best illustrated by applying the argument of the *Literary Digest* to the world of baseball. "Babe" Ruth, the most spectacular batter of all time, made 1,897 hits out of 5,476 times at bat during the period from 1915 to 1928, giving him an average of 0.346 (34.6 percent).[13] If he had been a perfect batsman, he would have made a hit each time he stood at the home base, and his average would have been 1.000 (100 percent). But "Babe" Ruth failed to score a hit 65 percent (100—34.6=65.4) of the times he was at bat; hence Ruth was an extremely poor ball player, being but 35 percent efficient as a batsman.

The fallacy of this conclusion, of course, is that the standard of performance by which Ruth's work is measured is unreal and far too high. To be sure, Ruth made hits but 35 percent of the time he was at the bat, but, though this was poor playing when measured against the impossible scale of perfection, it was superbly brilliant work when interpreted against the batting averages of the general run of baseball players.

In subtracting the 4.4 percent Hoover overprediction from 100 percent, the *Literary Digest* assumed that its straw vote could be in error by 100 percent. In practice, however, this would be incredible. Had Hoover been favored by every straw ballot returned to the *Literary Digest*, which is ridiculously improbable, the greatest possible overprediction would have been not 100 percent, but 41.2 percent, since Hoover actually secured 58.8 percent of all the official votes cast, (100—58.8=41.2 percent). But even the use of 41.2 percent as an index of the maximum possible error would be indefensible, since the magazine could not have conducted a normal referendum in which every ballot was marked for one candidate. The quest for a rigid yardstick of straw-vote perfection is thus an elusive one. Probably a more fruitful approach to the problem is to say with the *Literary Digest*: The straw returns gave Mr. Hoover 4.4 more votes per 100 than he officially received. Then, if an additional standard of performance be desired, it can best be sought, not in an absolute scale, but in a relative one determined by the predictive accuracy of competing straw votes.

[13] *World Almanac*, 1929, p. 774.

POLLS ON CANDIDATES

To go back now to the main question under discussion, namely, the legitimacy of characterizing straw-poll precision in terms of the error in predicting the proportion of the total vote received by the leading candidate, Dr. Franklin criticizes this practice on two counts. First, he declares, it is misleading to set the error for a single candidate against a background of the total vote cast. If the inaccuracy of a poll is to be stated in terms of candidates singly, he says, the proper procedure is to set the error in predicting the proportion of the vote received by each contestant against the background of that candidate's vote alone. Thus the Hoover error in prediction, according to this authority, should be stated:

$$\frac{63.2 \text{ percent Hoover predicted} - 58.8 \text{ percent Hoover official}}{58.8 \text{ percent Hoover official}} =$$

Hoover error of 7.5 percent of Hoover vote;

and not as the Digest expressed it:

$$\frac{63.2 \text{ percent Hoover predicted} - 58.8 \text{ percent Hoover actual}}{100 \text{ percent total official vote}} =$$

Hoover error of 4.4 percent of the total vote cast.

But no matter what divisor is used, Dr. Franklin continues, the characterization of error in terms of a single candidate (*Digest*) conveys a misleading impression of the accuracy of the forecast, because it leaves out of consideration the error in predicting the vote of other candidates. The 5.5 percent underestimate of the Smith vote in the nation by the *Literary Digest* in 1928, he contends, was just as important as the 4.4 percent overestimate of the Hoover vote, for, by adding the predictive error of the two candidates, it means that the plurality predicted for Hoover was 9.9 percent (of the total vote) greater than the Republican candidate officially won.[14] The magnitude of this error, says Dr. Franklin, is demonstrated by the fact that if the *Literary Digest's* prediction had been fulfilled, Mr. Hoover's popular plurality in the nation (as of November 14, 1928) would have been 9,700,000 votes instead of 6,200,000, the actual figure.

The differences of opinion between Dr. Franklin and the *Literary Digest* on the proper way to express straw-vote error are wholly a matter of definition of terms. Each form of computation may have

[14] If no minor candidates had run in 1928, the Hoover overprediction would have been balanced by the Smith underprediction.

its legitimate use. Let us discuss, first, Dr. Franklin's contention that error should be stated in terms of plurality, instead of in terms of the vote of a single candidate. It is quite as logical to say that the *Literary Digest* predicted Hoover's proportion of the total vote at 63.2 percent, which was 4.4 more votes in every 100 cast than Hoover actually received, as it is to say that the magazine gave Hoover a plurality of 9.9 votes per 100 greater than he actually polled. This Dr. Franklin admits. Experimentally, it may be advantageous to have error stated in terms of a single candidate for, in the search for the factors that cause inaccuracy, the configurations of error stand out more clearly when stated in this way than when expressed in terms of pluralities. Error of single candidates need not be misleading, for anyone who is competent to interpret straw votes is well aware that overprediction of the proportion of the total vote to be received by one or more candidates must be balanced by underprediction for the remaining contestants. Single-candidate error does not state the misprediction for other candidates, to be sure, but neither is plurality error perfect in this respect, for it deals only with the predictive inaccuracy of the winner and the runner-up, but not with the misprediction of the remaining candidates. By and large, statement of error in terms of the winning candidate does give a pretty fair picture of the accuracy of a straw poll.

Whether the error of a single candidate should be stated as a percentage of the total vote cast or as a percentage of the vote of that candidate, is the second issue raised by Dr. Franklin. It is just as logical to say that Hoover received 4 more votes per 100 cast for all candidates than the *Literary Digest* predicted, as it is to say that Hoover polled 7.5 more ballots per 100 Hoover votes cast than were foreshadowed. When the two methods are put to experimental trials, the expression of error against the background of total vote cast for the individual candidate appears to be the less serviceable. At least four disadvantages can be cited as follows:

1. It involves additional labor in calculation.

2. It introduces extreme numbers into the computations which upset averages, correlation coefficients, etc., thereby making straw-vote data more difficult to analyze. In 1924, for example, the Coolidge error for South Carolina, expressed in terms of the total vote cast was 8 percent, but in terms of Coolidge's own vote it was 377 percent.

3. It does not allow direct translation into terms of plurality

POLLS ON CANDIDATES

error. When two candidates alone are running and when error is expressed in terms of each candidate against a background of the total vote cast, plurality error is double the error of a single contestant.

4. It does not allow rapid check for accuracy of computations. When error is expressed as percentage of total vote cast, over and underpredictions balance.

A serviceable definition of straw-vote accuracy can now be made. Straw votes are accurate according to the degree of precision with which they predict the division of the total official vote between candidates.[15] The degree of precision, or "error in prediction," may be described in two ways, as plurality error or as error of single candidates. Plurality error is the difference between the predicted and the official plurality, divided by the total vote cast. Error for a single candidate is the difference between the predicted and the official proportion of the total vote for a given candidate—the winner usually—divided by (1) the vote of that candidate or (2) the total vote cast for all candidates. The selection of one of these methods for describing straw-vote error is a matter for each experimenter or critic to decide according to his own judgment.

In Chapters I and II, the forecasting accuracy of politicians and newspapermen was set forth in terms of plurality error. This method of description was adopted, because it is the custom of these men to make their predictions in terms of pluralities. In the summary of straw-vote accuracy to follow, consistency of statement will be maintained by giving plurality error. For some of the analytical demonstrations, however, error of the winning candidates, expressed according to the *Literary-Digest* formula, will be used. The reasons for preferring the *Digest* statement over that advanced by Dr. Franklin have been noted in a previous paragraph.

STRAW-POLL ACCURACY—EXPERIENCE

With the definition of accuracy agreed upon, what is the record of forecasting precision achieved by straw polls? The evidence on this question is presented in Tables 8-11. These tables show the plurality error, *i.e.*, the number of votes per 100 cast by which the

---

[15] By this definition, the reader will recall, a straw poll may, at the time it is held, reflect public sentiment perfectly yet be proved "inaccurate" by the official election returns because of change of voting intention following the marking of the straw ballots. Error in prediction, therefore, may be a result of bad sampling or of change of sentiment over a period of time. See p. 57.

plurality prediction missed its mark, for all the principal polls for which the author has been able to gather data. The tabulations give error by states for nine nation-wide straw votes, depict the predictive record of four middle-western newspapers over a period of years, and present figures on error for a substantial number of other polls under miscellaneous sponsorship. The straw polls included in the survey represent all types of canvassing technique, ballot-in-the-paper, personal canvass, and canvass by mail, as well as combinations of these methods. While most of the experience deals with presidential campaigns, a liberal number of polls from gubernatorial, senatorial, and mayoralty contests are also included. The data span a period of about two and one-half decades; hence the predictive precision of straw polls under widely different political circumstances is shown.

Because the survey covers the major portion of the nation's straw-vote experience, including polls by many sponsors, taken by different methods, in different campaigns in almost every conceivable political situation, an adequate answer can be obtained to the question: How accurate have straw polls been in the past? It must not be presumed, however, that the present demonstration offers, as well, an answer to the question: How accurate are straw polls likely to be in the future?—for old standards of performance should be excelled in time to come. A great deal of predictive error shown in the accompanying tables has been plainly due to careless management and lack of understanding of correct sampling technique. As the peculiarities of the straw-poll device become better known, and as sponsors become more skilled in the handling of this measuring tool, there is little question but that error in prediction will be materially reduced. The remarkably accurate forecasts here shown for some of the better-managed polls afford support for this belief.

Let us look first at the predictive results achieved by the nine nation-wide presidential polls. The plurality error by states is shown for each poll in Table 8. At the bottom of each column, the error by states is averaged to give a single figure whereby the accuracy of each enterprise may be characterized. In Table 11 these averages are recapitulated for the purpose of ranking the nine polls according to their error in prediction.

TABLE 8
Plurality Error by State for Nine Nation-wide Presidential Straw Polls

State	Literary Digest			Hearst Newspapers		Path-finder 1928	Farm Journal 1928	Rexall drug store 1928	New York Herald	
	1924	1928 Uncorrected*	1928 Corrected*	1924	1928				1912	1916
Ala...	8	9	1	9	0	39	..	18	..	..
Ariz...	21	4	17	10	34	33	..	4	3	15
Ark...	4	23	19	..	..	15	..	4	..	..
Cal...	17	5	12	23	7	4	7	13	3	31
Colo..	12	11	1	15	41	1	2	2	9	16
Conn..	29	30	1	0	4	1	30	3	8	10
Del...	12	18	6	21	2	29	36	13	23	10
Fla...	18	15	3	19	1	69	..	5	..	..
Ga....	10	6	4	11	6	5	..	16	..	..
Idaho.	10	4	2	9	0	22	13	0	1	8
Ill....	15	9	6	12	4	13	5	7	7	17
Ind...	24	17	7	7	0	7	5	5	9	7
Iowa..	3	18	15	7	15	9	20	11	11	2
Kan..	7	12	5	..	11	3	6	5	14	8
Ky...	3	1	4	31	1	14	13	18	16	26
La....	41	36	5	..	..	41	..	38	..	..
Me...	15	11	4	6	5	24	1	2	7	4
Md...	8	8	0	0	1	22	26	10	10	4
Mass..	28	34	6	16	10	4	52	2	1	2
Mich..	1	6	7	3	32	14	26	4	2	24
Minn..	16	22	17	62	8	18	16	7	22	8
Miss..	22	28	6	25	25	30	..	16	..	..
Mo...	12	18	6	5	1	4	12	11	19	1
Mont.	18	19	2	20	7	5	10	4	1	3
Neb...	13	9	4	15	4	2	10	6	5	13
Nev...	8	20	14	12	17	66	..	18	6	23
N. H..	34	27	7	14	17	47	37	15	10	13
N. J..	23	25	2	16	5	15	26	2	11	7
N. M.	12	9	3	9	1	14	..	4	5	12
N. Y..	23	6	17	8	3	2	23	38	3	8
N. C..	3	7	10	11	1	13	..	20	..	..
N. D..	16	18	15	39	2	14	36	15	3	18
Ohio..	11	11	0	3	5	17	11	22	7	2
Okla..	13	13	0	..	3	30	4	14	22	3
Ore...	13	5	8	5	9	5	10	1	4	8
Pa....	5	2	3	24	0	21	7	1	1	..
R. I...	45	35	10	10	7	15	58	17	10	2
S. C..	21	39	18	19	29	4	..	19	..	..
S. D..	1	20	17	21	14	6	24	8	40	7
Tenn..	3	8	11	11	1	18	39	20	..	10
Texas.	34	16	18	42	3	28	21	8	..	..
Utah..	13	12	1	3	13	9	27	5	1	..
Vt....	11	20	9	44	1	10	23	1	15	5
Va....	7	12	5	17	7	35	18	6	..	..
Wash.	5	6	4	12	0	13	1	11	6	7
W. Va.	6	12	6	19	8	20	34	12	5	20
Wis...	4	9	5	17	8	8	5	33	12	17
Wyo..	11	10	0	..	21	40	..	19	8	3
Md.av. plurality error per state..	12	12	6	12	5	14	17	9	7	8

*See pp 72–73, including n. 17.

TABLE 9
Plurality Error of Straw Polls of Four Middle-western Newspapers Over a Period of Twenty-Five Years—Also Plurality Error by State, Literary-Digest Polls, 1916 and 1920

Cincinnati Enquirer

Year	Office	Area covered	Plurality error
1908	Pres.	Ohio	3
1910	Gov.	Ohio	13
1912	Pres.	Ohio	7
1914	Gov.	Ohio	2
1916	Pres.	Ohio	2
1918	Gov.	Ohio	14
1920	Pres.	Ohio	1
1922	Gov.	Ohio	12
1924	Pres.	Ohio	0
1928	Pres.	Ohio	7
1930	Gov.	Ohio	8

Average* plurality error of 11 Enquirer polls of Ohio........ 7

Year	Office	Area covered	Plurality error
1908	Pres.	Ind.	2
1912	Pres.	Ind.	8
1916	Pres.	Ind.	5
1920	Pres.	Ind.	1
1924	Pres.	Ind.	9
1908	Pres.	Ky.	16
1912	Pres.	Ky.	16
1916	Pres.	Ky.	26
1920	Pres.	Ky.	10
1924	Pres.	Ky.	0
1908	Pres.	W. Va.	10
1912	Pres.	W. Va.	5
1916	Pres.	W. Va.	17
1920	Pres.	W. Va.	11
1924	Pres.	W. Va.	2

Average plurality error for 15 units of 5 Enquirer polls of neighboring states.......... 9

Chicago Journal

Year	Office	Area covered	Plurality error
1905	Mayor	Chicago	6
1907	Mayor	Chicago	15
1908	Pres.	Chicago	16
1915	Mayor Pri.	Chicago	14
1916	Pres.	Chicago	12
1919	Mayor Pri.	Chicago	10
1919	Mayor	Chicago	7
1923	Mayor	Chicago	4
1926	U. S. Sen.	Chicago	4
1927	Mayor Pri.	Chicago	4
1927	Mayor	Chicago	2
1928	Pres.	Chicago	1

Average plurality error of 12 Journal polls................ 7

Columbus Dispatch

Year	Office	Area covered	Plurality error
1906	Sec. State	Columbus	11
1908	Pres.	Columbus	2
1916	Pres.	Ohio	11
1920	Pres.	Ohio	10
1922	Gov.	Ohio	10
1924	Pres.	Ohio	4
1926	Gov.	Ohio	7
1928	Pres.	Ohio	0
1930	Gov.	Ohio	0

Average plurality error of 9 Dispatch polls.............. 7

Chicago Tribune

Year	Office	Area covered	Plurality error
1915	Mayor	Chicago	19
1919	Mayor Pri.	Chicago	13
1919	Mayor	Chicago	9
1923	Mayor	Chicago	6
1924	Pres.	Cook Co.	7
1924	Pres.	Ill. down-state	10
1924	Pres.	Ind.	20
1924	Pres.	Wis.	6
1924	Pres.	Iowa	2
1927	Mayor	Chicago	1
1928	Pres.	Chicago	3
1928	Pres.	Ill. down-state	3
1928	Pres.	Wis.	5
1928	Pres.	Ind.	5
1931	Mayor	Chicago	6

Average plurality error for 15 units of 8 Tribune polls...... 6

Literary Digest

Year	Office	Area covered	Plurality error
1916	Pres.	Ill.	5
1916	Pres.	Ind.	22
1916	Pres.	N. J.	19
1916	Pres.	N. Y.	28
1916	Pres.	Ohio	20

Average plurality error by state for 1916 Digest poll......... 20

Year	Office	Area covered	Plurality error
1920	Pres.	Cal.	9
1920	Pres.	Ill.	19
1920	Pres.	Ind.	18
1920	Pres.	N. J.	24
1920	Pres.	N. Y.	23
1920	Pres.	Ohio	27

Average plurality error by state for 1920 Digest poll.......... 21

*All averages used in this table are medians.

TABLE 10
Plurality Error of Straw Polls under Miscellaneous Sponsorship

Year	Office	Sponsor	Area covered	Method	Plurality error
1924	Pres.	Iowa Magazine	State of Iowa	Ballot in paper	2
1924	"	Omaha Daily News	Omaha, Neb.	" " "	14
1928	"	Atlantic News-Telegraph	Cass Co., Iowa	" " "	7
1928	"	Dansville Breeze	Dansville, N. Y.	" " "	3
1928	"	Erie Dispatch-Herald	Erie Co., Pa.	" " "	8
1928	"	Ft. Madison Democrat	Ft. Madison, Iowa	" " "	31
1928	"	Sheboygan Press	Sheboygan, Wis.		49
1906	Gov.	New York World	New York City	Personal canvass	3
1908	Pres.	Chicago Record-Herald	State of Iowa		4
1908	"	Chicago Record-Herald	State of Ill.	" "	9
1908	"	Chicago Record-Herald	State of Minn.	" "	7
1908	"	Chicago Record-Herald	State of Mich.	" "	9
1908	"	Chicago Record-Herald	State of S. D.	" "	18
1908	"	Chicago Record-Herald	State of Wis.	" "	5
1908	"	Chicago Record-Herald	State of N. D.	" "	8
1911	Mayor	Chicago American	Chicago, Ill.	" "	6
1919		Chi. Herald and Examiner	Chicago, Ill.	" "	5
1920	Pres.	New York Eve. Telegram	State of Conn.	" "	1
1920	"	New York Eve. Telegram	State of N. J.	" "	5
1920	"	New York Eve. Telegram	Up-state N. Y.	" "	14
1920	"	New York Eve. Telegram	New York City	" "	12
1923	Mayor	Chicago American	Chicago, Ill.	" "	3
1924	Pres.	Adrian Telegram	Lenawee Co., Mich.	" "	12
1924	"	Cleveland News-Leader	Cuyahoga Co., Ohio	" "	1
1924	"	Des Moines Tribune	Des Moines, Iowa	" "	24
1924	"	Ft. Wayne Sentinel	Ft. Wayne, Ind.	" "	16
1927	Mayor	Chi. Herald and Examiner	Chicago, Ill.	" "	8
1928	Pres.	Adrian Telegram	Lenawee Co., Mich.	" "	1
1928	"	Ossining Citizen-Sentinel	Ossining, N. Y.	" "	22
1928	"	New York Daily News	New York City	" "	18
1928	"	New York Daily News	Up-state N. Y.	" "	23
1928	"	New York Daily News	State of N. J.	" "	18
1928	"	Yonkers Herald	Yonkers, N. Y.	" "	19
1928	"	Youngstown Vindicator	Youngstown, Ohio	" "	21
1905	Mayor	Chicago American	Chicago, Ill.	Mail poll reg. voters	7
1912	Pres.	California Outlook	Los Angeles, Cal.	" " " "	23
1928	"	Cincinnati Times-Star	Cincinnati, Ohio	" " " "	9
1928	"	Cleveland News	Cuyahoga Co., Ohio	" " " "	11
1929	Mayor Pri.	Buffalo Courier-Express	Buffalo, N. Y.	" " " "	4
1929	"	Buffalo Courier-Express	Buffalo, N. Y.	" " " "	15
1929	" Pri.	Pittsburgh Sun-Telegraph	Pittsburgh, Pa.	" " " "	6
1915	"	Chi. Herald and Examiner	Chicago, Ill.	Ballot in paper and mail poll of registered voters	16
1922	Gov.	New York Globe	New York City	Poll of theater audiences	16
1928	Pres.	Altoona Tribune	Altoona, Pa.	Voting machines in public places	25
1928	"	Buffalo Evening Times	Buffalo, N. Y.	Ballot in paper and personal canvass	13
1928	"	Canton Daily News	Canton, Ohio	Ballot boxes left in public places	44
1928	"	Cleveland Press	Cuyahoga Co., Ohio	Voting machines	36
1928	"	Ft. Wayne Sentinel	Ft. Wayne, Ind.	Ballot in paper and personal canvass	19
1928	"	Long Island Daily Press	Queens Co., N. Y.	Voting booths	12
1928	"	Omaha World Herald	Omaha, Neb.	Ballot in paper and personal canvass	19
1928	"	St. Louis Times	St. Louis, Mo.	Ballot in paper, ballot boxes left in stores, etc.	27
1928	"	Philadelphia Press	Philadelphia, Pa.	Post cards to registered voters in every fifth precinct of four wards supposed to be "typical"	25
1928	"	Trenton Sunday Times-Advertiser	Trenton, N. J.	Ballot in paper and personal canvass	3

Median average error for all (53) polls under miscellaneous sponsorship........... 12

TABLE 11
Average Plurality Error by State for Nation-wide Straw Polls

Sponsor	Year	No. of states	Median average plurality error per state
Hearst Newspapers.......................	1928	46	5
New York Herald and collaborators........	1912	37	7
New York Herald and collaborators........	1916	36	8
Rexall drug stores.......................	1920	48	9
Literary Digest..........................	1928	48	12
Literary Digest (corrected)*..............	1928	48	6
Hearst Newspapers.......................	1924	43	12
Literary Digest..........................	1924	48	12
Pathfinder..............................	1928	48	14
Farm Journal...........................	1928	36	17

*See pp. 72-73, including n. 17.

Here are shown some very remarkable predictions. On the face of the straw returns alone, without interpretive correction, the *Hearst Newspapers* forecast the 1928 presidential pluralities in 46 states with an average error of only 5 percent, *i.e.*, 5 votes per 100 cast. Expressed in another way, in terms of the error of single candidates, this means that the proportion of the total official vote polled by Mr. Hoover and Mr. Smith was predicted correctly within less than 3 percent for the two major candidates. The prediction for Ohio is typical in this respect. The straw-poll returns from this state indicated that the Republican candidate would receive 62.6 percent of the total vote and the Democratic candidate 37.4 percent. Actually Mr. Hoover polled 65.3 percent of the total official vote and Mr. Smith won 34.7 percent. In 13 of the 46 states in which the Hearst canvass was conducted, the plurality prognostication was in error 1 percent or less, which is virtually perfect prediction. The 1928 *Literary-Digest* poll, under interpretive correction, showed virtually as good average results as the *Hearst-Newspapers* poll of the same year, but discussion of this will be deferred until a later paragraph when the polls of this magazine will be specifically dealt with.

The Hearst poll in 1928 was conducted by twenty daily papers widely scattered over the country. The methodology used was largely that of a postal-card canvass. The mailing lists were drawn from various sources. In some states, telephone directories or automobile registration lists were employed; in others, names

POLLS ON CANDIDATES

were compiled from the registry of voters, from tax-assessment rolls, or from other available sources such as city directories. In large cities the personal-canvass technique was frequently used.[16]

The 1924 *Hearst-Newspapers* poll, with an average state-plurality error of 12 percent, was not as accurate as that of 1928. The apparent reason is that the Hearst organization did not go to work as systematically and as thoroughly in the earlier enterprise as it did in the one of more recent date. Many of the 1924 straw votes were gathered by the ballot-in-the-paper method, and metropolitan areas received representation out of proportion to their official voting strength.

The *New York Herald*, with the collaboration of the *Cincinnati Enquirer*, the *Chicago Record-Herald*, and other daily newspapers, made very good predictions in 1912 and 1916, showing an average state plurality error of 7 percent and 8 percent respectively, for these years. The *Herald* and its collaborators used the personal-canvass technique almost exclusively for the gathering of its straw ballots.

The Rexall drug stores poll of 1920, gathering ballots through its far-flung chain of merchandising stores, shows an average state-plurality error of 9 percent, which is a surprisingly good record considering the polling technique employed. Ordinarily the collection of straw votes from permanent booths located in stores or other public places allows large opportunity for ballot box stuffing and consequent error in the returns. According to newspaper reports on this poll, the Rexall management hired special clerks to superintend the ballot boxes and to keep a record of the people who had voted, which may have reduced duplication to a minimum. The author does not have searching information on the Rexall poll and does not know whether there is an inside story to it, *i.e.*, whether independent check-ups were made or other special guidance given to the collection of the straw returns.

The 1928 poll of the weekly magazine, the *Pathfinder*, taken by the ballot-in-the-paper method, erred, on the average, 14 percent in predicting state presidential pluralities. With this enterprise the spread of error between the best and worst state prediction was very large, the forecast for the state of Florida showing the enormous

[16] In Colorado, the poll was taken by ballot-in-the-paper technique under sponsorship of the independently-owned *Denver Post*. The plurality error for the Colorado return was 41 percent, the largest error for any state in the Hearst nation-wide poll. The Utah poll was taken by the independently-owned *Salt Lake City Tribune*.

plurality error of 69 percent. The *Pathfinder* circulates largely among farm people; hence the poll of this magazine is probably more a reflection of farm sentiment than of public sentiment at large.

The *Farm-Journal* poll of 36 states in the 1928 presidential campaign shows an average state-plurality error of 17 per cent. The returns for this enterprise were gathered by means of ballot-in-the-paper technique and by personal canvass at state fairs or other points of contact with farm people. A goodly portion of this error in prediction was no doubt due to the political complexion of the classes from which the participants were drawn, but also the lack of system in canvassing probably contributed to the inaccuracy of the forecast.

The *Literary-Digest* returns, on their face, show an average state-plurality error of 12 percent in both 1928 and 1924. In comparison with other national polls, this can be described as average performance, neither the best nor the worst. If the *Literary-Digest* figures are specially interpreted, however, the 1928 poll shows less error than any national undertaking except the *Hearst-Newspapers* poll of the same year. A legitimate basis for such interpretation probably exists in the consistent overprediction of the Republican vote shown by the polls of this magazine. In 1928 the *Literary Digest* overestimated the Hoover vote in every state, and in 1924 it gave Mr. Coolidge a greater proportion of the vote than he officially received in all states but 7. If La Follette had not run in 1924, these 7 states would probably have been overpredicted for the Republican candidate as well. From this consistent overestimation of the Republican vote, arises the hypothesis that the "tel-auto" population (owners of telephones and automobiles) which forms the *Literary-Digest* "electorate" is more Republican than the voting population at large; hence, under the *Digest* sampling methodology, overprediction for this party can be expected from year to year, and the predictive error shown by one poll can be used to correct the bias of the succeeding poll. When the 1928 straw returns are thus corrected on the basis of the error revealed in the 1924 poll, the average *Digest* plurality error by states is reduced from 12 percent to 6 percent.[17] Whether or not similar corrections would improve

---

[17] In Connecticut, for example, the 1924 *Literary-Digest* poll overestimated Coolidge's plurality over Davis 29 votes per 100 cast. On the face of the returns, the 1928 poll foreshadowed a Hoover plurality over Smith of 38 per 100 votes in this state. Adjusting this figure on the basis of the experience in the poll four years previously, the Hoover plurality is deflated 29 votes to 9, the corrected forecast. Actually Hoover carried Connecticut with a plurality of 8 per

the predictive accuracy of future polls—granted that such be undertaken—is, of course, an open question. In Chapter V the scientific basis for the correction will be discussed in more adequate detail.[18]

The earlier polls of the *Literary Digest*, taken in a handful of states in 1916 and 1920, were not as accurate as the later ones. In the former year a post-card canvass of *Digest* subscribers in 5 states showed an average plurality error of 20 percent. In 1920 a mail canvass in 6 states resulted in an average plurality error of 21 percent. The detailed figures on these undertakings are given in Table 9.

Turning now to the predictive achievements of the four middle-western newspapers that have long conducted personal canvass polls in local and state elections, we find in Table 9 a uniformly high record of performance. In 11 presidential and gubernatorial polls of Ohio since 1908, the *Cincinnati Enquirer* shows an average plurality error of 7 percent. For the polls of the neighboring states, which the *Enquirer* undertook in presidential campaigns, the average plurality error was somewhat higher, being 9 percent. This increased error is due, no doubt, to laxity in canvassing, for, the *Enquirer* never gathered ballots in these bordering states as systematically and as thoroughly as in the home state of Ohio.

The *Chicago Journal*, in 12 polls, mostly in local mayoralty campaigns, shows an average plurality error of 7 percent.

The *Columbus Dispatch*, in 9 polls, mostly in presidential and gubernatorial campaigns, shows an average plurality error of 7 percent.

The *Chicago Tribune*, in 8 polls in mayoralty and presidential campaigns, erred in predicting pluralities, 6 percent on the average.

These four middle-western newspapers, by means of their straw votes, have thus been able to predict the pluralities of two score elections with average error of from 6 to 7 percent. This is a very significant demonstration, for it shows that year in and year

---

100 votes cast. The corrected *Digest* prediction, therefore, showed a plurality error of 1 vote per 100, whereas uncorrected this error was 30 votes per 100. Strictly speaking, the logic of this corrective technique requires that the political campaign be fought out by the same parties in the two elections involved. In 1928 there was no counterpart to the independent candidacy waged by Robert M. La Follette four years previously; hence in those states where the La Follette vote was largest, the corrections tended to be less reliable. In Table 8 the 1928 Hoover plurality is corrected for each state on the basis of the plurality error of Coolidge over Davis, though La Follette was actually the winner in one and the runner-up in eleven states. In those states in which the Coolidge pluralities were underestimated in 1924, the 1928 correction, of course, calls for inflation, rather than deflation, of the Hoover-plurality predictions.

[18]See pp. 116-7.

out, in all types of campaigns and in widely varied political circumstances, straw-vote measurements made by responsible organizations have foreshadowed the official election returns with a high degree of faithfulness.

The final evidence on forecasting precision achieved by straw votes is furnished by the predictive record of 53 polls under miscellaneous sponsorship, as listed in Table 10. The average plurality error for these polls is 12 percent. This compares favorably with such national undertakings as those of the *Literary Digest* (uncorrected) or the 1924 Hearst poll, but does not constitute as good a showing as that made by the four sponsors of long experience in the Middle West. It is to be expected that the miscellaneous group would show a relatively high average-plurality error, because this classification includes many polls by sponsors who were unskilled in the technique of gathering straw ballots, or who did not give their polls the serious thought that is necessary to the success of these preëlection tests. In presenting the predictive error for miscellaneous polls in Table 10, the canvassing technique employed in each undertaking has been indicated. For convenience in printing, polls using the same canvassing method have been grouped together. No attempt has been made, however, to summarize the predictive accuracy of each type of poll by averaging the plurality error, because of the small number of cases in each group, and also because error is not alone a matter of the kind of polling machinery employed, but also of the skill in handling this machinery and of other special circumstances incident to the operation of the polling mechanism not here known.

Predictive Record of Straw Polls, Politicians and Newspapermen Compared

With the forecasting record of straw polls now before us, what can be said of the accuracy of this predictive device when compared with that achieved by the politicians and by the newspapermen? Are predictions based upon straw-poll returns more, or less, reliable than those made by forecasters employing other techniques? Figures for such a comparison are available for the presidential campaign of 1928.

From Chapter I the reader will recall that the average plurality error for Republican predictions in 16 states was 7 percent. For Democratic forecasts in 8 states, plurality error averaged 18 per-

POLLS ON CANDIDATES 75

cent. These figures characterize the politicians' predictive skill under the conditions of 1928.

For an index of the newspapermen's prognosticative ability under the same political circumstances, the average plurality error revealed by the *Editor-and-Publisher* poll may be taken. As described in Chapter II, this canvass of editors revealed an average plurality error of 13 percent.

The average state-plurality error of the four 1928 nation-wide straw polls, as given in the preceding section, was: *Hearst Newspapers*, 5 percent; *Literary Digest*, 12 percent; *Literary Digest* (corrected), 6 percent; *Pathfinder*, 14 percent; *Farm Journal*, 17 percent. It would seem fair to eliminate the *Pathfinder* and the *Farm-Journal* indices from the comparison on either one of two grounds. In the first place, these publications gathered their ballots almost exclusively among farm people; hence their polls do not represent the performance of the straw-vote device as applied to the measurement of preëlection sentiment in the large. Secondly, the straw preferences were gathered largely by the ballot-in-the-paper method, which is the most untrustworthy of the three principal polling techniques. Knowing the polling methodology of these two magazines, a skilled interpreter would be extremely cautious about accepting their tabulated returns as portraying the facts. Forecasts based on straw polls have this advantage over other forms of prediction in that the wheat can be separated readily from the chaff. Given a room filled with politicians or newspapermen with different opinions as to how the people will vote in a coming election, a disinterested person would have no way of choosing the opinion that is most likely to represent the facts. The inability of a party board of strategy to resolve a clash of opinion as to the status of preëlection sentiment is sufficient illustration of this. Given a dozen straw-vote measurements, however, it would be possible to choose the predictions that could be relied upon. One would need only to examine the methods used in the canvass and select the poll that employed the best sampling technique. If this were done for the nation-wide polls of 1928, the *Pathfinder* and the *Farm-Journal* returns would certainly be rejected in favor of those from the *Literary Digest* and the *Hearst Newspapers*.

If the reader allows this contention, we have a comparison of predictive ability as given in Table 12, which shows that the *Hearst-Newspapers* poll and the corrected poll of the *Literary Digest* predicted the outcome of the Hoover-Smith campaign more accurately than the Republican leaders and very much more accurately than Democratic chieftains and the newspaper editors. Uncorrected, the *Literary-Digest* poll yielded less accurate forecasts than those made by the Republicans but more accurate than those of the Democrats and of the newspaper editors.

TABLE 12

PLURALITY ERROR OF 1928 STATE PRESIDENTIAL PREDICTIONS BY POLITICAL LEADERS, NEWSPAPERMEN AND STRAW POLLS

	Average state plurality error
Political leaders	
Republican—16 States	7
Democrat — 8 States	18
Newspapermen	
Editor-and-Publisher poll of 925 editors of American daily newspapers—48 States	13
Straw polls	
Hearst Newspapers—46 States	5
Literary Digest—48 States	12
Literary Digest (corrected)—48 States	6

A similar comparison of 1928 predictions for the state of Ohio, as given in Table 13, tells the same story, the predictions resulting from the straw polls of the *Columbus Dispatch* and the *Cincinnati Enquirer* being superior to those of the local politicians and newspapermen.

TABLE 13

PLURALITY ERROR OF 1928 PRESIDENTIAL PREDICTIONS FOR OHIO BY POLITICAL LEADERS, NEWSPAPERMEN AND STRAW POLLS

	Plurality error
Political leaders	
Republican	14*
Democrat	24*
Newspapermen	
Editor-and-Publisher poll of 56 Ohio editors (concensus of opinion)	19
Straw polls	
Columbus Dispatch	0†
Cincinnati Enquirer	7†

*See Table 1. †See Table 9.

The unusual circumstances of increased registration, religious intolerance, and the prohibition issue, in the presidential race between Hoover and Smith may have made it exceptionally difficult for newspapermen and politicians to gauge voting sentiment in the

1928 campaign, and, in more normal times, forecasts from these sources may appear in a more favorable light when compared with the predictions based on straw polls. But the position of the straw poll as an accurate predictive device, it would seem, is secure, because a straw poll goes directly to the people for information on voting intention, and because the technique can be objectively controlled, and thus freed from the subjective biases that sometimes distort the observations of the politicians and newspapermen.[19]

Causes of Straw-Poll Error

The nation's experience with straw polls, the major part of which is included in the foregoing survey, shows many instances of remarkable accuracy in prediction and others of great inaccuracy. Since straw-poll forecasts are serviceable only as they are precise, and since any competent understanding of the technique of straw votes requires a knowledge of the influences that affect precision, we must next inquire about the factors that cause straw polls to be inaccurate.

Eight distortive factors can be distinguished. As the technique of preëlection polling becomes better known and more completely analyzed, some of these categories may be added to, broken down or combined, but they can be accepted here as affording a descriptive beginning. They are as follows:

(1) Manipulation: The count of the straw ballots may be dishonest. The sponsors of the poll may manipulate the returns to aid a candidate in whom they are interested.

(2) Stuffing the ballot box: The safeguards thrown around the poll may be insufficient to prevent duplication in voting by lazy canvassers or by enthusiastic friends of a candidate.

(3) Geographical bias: A straw poll in a city may neglect a strong Democratic or Republican ward, or a poll of a state may be taken in the cities and fail to include the farm vote.

(4) Class bias: A straw poll may cover a geographical territory inclusively, but the ballots may be gathered disproportionately from one economic or social class, thus coloring the poll with the political views of this class.

[19] In 1928, when the *Hearst Newspapers* printed straw-vote returns showing that Hoover would carry Missouri and certain other states, the poll managers in Chicago were bombarded with telegrams from able newspapermen in these states, declaring that when the officia votes were counted the Hearst people would be "the worst discredited forecasters in Christendom"; but events proved that the straw-vote figures were right and the protesting journalists wrong, the latter apparently having been misled by the vociferous demonstrations for the Democratic candidate in the metropolitan centers.

(5) Bias of selection in cooperation: All classes may be given an opportunity to participate in a poll, but one class may coöperate with the sponsors more than another.

(6) Bias of participation—nonparticipation: People may vote in a straw poll, but because of age, citizenship ineligibility, or disinclination, fail to vote in the official election.

(7) Adequacy: The number of straw ballots gathered may be too small to provide a perfect sample.

(8) Change of sentiment over time: People may honestly vote for candidate Brown in a straw poll, then change their minds and vote for candidate Jones in the official election.[20]

In the sections that immediately follow, insight into the operation of each of these factors causing sampling distortion, will be sought.

Manipulation of Returns by Sponsors

Few straw polls escape the charge of dishonesty in sponsorship. In 1924 Senator Pat Harrison, Democrat, of Mississippi, saw, for publicity purposes at least, a dire plot in the *Literary-Digest* presidential poll of that year. To him the *Digest* undertaking was part of the plan of the Republican campaign managers to deceive the public into believing that President Coolidge was a sure winner and thus to capture the "band-wagon" support.[21] A newspaper editor writes the author that he has never known a straw vote that was conducted honestly, *i.e.*, without deliberate endeavor to influence votes in the official election. Particularly difficult is it for critics to credit the large expenditure of money entailed in straw-poll sponsorship with honest intention. Why, for example, it is frequently asked, should the *Literary Digest* spend close to one million dollars for a nation-wide straw vote if it has no ulterior political motive? This enormous expenditure of money for the 1930 poll on prohibition the *American Issue*, the official organ of the Anti-Saloon League of America, suggested, was not of disinterested character. "Evidently," said the *Issue*, "those who are responsible for the *Literary Digest* poll are against prohibition.[22]

The general answer to these charges of dishonesty on the part of sponsors of straw polls is that practically without exception straw

---

[20]Change of sentiment is primarily thought of here as change in conviction. A somewhat variant type might be recognized, however, in the man who votes his true preferences in a straw poll, but, though unchanged in conviction, yields to social pressure and votes the customary ticket at the election. See pp. 95-96 for an example.

[21]*New York Times*, Oct. 10, 1924.   [22]*American Issue*, March 1, 1930.

returns are gathered with honest intent, and that inaccuracies of measurement are due, not to deliberate faking, but are almost always chargeable to faulty sampling technique. The simple guarantee of this is the fact that the cost of such dubious form of support for either candidates or issues is far greater than any sponsor can afford to pay. One of the most jealous possessions of a newspaper or a periodical is reader confidence. People do not buy publications which they feel they cannot trust. Reader confidence is an essential foundation for circulation, and circulation attracts advertising; hence the lifeblood of a paper is to a high degree dependent on the faith the editors keep with the public. It requires long years of patient and costly toil to build up reader confidence, and no editor in his right senses would jeopardize this asset for such a paltry sum as the few votes he might influence by faking his straw returns. The day of reckoning is never far removed in a situation of this kind, for should an editor falsify a straw vote to help his candidate, despite indications pointing to victory for the opposition, he would need to wait only until election day to be exposed. His own readers would notice the discrepancy, and rival editors might also make some observations on the difference between the straw and official returns. The offending editor would shortly be accused of dishonesty and double-dealing, and reader confidence in his paper would be correspondingly shaken.

Newspaper editors are well aware of these facts and, for the most part, they are exceedingly scrupulous in preserving the honesty of their polls. Some papers hire certified public accountants to guarantee the fairness of their count. A middle-western newspaper assigns one of its most trusted political reporters to the responsibility of conducting its straw polls, and relieves him of his regular round of contacts with the political world lest some factors of prejudice creep into the unofficial returns.

The managing editor of another middle-western newspaper considers the job of straw polling so important to the interests of his journal that he refuses to delegate the responsibility of management to a subordinate, preferring to direct the undertaking himself. At the commencement of the work he calls into his private office several of the best men on his staff, informing them that he is assigning to them the most important task that the newspaper has to perform this year, the faithful gathering of ballots for its straw poll. Each morning the men come to the office of the managing editor for their blank ballots, and each evening they hand the marked votes to him personally. "If there is one sure way for a newspaper to commit suicide," this editor told the author, "it is to conduct a fake straw vote."

Many newspapers that sponsor straw polls occasionally find themselves in the strange position of editorially urging the election of candidate Brown in one column and predicting his defeat in another. In the 1924 campaign for the governorship of Illinois between Len Small, Republican, and Norman L. Jones, Democrat, the *Chicago Tribune* was saying editorially, "Small, in our opinion, is the worst Governor the state has ever had." To elect him would be "an unpleasant lowering of community ideals."[23] Yet in the news section, the paper was reporting that "All straw votes taken by the *Tribune* indicate that Small will win.[24] Another illustration of the same point—and there are many—comes from the *Cincinnati Enquirer*. At the close of the 1930 gubernatorial campaign in Ohio, the *Enquirer* printed a two-column, large type editorial on the front page calling for the election of Myers Cooper, Republican, to the governorship of the state. In an adjoining column appeared a news article which declared that Cooper, on the basis of the *Enquirer* straw poll, would be defeated by a minimum plurality of 75,000 votes. Newspaper editors, of course, are fully aware of the beneficial effect of such a display in convincing the reader of the divorcement of the news and editorial departments of the paper; perhaps, even, they take special pains to emphasize the circumstance for its subtle effect on the reader, but the fact remains that straw polls are seldom deliberately influenced by editorial policy.

The loose accusations that partisan interests pay the bills of the leading straw polls are also groundless. It is doubtful if there is a single case of this on record in straw-voting experience. Sponsoring institutions pay their own bills, because their polls are business undertakings properly chargeable to the account of news gathering or to the advertising or circulation budgets. William Seaver Woods, editor of the *Literary Digest*, effectively answered all criticisms of this nature when, in meeting the challenge of Representative Tom Connally, Democrat, of Texas, on the honesty of the 1924 *Literary-Digest* presidential poll, he said:

> The Congressman wants to know who is paying our bill for this straw vote. The answer is that the bill is paid by the *Literary Digest*. It is a business propo-

[23]Ed., "Vote for Jones," Oct. 30, 1924. [24]*Chicago Tribune*, Nov. 3, 1924.

sition. Attached to each post card sent for balloting is a subscription blank for the magazine. The returns in subscriptions have been enormous and they have paid the expenses of the poll.[25]

One exception only must be taken to the proposition that straw-poll sponsors practically never manipulate their returns for dishonest purposes. A few editors contend that reader interest demands simulation of a hot race. If one candidate springs into a decisive lead from the beginning of the poll, interest, they say, tends to lag. Some newspapers, therefore, report their returns in such a manner as to indicate a close struggle, now giving one candidate the advantage, now another, finally, in the closing days of the campaign, feeding the true figures into the totals, thus allowing the real winner to bound out ahead on the home stretch. The editor who holds this theatrical view of his responsibilities takes care that his final printed figures are correct, for to do otherwise would be to risk exposure when the official election returns become available for comparison. The manipulation is thus of temporary nature, and falsifies only the picture of change of sentiment during the campaign. Most newspapers, however, do not make even this concession to a dubious practice.

STUFFING THE BALLOT BOX

The second factor that operates to produce inaccuracy in a straw poll is stuffing the ballot box. Every referendum, whether official or unofficial, must be protected from this form of tampering. With the former, the strong arm of the law and the watchfulness of the authorities are the deterring forces; with the latter, the ingenuity and vigilance of the sponsors alone guards the integrity of the ballot box.

There are three types of ballot-box stuffing in straw polls. First, there are the frauds perpetrated by lazy and unfaithful employees who prefer to concoct figures out of their heads rather than to gather them in the prescribed way; second, there are the distortions due to amateur enthusiasts who duplicate but a few times at most; and, third, there are the major conspiracies, chiefly of local character, that are engineered by professional politicians or persons interested in the candidacy of some aspirant to public office. The three types of polling technique described heretofore offer varying degrees of opportunity for fraud.

[25] *New York Times*, Oct. 9, 1924.

The polling procedure that is most vulnerable to ballot-box stuffing is the ballot-in-the-paper type. With this method of gathering straw votes, interested persons may buy several copies of the newspaper in which the blank votes are printed and clip, mark, and mail them in quantities to the sponsoring organization. Some enthusiasts confine their activities to mailing one vote per day, although the cost of postage exercises a deterrent effect. The defense which sponsors of this type of poll set up against these distortive activities usually consists of editorial appeal for fair play, and also a rule requiring each participant to sign his name or address, to his ballot, it being promised by the sponsor that under no circumstances will the voting intention of the participant be revealed. The idea is then to scrutinize the handwriting on ballots and discard duplications. But this safeguard never works, because repeaters that reach the sponsoring office a day apart cannot be detected without careful scrutiny of all ballots received up to that time, and no newspaper would go to that trouble to eliminate such duplications. Detection of repeating can only be made where large numbers of ballots, all signed in the same handwriting reach the straw-vote editor at one time. Moreover, the signature safeguard will not work because most people refuse to sign their names to a straw ballot. Especially is this true if the participant is planning to bolt from the party of his customary loyalty, for thus to reveal his intentions of deserting the party would be to risk imparting that fact to the local politicians, who might retaliate with some form of political recrimination. Many papers have started their ballot-in-the-paper polls with the demand for signatures, but almost invariably this requirement has been softened or disregarded entirely before the close of the referendum, because few people would coöperate on that basis. The ease with which a ballot-in-the-paper poll can be stuffed is one of the chief drawbacks of this type of polling technique.

The personal canvass poll is padded or not according to the quality of the personnel employed as canvassers and according to the method used in collecting the ballots. Many papers employ only trusted men from their regular staffs on their canvassing crews and inflict the swift and sure penalty of discharge if there is a suggestion of cheating. The papers that pick up temporary and lowgrade help for their straw canvass have more difficulty, of course, on this score. Given faithful employees in a personal canvass, distortion of the straw returns on account of ballot-box stuffing becomes a matter of how the votes are collected. Where stationery booths are set up in public places, the admirers of one candidate may vote as often as they please. In this regard one middle-western editor told the author that he had conducted a scientific experiment on a rival's straw vote. He instructed his men to vote as many times as they were able in the competing poll, and to keep account of the number of ballots they had cast. During the one lunch hour, one subordinate declared that he had voted fifteen times.

In its presidential poll of 1928, the *St. Louis Times* left ballot boxes and blank ballots at drug stores, cafeterias, and small shops around the town, collecting the straw votes at the end of every day or two. This technique offered great opportunity for duplication. The *Chicago Herald and Examiner*, in its presidential poll of 1924, distributed thousands of multiple ballots, each containing space for twenty signatures, to pedestrians and customers in small stores. The temptation to individual partisans to essay twenty different names in twenty different handwritings must have been very great indeed.

Well conducted personal canvass polls like those of the *Columbus Dispatch* and *Cincinnati Enquirer* endeavor to avoid duplication by "spot" canvassing. The straw-vote solicitors of these papers descend upon an operating point without warning, systematically collect their ballots, and leave. Little opportunity is thus offered to repeaters to get in their work. The same end is also achieved by avoiding public places and confining the canvass so far as possible to offices, factories, residences, etc., where men and women work.

Of the three canvassing techniques, the mail poll is the most difficult to stuff. With this method, the address list controls the selection of participants. Where the sample comprises 5 percent of the voting population, say, the cards are scattered so sparingly that it is exceedingly difficult for repeaters to make collections of them.

A very amusing and interesting example of an attempted mail-poll conspiracy on a large scale occurred in the 1929 mayoralty primary straw vote conducted by the *Buffalo Courier-Express*. In this undertaking the *Courier-Express* mailed a ballot card to every tenth person listed on the registry of voters. After the poll had been in operation for two weeks, a torrent of ballots, all marked for Frank X. Schwab, the irrepressible mayor of Buffalo, who was seeking renomination on both the Republican and Democratic tickets, began coming in. For such eventualities, however, the *Courier-Express* was prepared. It had kept a record of the wards sampled, and had also instructed the addressograph company to mutilate the second f of the word "Buffalo" in the address on the return post card. When the ballots began pouring in from wards to which cards had not yet been mailed, all bearing a perfect f in the word "Buffalo," the *Courier-Express* knew that a conspiracy was afoot, and nonchalantly proceeded to sort out the spurious ballots, 3,902 in all, and preserve only the legitimate ones for the final count. In announcing that the villains had been foiled, the newspaper had its laugh on the politicians, declaring that they were "a little dumb" in allowing their plot to be so easily discovered.

The great number of ballots distributed in the mail polls of the *Literary Digest* encourages more duplication by partisan enthusiasts than in polls employing less numbers. In handling the *Literary-Digest* post cards the author has found a few instances of a dozen to eighty cards marked in the same handwriting with the same writing instrument, and canceled from the same post office at an identical hour, which is pretty good evidence that some master hand was at work. But the influence of this type of distortion in the *Literary Digest* returns must be adjudged negligible for at least four reasons:

(1) According to *Literary-Digest* estimates, the proportion of undeliverable ballots in its polls is very small, being about 1.3 percent of the total mailed.[26]

(2) The magazine employs men to scrutinize all ballots received and to eliminate those that bear identical handwriting and cancellation marks.

(3) The number of preferences collected in a *Digest* poll are so large as to minimize the influence of a few fraudulent votes.

(4) A compensating influence is always at work in connection with fraud, since the duplication of votes by an amateur of one political persuasion may be offset by the activity of another of opposite faith. This last argument, of course, applies to all straw polls.

To prevent major conspiracies looking to wholesale duplication of its ballots, the *Literary Digest* uses a special brand of paper that has a layer of color between the outer and inner ply of the paper. By tearing the card this inner streak of color is visible. Only a

[26]See p. 57.

few machines are prepared to manufacture paper of this sort and, during the progress of a *Digest* poll, their output is strictly accounted for. Curiously enough, the only major plot against the integrity of the *Literary-Digest* ballot box which has been discovered was engineered in the 1922 prohibition poll by members of a Massachusetts religious society who copied the magazine's straw ballot form more or less perfectly and canvassed for votes among their friends, because they thought the drys had been slighted in the distribution of ballots.[27]

Geographical Bias

To constitute a valid sample of preëlection voting intention, a poll must include voters holding all shades of political opinion in direct proportion to their numerical importance in the electorate. When one politically dissimilar group is given greater representation in the straw sample than it commands in the election, the unofficial returns are said to be biased in favor of that group. Disproportionate representation of one social class, however, is not synonymous with straw-poll error, for the accuracy of a poll is affected only if the favored class holds different voting intentions from those of the neglected class. The establishment of inaccuracy due to bias, therefore, requires proof, first, that one class is disproportionately represented in the straw sample and, second, that this favored class is politically different from the main body of voters. Four types of biasing factors which may operate to distort straw-poll returns have been named. The first to be discussed here is geographical bias.

With ballot-in-the-paper polls, geographical bias often has free play, because returns are classified by political subdivisions, whereas the ballots are actually collected in trade areas which have no necessary relation to voting districts. To offset this difficulty, participants are often asked to specify the county or state in which they are legal voters, but this system does nothing to prevent improper geographical selection within political boundary lines.

Personal canvass polls of states are frequently subject to geographical bias, because solicitors tend to collect votes only in accessible places. Towns usually form the loci of such polling activities and, in these, the main street most often receives the major share of attention, the tendency being to neglect the rural vote because of

[27]*Literary Digest*, Sept. 9, 1922.

its inaccessibility. The large plurality error of 32 percent for Michigan in the Hearst poll of 1928 probably originated in this manner.

Geographical bias is most easily controlled in a mail poll, because inaccessibility holds no terror for the United States post-office system. Once a complete mailing list is compiled, territorial coverage is assured, so long as the mails are delivered.

The *Literary-Digest* polls are frequently criticized on the score of geographical bias, the charge being made that names of city people are more readily obtainable for mailing lists than are those of country dwellers, and that, as a consequence, the urban classes are favored unduly in the distribution of the blank ballots. In the popular discussion of the 1930 *Literary-Digest* prohibition poll much was made of this point, dry spokesmen declaring that underrepresentation of the dry rural vote in the sample gave the straw returns a pronounced wet bias.

On their face, figures descriptive of the urban-rural composition of the *Digest* mailing list show urban favoritism. In "The Lord of Telephone Manor,"[28] a small booklet printed by the *Literary Digest* for the purpose of acquainting its advertisers with the circulation-getting methods of the magazine, data are given which show that the telephone list used in the straw polls reaches one person in 8 in cities of 2,500 and over, but only one person in 24 in communities with fewer than 2,500 inhabitants. The automobile list employed by the magazine was less urban in complexion, but still favored the city people by reaching one in 5 of this class of the population and only one in 7 of rural folk. These figures, showing greater urban than rural representation in both the telephone and automobile lists, would appear to clinch the contention of city bias in the *Digest* sample, but this conclusion cannot be accepted too hastily, because there is some reason to believe that, in terms of ballot cards actually returned—and this is all that counts—the farm people are virtually as well represented as the residents of cities. This fact is suggested by the following experiment.

The 1928 ballot cards returned to the *Literary Digest* from six states, Iowa, Kansas, Louisiana, Oregon, Virginia, and Wisconsin, were distributed into county of origination by reading the cancellation mark on the back of each card.[29] The number of people who

---

[28] 1927 ed., p. 43.

[29] The cancellation mark revealed the town from which the card was mailed. Reference to the United States Official Postal Guide made it a simple matter to group the towns by counties.

participated in the *Literary-Digest* poll to each 100 who voted in the official 1928 election was calculated for those counties 75 percent and more urban, and for those counties less than 75 percent urban. In the urban counties of the six states considered, it was found that 8.4 people participated in the straw poll to every 100 who voted in the actual election, while in the rural counties the comparable figure was 6.6. This demonstration would appear to indicate that the *Literary-Digest* returns do include city residents more than country dwellers, but that such bias is very small, and certainly is not the distortive influence that the critics of the *Literary-Digest* polls have supposed it to be.[30]

That this conclusion is sound is indicated by a second experiment

---

Tabulation of ballots by counties in this manner proceeds on the assumption that a voter mails his card in the county in which he votes. This may not always be true. Commuters to big cities often mail their letters where they work. Farmers deposit mail in their trading centers, many of which are across the county line. Letters gathered on R. F. D. routes may be canceled in a town situated in a county other than that in which the postal matter originated. In spite of these specific objections, however, figures derived from county sorting by cancellation marks are highly reliable. Several tests indicate this. In the 1928 Hearst mail poll of the state of Virginia, the participants were asked to designate the county in which they vote. By comparing these declarations with the cancellation marks on the returned ballots, it was found that 95 percent of the postal cards were canceled in the counties in which the citizens cast their legal vote. In the 1928 presidential poll of the *Literary Digest*, about 2.5 percent of the New Jersey straw votes were carried to New York City to be mailed. About 4 percent of the cards returned from the environs of Philadelphia were canceled in the metropolitan area. Both New York and Philadelphia, of course, draw an exceptionally large commuting public. The proportion of straw ballots canceled outside the county where the citizen votes is here shown to be very small. Since contiguous areas are most likely to be politically likeminded to a high degree, and, since a county both gains and loses ballots in the process of mail collection and cancellation, the total effect of drainage on county figures, derived from cancellation sorting, is wholly negligible. In a special study of R. F. D. routes in Yamhill county, Oregon, for example, the author estimates that "mail drainage" in the 1928 *Literary-Digest* poll caused an error in the straw returns for this county of only one vote in 1,000.

[30]The large urban bias on the face of both the *Digest* telephone and automobile lists, and its subsequent reduction to very small proportions in the straw poll returns needs to be reconciled. If the rural people coöperated with the magazine more than the urban folk, a ready explanation would be afforded since it could then be said that though the rural areas are less represented than the urban in the *Digest* mailing list, the farm class makes up for the discrimination by returning a greater proportion of their ballot cards. This explanation is not tenable, however, since one class appears to coöperate to about the same extent as the other. (See p. 99.) A second hypothesis is that city people tend to own both automobiles and telephones, whereas the country people tend to own one convenience to the exclusion of the other. If this were true—the author has no data with which to verify this suggestion—the coverage failure of one type of mailing list in the rural sections would tend to be made good by the other list, and the combined tel-auto list would tend to canvass the rural voters as extensively as the urban voters. The operation of this process may be illustrated as follows:

Make-up of sample for area where urban and rural population is equal:

Names	Rural	Urban
Names on telephone list	xx	xxxxx
Names on automobile list	xxx	xxxxx
Names on combined tel-auto list	xxxxx	xxxxx

in the six states for which the *Digest* ballot cards had been sorted by counties. Each county was weighted according to the percentage of the total state vote that that county cast for presidential electors in 1928. The Hoover percentage of the total straw ballots from each county was then calculated and a weighted Hoover prediction was made for each of the six states. By this manipulation, disproportionate representation of counties, *i.e.*, geographical bias as expressed in county units, was eliminated from the *Digest* sample. If this disruptive influence were operative to any great extent, we should expect its elimination to make a marked change in the state forecasts. As a matter of fact, the weighted and unweighted predictions, as shown in Table 14, give practically identical results. Hence again it can be concluded that geographical bias had very little effect on the reliability of the *Literary-Digest* straw vote.

TABLE 14

WEIGHTED AND UNWEIGHTED LITERARY-DIGEST PRESIDENTIAL POLL PREDICTION FOR SIX STATES, 1928

State	Predicted Hoover percent of total vote, weighted	Predicted Hoover percent of total vote, unweighted	Difference weighted and unweighted
Iowa	70.4	70.7	0.3
Kansas	78.4	77.9	0.5
Louisiana	41.6	41.6	none
Oregon	67.3	66.9	0.4
Virginia	59.2	59.9	0.7
Wisconsin	59.2	57.9	1.3

In this second experiment, the similarity between the weighted and unweighted state predictions has been interpreted to mean that there was very little disproportionate representation of counties in the *Literary-Digest* sample. While this conclusion is, no doubt, the correct one to draw from the figures, a second interpretation is theoretically possible. The counties of A, B, and C, for example, may have been overrepresented in the straw sample for a given state, and the counties of X, Y, and Z underrepresented, relative to their numerical importance in the official state vote, yet no error occurs in the *Digest* prediction for that state because of the similarity of political sentiment in the two county groups. This alternate interpretation suggests the desirability of a study of the homogeneity of voting behavior as between election districts. If it were found, for example, that a sample of voting intention in one county could be made to stand for a dozen contiguous counties, the labor of straw polling could be greatly diminished. In that case, the gathering of straw votes could proceed by homogeneous voting areas, and would not need to be inclusive, the typical or key county in each area alone receiving the attention of the canvass.

This idea, in one form or another, has long been current in election forecasting, but little attempt has been made at rigorous verification. The state of Maine, as has been pointed out in Chapter III, has been regarded as a political barometer for the nation for almost a century. In Illinois, according to Oscar Hewitt of the *Chicago Tribune*, Macon is the key county, the political views of Macon's citizenry having been "truly typical of Illinois for thirty-two years without a break."[31] In Indiana, says Mr. Hewitt, Decatur county is representative of the state, and in Wisconsin, according to our authority, this distinction goes to Fond du Lac and Outagamie. In personal canvass polls of states, sponsors continually use the idea of homogeneous political areas since, in mapping out the routes for their solicitors, they often select one town to represent the wheat interests, another to stand for the mining interests, and so on. Within recent years several careful students of politics have been impressed by regional similarities of election returns and have examined the economic and social characteristics of these areas with the view to throwing light on voting motivation.[32]

As we have seen in Chapter III, the proposition that "As goes Maine, so goes the nation," when put to a scientific test, falls to the ground. The political heterogeneity of the nation is such that one state could hardly be expected to be representative of all. With single states or portions of states, however, the hypothesis that political sentiment in one county may be typical of sentiment in other counties is more plausible, and seems worthy of further research attention.

[31]*Chicago Tribune*, July 16, 1928.

[32]See Stuart Rice, *Farmers and Workers in American Politics*, pp. 143-183, and *Quantitative Methods in Politics*, pp. 125-175, by the same author; also Jerry Alvin Neprash; *The Brookhart Campaigns in Iowa, 1920-1926;* also George A. Lundberg, "The Demographic and Economic Basis of Political Radicalism and Conservatism," *American Journal of Sociology*, March, 1927.

Chapter V

STRAW POLLS ON CANDIDATES (*Continued*)

Class Bias

A second source of straw-poll bias is class favoritism in the collecting of the ballots. Theoretically, a straw poll should be a random sample of the effective electorate,[1] the opportunity to participate now falling to the lot of the butcher, now to the day laborer, now to the banker, without discrimination. But, in practice, this dispassionate selection of straw-vote participants is difficult to achieve, because people are most easily reached for sampling purposes through groups, *i.e.*, reader clientele, factory workers, farmers, and other occupational groups, owners of telephones and automobiles, etc., which opens the door to disproportionate class representation.

A ballot-in-the-paper poll presents immediate possibilities for class bias, because, at best, it can only reflect the voting intentions of the readers of the sponsoring newspaper or periodical, who may or may not be typical of the electorate as a whole. A sample of preëlection sentiment derived from tabloid readers, for example, would doubtless give very different results than a sample taken from the readers of the *New York Times*. In 1928, the *Nation*, a weekly devoted to liberal thought, conducted a poll among its readers, with the result that Smith received 53 percent of all the straw votes cast.[2] The magazine, in setting forth the returns, plainly labeled them as an expression of liberal-voting intention, and declared that the figures were not typical of sentiment in the large; but many sponsors of ballot-in-the-paper straw polls do not make discriminations of this kind. They assume that their readers are a fair cross section of the voting public, whereas, in truth, the subscribers to their publication may carry considerable class bias.

Personal canvass polls are often distorted by class bias, because the collection of ballots is usually made along the lines of economic or social *blocs*. The canvassers are sent to the factories for the labor vote, to the offices for the white-collar vote, to the churches for the religious vote, to the foreign quarters for the Italian vote, etc. If each class is sampled in correct proportion to its importance in the

[1] See p. 102. [2] *Nation*, Vol. 127, no. 3305, p. 470, Nov. 7, 1928.

POLLS ON CANDIDATES 91

electorate, no bias can result from this source, but, in so far as this sampling requirement remains unmet, the straw-vote returns may fall short of the goal of representativeness.

A mail poll using a random selection of names from a qualified voter list presents the best opportunity to avoid class bias, but it is not always possible to employ this type of canvass. Registration practice varies widely with different states and with separate localities in these states, and, in large polling undertakings, the trouble and expense of compiling mailing lists of qualified voters is virtually prohibitive. As a consequence, sponsors of mail polls use names derived from more available sources, such as tax-assessment rolls, telephone directories, or automobile-registration files, with the result that their unofficial returns may be tinted with class bias.

The mailing list of the *Literary Digest*, derived from telephone directories and automobile registers, carries class bias of three descriptions. The first is economic in character. Before a man's name appears in a telephone book or in the automobile records of a state, he must have sufficient means to own one of these conveniences. Great numbers of factory workers and laboring people are unable to meet this qualification, and hence are automatically barred from participation in a *Literary-Digest* straw vote. This imparts to the *Digest* straw returns an economic class bias which may impair to a certain extent the representativeness of the sample. It does not follow from this, however, that the *Digest's* straw measurements are untrustworthy, for the tel-auto population is representative, within certain limits, of the population that owns neither telephone nor automobile. What this fact does suggest is that on questions markedly involving economic class interests, straw polls based on a tel-auto mailing list can be expected to favor unduly the side of wealth.

The second type of class bias that creeps into the *Literary-Digest* returns is that pertaining to sex. Ownership of telephones and automobiles is largely declared in the name of the male member of the household, hence men have the opportunity to participate in the straw poll in larger numbers than women. According to a statement made by the magazine in 1922, the sex composition of the mailing list derived from telephone directories is about 90 percent male and 10 percent female.[3] No statement has been made as to the proportion of males and females listed in the combined telephone

[3] *Literary Digest*, Sept. 9, 1922, p. 15.

and automobile compendium, but the same sex factors are operative in both types of ownership, and it can be assumed that the 90-10 percent division holds for this list as well. This is on the basis of cards mailed out. With the ballots actually returned to the magazine, male representation is probably greater even than 90 percent, because men are more coöperative in indicating a voting preference than are women.[4] The electorate is usually thought of as 50 percent male and 50 percent female, but perhaps on account of the relative youth of woman suffrage, the men cast about 60 percent of the vote.[5]

If the women vote as do their husbands and sweethearts, this disproportionate sex representation in the *Literary-Digest* polls would cause no inaccuracy in the straw-vote returns. Probably no single generalization can be made on this point, however. What evidence there is seems to indicate that in some elections the women divide on candidates the same as the men, while in others there appears to be difference. In Chicago, owing to litigation over state suffrage for women, official returns were tabulated by sex in 1919 and 1920. In the mayoralty contest of 1919, 52 percent of the men and the same proportion of the women voted for "Big Bill" Thompson, the Republican candidate. In the presidential election of the following year, the favor of the two sexes differed only slightly. In Chicago, Harding received 76 percent of the men's vote and 77 percent of the ballots cast by women.

Straw-poll returns that have been tabulated by sex show a wider variation. In 1928, the Hearst presidential poll indicated that 56 percent of the men and 60 percent of the women of the nation were for Hoover. In the 1930 gubernatorial poll of the *Columbus Dispatch* in Ohio, 54 percent of the men and 48 percent of the women favored the Democratic candidate, George White. A sex difference of about the same proportion was revealed in the 1929 mayoralty primary poll of the *Pittsburgh Sun-Telegraph*. These returns gave Kline, the winner on the Republican ticket, 46 percent of the male vote and 41 percent of that cast by women.

The distortion in the 1928 *Literary-Digest* returns, caused by male bias in the sample, was probably small. If the Hearst straw-poll figures for this election are descriptive of sex differences in voting

[4] See pp. 99-100. There is no way of knowing how many ballots addressed to men are voted by their wives.

[5] This is the figure most frequently used by politicians in their calculations. Official tabulation of the vote by sex in Chicago for the 1919 mayoralty and 1920 presidential elections shows that 37 percent of the ballots in each election were cast by women.

intention, the *Digest* sample of 9 males to one female, would have given Hoover 56 percent of the national vote. Had the sex ratio in the sample been 6 males to 4 females, as it probably was in the official returns, the *Digest* prediction would have been 57 percent for Hoover. This is a difference of but one vote per 100, which is probably a fair measure of the distortive influence of sex bias in the 1928 *Digest* straw vote. In future polls conducted by this magazine, male bias in the sampling list may affect the returns to greater or less degrees than in 1928, depending upon how closely the election issues parallel the interests of the sexes, but upon most public questions the views of men and women are much alike; hence disproportionate male representation in the *Digest* sample may not seriously prejudice its reliability.

The third type of bias carried by the *Literary-Digest* mailing list has to do with party membership. In the presidential poll of 1928, as has been pointed out in a previous section on straw-poll accuracy, Hoover received a larger proportion of the straw vote in every state than he later commanded in the election. Similarly in the 1924 poll, Coolidge, in all states but seven, showed more strength in the straw test than he subsequently demonstrated in the official count. In these seven states, as well, it is probable that the Coolidge strength would have been overstated in the straw poll had not the insurgent candidacy of La Follette appeared to divert a portion of the vote that would customarily have gone to the two major parties. Moreover the degree of overstatement of the Republican vote in the two presidential polls also tended to be similar. This is forcefully demonstrated by the fact that the average plurality error by state was reduced from 12 to 6 percent by correcting the 1928 pluralities in the light of the plurality error of four years previous.[6] Apparently the *Literary-Digest* mailing list of telephone and automobile owners contains a larger proportion of Republicans than the electorate which casts the official vote.

This view is suggested by the consistency of the Republican bias in the straw returns noted above, and also by experimental data. Through the generous coöperation of the *Literary-Digest* officials, the name and address of every tenth person on the magazine's mailing list was secured for Multnomah County, Oregon—largely the city of Portland—where official data were available for the desired

[6] See p. 72. The coefficient of correlation between the 1924 Coolidge error and the 1928 Hoover error in prediction is $r = .66$.

test. This list was then sent to research assistants in Portland, who checked the *Literary-Digest* names against the official registry of voters, in order to secure the party affiliation of each *Digest* addressee. Fifty-nine percent of the sample names from the mailing list of the magazine were identified.[7] If there were no party bias in this mailing list, the *Digest* addressees would divide proportionately between the Republican and Democratic parties the same as all the registered voters in the city. The test reveals, however, that there were about 2 more Republican voters per 100 on the 1928 *Digest* Multnomah-County list than there were in the qualified electorate, as shown in Table 15.

TABLE 15

PARTY COMPLEXION OF THE 1928 LITERARY-DIGEST MAILING LIST AND REGISTERED ELECTORATE IN MULTNOMAH COUNTY, OREGON, IN PERCENTAGES

	Digest Multnomah County mailing list	All registered voters in Multnomah County	Bias in *Digest* list
Democrat	23.55	25.50	—1.95
Republican	76.45	74.50	+1.95
	100.00	100.00	

In the 1928 presidential poll, Hoover was favored on 65.5 percent of all the ballot cards, exclusive of those carrying minor preferences, which were mailed from the County of Multnomah. In the subsequent election, the Republican candidate polled but 62.6 percent of the official Hoover-Smith vote cast in this area. The *Literary-Digest* poll in Multnomah County, therefore, overstated Hoover's strength by 2.9 percent of the total Hoover-Smith vote. Here, then, we find a Republican bias of 1.95 names per 100 in the *Digest* mailing list, and a subsequent Republican bias of 2.9 votes per 100 in the straw poll. This gives strong corroborative evidence for the belief that party bias in the magazine's mailing list largely accounts for the predictive error of its straw polls.[8] The possibility of allowing

[7] The remaining 41 percent of the names either could not be located, owing to change in address, varied spelling and initialing, or because the addressee was not a registered voter. Every straw poll, of course, no matter what the source of its mailing list, counts preferences from people who may not cast an official vote. The possible sampling distortion that may spring from participation in a straw poll and nonparticipation in the official election is discussed on pp. 101-3.

[8] The customary statistical tests for significance are as follows:
Republican percentage of the sample *Digest* mailing list $= 76.45 \pm .47$.
Republican percentage of the *Digest* straw-vote sample $= 65.5 \pm .32$.
Difference between Republican bias in mailing list and straw vote: $2.9 - 1.95 = .95 \pm .89$.

POLLS ON CANDIDATES 95

for this form of sampling distortion by special interpretation will be considered in a subsequent section on "recurrent bias."

In suggesting that party bias in the mailing list is the chief cause of the predictive error of the *Literary-Digest* presidential polls, one seeming inconsistency must be resolved. In the southern states, the tel-auto population is avowedly Democratic, yet in these states, as elsewhere, the *Digest* polls have consistently overstated the strength of the Republican candidates. If it is true that the *Digest* straw poll carries the political bias of the tel-auto population, then Democratic candidates should be overpredicted in the South just as Republican candidates are overpredicted in the North.

In seeking an explanation for this apparent inconsistency, the opinion of more than a score of southern newspaper editors and political writers was canvassed. It is the belief of those observers that part of the *Digest* Republican overstatement was caused by the ownership of telephones and automobiles by negroes who cast a Republican vote in the straw poll but, because of race pressure, did not register their voice in the official election. Of greater importance, however, the editors suggest, is the fact that many southern business men—bankers, manufacturers, oil and wool producers, etc.—are in sympathy with the Republican party on national economic questions. These men, according to our authorities, express their true wishes in a straw poll, but in the official election remain at home or conform to the strong urge of custom and vote Democratic. To ballot otherwise in a legal poll would be to risk the terrible penalty of social ostracism, and, in many states, virtual disfranchisement, since voting the Republican ticket would disqualify the citizen from participating in a Democratic primary where local officers are elected in fact. In 1928 religious intolerance may have influenced some citizens in the South to vote for Hoover in the straw poll, then remain at home on election day or vote the customary Democratic ticket, but this does not explain Republican overprediction in 1924 when the factor of religion was absent. The sympathy of many southern business men with the national economic views of the Republican party, therefore, appears to be the most logical interpretation.

This explanation by local newspaper editors resolves the apparent inconsistency of Republican overstatement in the *Digest* straw polls of the Southern states. The political bias of the tel-auto population does color the magazine's straw returns, but only if the participants vote officially as they vote unofficially. In the South, where the race question always looms in the background of politics, this provision remains unmet, many citizens voicing their true preferences in one test and their customary ones, if at all, in the other.

Bias of Selection in Coöperation

The next form of bias to be dealt with here is selection in coöperation. By way of introduction to this distortive influence, it is first necessary to describe coöperation, or the willingness of citizens to express their voting intentions in an unofficial poll. No straw vote ever achieves 100-percent coöperation, for many people, because of suspicion, lack of interest, or opposition, refuse to reveal their political preferences. The extent to which citizens are willing to mark ballots depends a good deal on the polling technique employed, the publicity given to the undertaking, the intensity of public interest in the current political campaign, and the acquaintance of the people with the agency that is sponsoring the test.

With a ballot-in-the-paper poll, coöperation is voluntary to the highest degree. In order to vote, a person must on his own initiative, clip and mark the printed ballot, and send it to the straw-vote headquarters at his own expense. This is an effective barrier to coöperation, and only a very small percentage of the blank ballots appearing in the columns of a sponsoring newspaper are ever returned to the straw-vote editor.

In a personal-canvass poll a larger number of people will mark a ballot, for the reason that a spoken request is more forceful than a printed one. Sponsors of personal canvasses do not ordinarily keep account of the number of people who refuse to divulge their voting intentions; therefore it is difficult to determine the exact extent of coöperation in this type of straw poll. The two examples that follow, however, are suggestive. In its poll in the mayoralty primary of 1919, the *Chicago Tribune* states that on one day of its canvass, 300 out of 1,400 people approached refused to participate. This would be 78 percent coöperation. Four years later, in the mayoralty campaign of 1923, the *Tribune* called 8,145 people on the telephone and made inquiry as to their preference of candidates. Those who gave reply numbered 5,794, which was 71 percent coöperation, somewhat less than in the previous canvass involving face to face contacts. A smaller degree of coöperation would be expected in this type of canvass, of course, because a request for information loses some of its force when made over the telephone, and because the people who were called had no guarantee that a *Tribune* representative, and not the local precinct leader, was on the other end of the wire.

In a mail poll, coöperation is voluntary and depends upon the willingness of the individual to mark and mail a card. The barrier is less formidable than that of a ballot-in-the-paper poll, because a person is addressed directly and is not required to pay postage on the returned card; but it is a greater deterrent than that of a personal canvass because a request conveyed by means of correspondence is much less forceful than one carried by the spoken word. Figures on coöperation in mail polls are usually available. In general, they show a return of from 10 to 30 percent. The *Columbus Dispatch*, in its mailings to R. F. D. box numbers in Ohio, gets a return of about 9 percent. In a recent mayoralty poll in the city of Columbus, this paper secured a 15 percent return on cards addressed simply to "Householder." In the Hearst presidential poll of 1928, the *Atlanta Georgian*, covering seven states in the South, enjoyed a return of about 20 percent; the coöperation figure for the *Washington Herald* in Virginia was 19 percent, and for the *Pittsburgh Sun-Telegraph* in Pennsylvania, 30 percent. The last paper conducted a postal-card poll in the 1929 Pittsburgh mayoralty primary, which commanded a return of 24 percent.

With the *Literary-Digest* polls, the proportion of cards returned, relative to the number sent out, varies by states. For the 1924 and 1928 presidential polls, the average coöperation for the forty-eight states was 15 percent and 13 percent respectively. For the three prohibition polls conducted by the magazine, the average coöperation by state was 12 percent in 1922, 24 percent in 1930, and 22 percent in 1932. The increased willingness of the public to participate in the latter referenda was due, no doubt, to the nation-wide radio publicity given the poll, and also to the heightened interest with which the liquor question has been debated in recent years.

The fact that no preëlection poll achieves 100 percent coöperation from the voting public is not in itself a cause of inaccuracy in straw-vote returns. A poll might receive expressions of voting intention from one percent or 75 percent of the people approached, yet be extremely precise. Inaccuracy creeps in only when those who do not mark straw ballots hold different political views from those who do coöperate, or, in other words, where there is present selection in coöperation. This biasing factor may be operative in any preëlection poll, and if not understood may lead to serious confusion in interpreting straw returns.

In Chapter I, in the discussion of the inclusive-canvass technique employed by the politicians to gauge public sentiment before an election, it was shown how unwillingness on the part of individuals to reveal voting intention to the precinct chairman or party worker resulted in a "doubtful" column in the returns. In political parlance, the "doubtful" portion of the electorate is called the "silent vote," this factor being the subject of unending speculation in the preëlection forecasts of the politicians. In a straw poll, the uncommunicative section of the electorate goes unreported, the assumption being made that the noncoöperative voter holds political views similar to those revealed by the straw-vote participants. In so far as this is true, the bias of selection in coöperation is absent, and no inaccuracy in the straw returns results. But the truth of this assumption can never be taken for granted, and intelligent straw-vote sponsors will always be on the alert to detect the presence of this form of bias.

The operation of selection in coöperation varies with the type of poll and with numerous special circumstances. With the ballot-in-the-paper poll, selectivity is a matter of enthusiasm, only those people coöperating who have enough interest to clip, mark, and mail or carry the ballot to the sponsoring agency. Too often this enthusiasm exceeds the bounds of normal participation and takes the form of stuffing the ballot box.

The personal canvass more successfully eludes the bias of selection in coöperation than either the ballot-in-the-paper or mail polls, because the force of a personal request tends to break down reluctance in marking a ballot. Also in this type of poll the solicitor has a chance to observe the type of people who are noncoöperative, which may provide clews for the proper interpretation of the returns.

In mail polls, selection in coöperation is very difficult to detect, because the sponsors ordinarily have no way of knowing who coöperates and who does not. If the supporters of one candidate or issue are more enthusiastic and more desirous of expressing their preferences through the medium of the straw vote, selective bias may creep in unnoticed. Straw-vote managers could learn who is coöperating and who is failing to respond to their request by numbering or "keying" ballot cards, but printed numbers on ballot cards are likely to arouse the suspicions of the prospective voters, and as for the use of secret reference marks, there is a certain element of deceit in the practice which, if exposed to the public, might seriously undermine confidence in the sponsoring agency. This objection, however, would not apply if classes, rather than individuals, were distinguished. A sponsor might well control the factor of selection by including in his mailing a number of special ballots to classes with known views, then by comparing the coöperativeness of test groups of differing partisanship, the presence of selection could be detected and its influence on the poll could be discounted. Because of the difficulty in controlling this element of bias, it remains as one of the gravest defects of the mail-poll technique.

Selection in coöperation may manifest itself in several sets of categories as, for example, rural people may coöperate more than city people, men more than women, Republicans more than Democrats, the educated more than the uneducated, adherents of reform more than defenders of the *status quo*, or any of these hypotheses may be reversed. For a thorough understanding of straw-voting procedure, it would be well to have decision on all these propositions, but it is not possible to give complete and definite answers, because the data necessary to proper analysis are largely unavailable, and also because so many factors are at work to influence coöperation that it is difficult to isolate one factor and weigh it. What information there is on the subject, however, may be presented here and certain tentative opinions may be advanced which will serve as a starting point for further research.

Between urban and rural people there appears to be little difference in coöperation. It is often held that the receiving of mail is more of a novelty to country than to city people, and that the desire to be in the swing of things stimulates greater coöperation among the farming class; but the evidence does not bear this out. In 33 states in which the population was 50 percent or more rural (1920 census), an average of 14.4 percent of the people who received ballot cards in the *Literary-Digest* presidential polls of 1924 and 1928, returned them to the magazine. In the remaining 15 states, more than 50 percent urban, the average return of ballots was 14 percent. The very slight difference in return between the urban and rural states here revealed is probably without significance.[9]

Between the sexes, men tend to coöperate more than women.

[9] A scatter diagram showing return by states in relation to degree of rurality reveals no correlation.

With personal-canvass polls taken on main streets, the gathering of straw votes is most often presided over by men, and some women would consider it bad manners to give heed to a request to mark a ballot. Sex selection in coöperation would result from this circumstance. In the case of mail polls, the evidence on the point is quite clear. In its prohibition referendum of 1922, the *Literary Digest* supplemented its principal undertaking, in which nine out of ten participants were men, with a special poll devoted exclusively to women. Coöperation for the nation as a whole in the predominantly male poll was 10 percent; in the poll of women the return was only 5 percent. The experience of the *Washington Herald* (D. C.) in its presidential poll of Virginia in 1928, shows the same tendency. In this straw vote 23 percent of the men, and but 12 percent of the women, who received ballot cards returned them to the newspaper. Between men and women, therefore, selection in coöperation operates in personal-canvass and mail polls to give the returns a male bias. The effect of sex selection on ballot-in-the-paper polls is not known.

While there is little data on the subject, it would be presumed from common observation that educated people would respond to a straw vote in larger numbers than uneducated persons. Accosted on the street or in a place of employment by a straw-vote canvasser, the literate man would quickly grasp the meaning of the request, whereas the illiterate person might look upon the solicitation with suspicion. This would be even more true of a mail poll. The educated classes are accustomed to receive mail, whereas the uneducated are not; the latter might view a straw ballot as a piece of trickery designed to take away the right to vote, or to spy on the individual's political intentions with the view to doing him harm. Newspapermen, who have conducted straw polls in large cities, have told the author that postal-card polls are not as successful as are personal canvasses in wards peopled by negroes, foreign-born whites, and others of limited education. In these circumstances, the latter technique, they hold, is to be preferred to the former.

Between Republicans and Democrats, as such, there is probably little selection in coöperation, because the bias of selection would depend upon the interest and enthusiasm uppermost at the moment and not primarily upon party membership. In one campaign the Republicans, enthusiastic, confident, and led by a vigorous personality, might show excess zeal in straw-vote coöperation, while in another election the Democrats might occupy this position. A test for party selection based on *Literary-Digest* data shows no significant difference between Republicans and Democrats on the point of coöperation. In 26 states in which the Republican vote averaged more than 55 percent[10] of the total vote cast in the presidential elections of 1920, 1924, and 1928, the average coöperation by state in the 1924 and 1928 presidential polls was 14.0 percent. In the remaining 22 states, where the Democratic proportion of the official vote averaged 45 percent or over for the three presidential elections from 1920 to 1928, the average state coöperation for the two *Digest* polls was 14.5 percent, practically the same as in "Republican" territory.

Reformers usually coöperate more in straw polls than defenders of the *status quo*, because they are more zealous in their partisanship. Men who are against the established order generally have an overflow of indignation, they are rebuffed in the achievement of their reforms, and they welcome an opportunity to vent their opinion in a straw poll. The advocates of the existing order, on the other hand, are more likely to be complacent, being content to rest behind the barriers of inertia that protect social arrangements as they are. People on this side of the fence are not so much interested in participating in straw votes; hence selection in coöperation, if operative in a straw poll at all, most often favors the reform side. In the discussion of polls on issues, which follows in a later chapter, illustrations of this proposition will be presented.

Bias of Participation-Nonparticipation

The final biasing factor that may operate to make a straw-poll sample unrepresentative of public sentiment is "participation-nonparticipation," which means that a person may register his choice in a straw poll, but fail to cast a vote in the official election. Contrary to popularly held notions, democracy's public officials are chosen, not by all the people, but by part of the people. Minors under twenty-one may not vote; immigrants who have not fulfilled citizenship requirements are denied the franchise, and people who have failed to qualify by registering are ineligible to mark a ballot. Moreover, the number of voices unheard on election day is swelled by the "stay-at-homes" who, though qualified, are disinclined to spend the

[10]The categories 55-45 percent were selected to divide Republican and Democratic territory, because the former party won the elections of 1920, 1924, and 1928 by large pluralities and a 50-50 percent division would have left only the South to the Democrats, giving the comparison a sectional aspect.

time and energy necessary to exercise the democratic privilege. In the 1928 presidential election, for example, when popular interest was aroused to an extraordinary extent, only 60 percent of the people twenty-one years and over (exclusive of the ten states in the Solid South) attended the polls. The effective electorate, therefore, is considerably less than the whole adult population.[11]

Since the purpose of a straw poll is to foreshadow the election behavior of the people who actually vote, the sample, theoretically, should be drawn only from this effective electorate. Practically, however, this is impossible, for even if a list of qualified voters were used as the basis for the unofficial canvass, there would still be no guarantee that every man who marked a straw ballot would subsequently participate in the official election. In mail polls, the use of registered-voter lists undoubtedly reduces the sampling distortion from the factor of participation-nonparticipation to the lowest level, but, with the exception of polls in restricted areas, it is neither possible nor financially practicable to derive all names from this source. Other criteria for selection, such as ownership of telephone or automobile, payer of taxes or mention in a city directory, are ordinarily employed. In a ballot-in-the-paper poll the qualification for participation is reader clientele; for a personal canvass it is chance meeting in workshop or street between the straw-vote solicitor and the person canvassed. No matter what form of polling technique is employed, therefore, the returns from a straw poll may include the choices of individuals who have no voice in the official election. If the preferences of these people are different from those of the voters who actually choose the officers of the government, then an element of bias may be introduced into the straw-vote sample.

Ordinarily one would think that this distortive influence would have little practical effect, because in the hit-and-miss selection of participants a very good representation of the voting public would be secured. Minors might hold the same political views as their fathers, aliens might follow the political divisions of their communities, and the desire to exercise the right of voting may be as

[11]The ten states in the Solid South are excluded from this calculation, because in these states the one-party system and the disfranchisement of the negro makes for an exceptionally small turnout in a general election. In the states with which the computation deals, no adjustment has been made for noncitizens; hence the indicated turnout is slightly smaller than it would be if such adjustment were made. For estimates of the "stay-at-home" vote in presidential elections from 1880 to 1920 see Simon Michelet, "Forty Year Growth of the Stay-at-Home Vote", *Current History Magazine*, November, 1924. For a study of the causes of non-voting, see Charles E. Merriam and Harold F. Gosnell, *Non-Voting: Causes and Control*.

strong in one party as in another. If this is true, the factor of participation-nonparticipation may cause little inaccuracy in straw-poll predictions. However, we cannot be sure. In the South the negroes are largely Republican, but they do not have a legal vote. In a city where a large number of aliens live, the political sentiment among the nonvoters may strongly side with one party. The ability of party leaders to turn out their vote may be different. We do not know how many elections are decided, not by dominant preferences in the public at large, but by the greater effectiveness of partisan groups in marshaling latent sentiment, and getting it registered at the polls, where it legally counts. Decision on these points must await further research on the general straw-vote problem.

Size of Sample—Adequacy

A great deal of confused thinking is found on the question of the number of unofficial ballots that must be collected before straw-vote figures can be relied upon. In a legal election, the opportunity to vote is given to all persons who can qualify. While this does not mean that all individuals twenty-one years and over actually cast a ballot,[12] it does mean that an official canvass generally includes more people than it excludes, and that large numbers of ballots are always dropped in the receiving boxes in major elections. In comparison with official totals, the number of straw votes collected in a preëlection poll seems small, indeed, and the inference that such a compilation cannot be trustworthy is difficult to resist. We find, as a result, straw-poll sponsors who send their agents out with orders to collect as many ballots as possible, in the belief that the more participants the more reliable the straw returns are likely to be. Also, we find critics of preëlection polls who point triumphantly to the small number of ballots gathered as a sure indication of the faithlessness of the tests. Literally scores of printed criticisms employed this argument to discredit the *Literary-Digest* presidential polls of 1924 and 1928.

Most of this confusion is no doubt due to a lack of understanding of formal sampling procedure. According to sampling theory, a reliable judgment of a population can be formed by observing a comparatively small part of that population, provided the individuals are chosen in a random manner so that every one has a fair chance of being selected for test purposes, and provided that the number of

[12] See p. 102.

individuals thus chosen is great enough to minimize the influence of chance variations. The reliability of a sample, therefore, depends, first upon whether it is typical or representative of the whole population, and second, whether it is adequate in size.

Without being aware of it, the critics who look upon straw-poll reliability as a question of the number of ballots gathered are voicing their objections both in the name of representativeness and in the name of adequacy. In thinking about the problem, however, these two factors should be dealt with apart. A sample may be adequate in size, yet be faithless because it is not representative; or, again it may be representative so far as it goes, but unreliable because it is not adequate in size. It is not enough to have numbers alone. The straw-poll sponsor who goes out for quantity without regard to the quality of his ballots has no guarantee of accuracy in his returns. Neither has the interpreter or critic of straw polls who fixes his attention solely on totals. The influences that affect the quality or representativeness of a sample have already been discussed. In the present section, the distortive influence of the size of the sample alone will be considered. Given the several methods for conducting straw polls, can their error in prediction be ascribed to the number of unofficial votes gathered? Also, how many ballots must be collected to give a reasonable degree of predictive reliability?

Practice has varied as to the size of the straw-vote sample. Some sponsors have collected more ballots, some less. In 11 polls of Ohio since 1908, the *Cincinnati Enquirer* has gathered an average of 18 straw votes for every 1,000 official votes cast in the subsequent election. The *Columbus Dispatch* has taken a slightly larger number. In 7 polls of Ohio since 1916, it has averaged 23 unofficial to every 1,000 official votes cast. In the nation-wide poll of the *Hearst Newspapers* in 1928, the number of straw preferences gathered was 32 to every 1,000 official votes. The *Literary Digest* has taken much larger samples than other straw-vote sponsors. In its presidential poll of 1924, the *Digest* total compared to that of the official returns was 81 to 1,000. In the presidential poll of 1928 this figure was 74 to 1,000.

A good rough test for adequacy is to increase the number of selected individuals to the point where additional increments do not materially change the complexion of the sample. Applied conversely to the present straw-vote problem, if, in specific instances, it can be shown that the collection of a smaller number of ballots would have yielded as good a forecast as the larger number actually gathered, then it can be said, in answer to our first question, that the size of the sample in these straw polls was adequate for predictive reliability. Our second question likewise can be answered by the same test, for by reducing the size of a poll to the lowest point, consistent with no increase in its predictive error, we can gain a fair idea of the, number of ballots a straw-poll sponsor should endeavor to collect.

The first grist for our mill is a comparison of the predictive reliability of the independent polls of the *Chicago Journal* and the *Chicago Tribune* in two local and one presidential campaign in the city of Chicago. Both newspapers used the personal-canvass polling technique, but the *Journal*, contenting itself with small samples, gathered an average of but 29 straw per 1,000 official votes subsequently cast in the three elections; whereas the *Tribune*, placing its dependence on larger numbers, collected an average of 108 unofficial preferences per 1,000 official votes in the three elections. The plurality error of the *Journal* for the three polls averaged 2 and that of the *Tribune* 3 per 100 votes cast. The *Journal* with a 29 to 1,000 sample, therefore, secured slightly better results than the *Tribune* with a sample of 108 to 1,000, which was three times as large. The figures for this comparison are given in Table 16.

TABLE 16
SIZE OF SAMPLE AND PLURALITY ERROR FOR STRAW POLLS OF CHICAGO JOURNAL AND CHICAGO TRIBUNE IN THREE CAMPAIGNS

Date	Campaign	Chicago Journal		Chicago Tribune	
		Straw per 1,000 official votes	Plurality error	Straw per 1,000 official votes	Plurality error
1923	Mayoralty.........	56	4	119	6
1927	Mayoralty.........	12	2	132	1
1928	Presidential........	20	1	74	3
	Mean average....	29	2	108	3

Further light is thrown on the question of adequacy by the experience of the *Literary Digest*. In its presidential poll of 1928, this magazine collected 74 straw preferences to every 1,000 official votes cast in the election. If this quantity of straw ballots can be decreased without prejudicing the accuracy of the forecast, it can be concluded that the size of the *Digest* sample was adequate and, also some idea of what constitutes adequacy can be gained. To deflate the size of the *Literary Digest* sample, the ballot cards for seven states were sorted according to the dates upon which the straw voters dropped their cards into the mail boxes for return to the magazine. These dates were readily ascertained by reading the post office cancellation mark printed on the back of each card. For each of the seven states, one day's returns (usually those for the second day following the distribution of the ballots to assure complete coverage of a state) were regarded as the straw sample. In size these one day samples averaged 10 straw to every 1,000 official votes subsequently cast, and constituted about one-tenth of the complete *Digest* sample. Based on the one day totals, the average plurality error of the seven state forecasts was 17 percent; based on the complete sample, the average plurality error for these states was 19 percent. Contrary to the assertions of many critics, therefore, the size of the *Literary-Digest* sample was not a cause of its predictive error, since in the seven states examined, one day's returns, amounting to 10 straw per 1,000 official ballots, on the average, gave as reliable forecasts as the complete sample, which numbered, on the average, 100 straw to every 1,000 official votes cast.[13] The figures descriptive of this experiment are displayed in Table 17.

TABLE 17

SIZE OF SAMPLE AND PLURALITY ERROR FOR ONE DAY'S RETURNS AND COMPLETE RETURNS FOR SEVEN STATES IN 1928 LITERARY-DIGEST PRESIDENTIAL POLL

State	*Literary-Digest* returns one day		Complete *Literary-Digest* returns	
	Straw per 1,000 official votes	Plurality error	Straw per 1,000 official votes	Plurality error
Iowa...................	4	20	64	18
Kansas.................	6	10	81	12
Louisiana...............	15	33	112	36
Oregon.................	8	1	75	5
South Carolina..........	19	32	182	39
Virginia................	8	8	131	12
Wisconsin..............	8	14	55	9
Mean average.......	10	17	100	19

[13] The coefficient of correlation between error in predicting the Hoover proportion of the total vote and the size of the *Literary-Digest* sample $\left(\dfrac{\text{Total } Digest \text{ returns}}{\text{Total official returns}}\right)$ for 47 states is $r. = .17$. South Carolina was dropped from this computation because the extreme Hoover error in this state would have imparted an element of spuriousness to the correlation coefficient. The relation between the Coolidge error in the 1924 poll and size of the *Digest* sample is expressed by the correlation coefficient $r = .14$. This, of course, corroborates the evidence given above.

If similar experiments could be carried on with the data from other straw polls, it would doubtless be found that the size of the sample was adequate. The cause of error in the forecasts, therefore, must be looked for in the other distortive influences affecting straw polls, such as fraud, or bias in the sample, or change of voting intention with the passage of time.

What, now, can be said of the number of ballots that should be collected in order to guarantee a straw-vote sample on the score of adequacy? In the foregoing discussion it was shown that the *Chicago Journal* achieved good results with a sample as small as 12 straw to every 1,000 official votes cast. With the *Literary Digest*, it was experimentally demonstrated that a sample of 10 to 1,000 would have produced maximum forecasting accuracy under its method of polling. The *Cincinnati Enquirer* and the *Columbus Dispatch* have achieved splendid forecasting records with samples of 20 to 30 per 1,000, while the Hearst nation-wide poll of 1928 gave a very remarkable prediction with a sample of 32 to 1,000. In polls of states or large cities, therefore, 30 straw preferences to every 1,000 votes expected to be cast in the official election would appear to constitute an adequate sample, and this number even might be safely reduced to 10 per 1,000. In polls of smaller electorates, the size of the sample may have to be increased to guarantee the returns on the score of adequacy. This is a matter for judgment in the light of specific circumstances. The guiding principle to be employed is, first, to gather straw preferences that are representative of the electorate as a whole; then, second, to increase the number of these preferences until additional choices make no material difference in the results. When this point of stabilization is reached, the size of the sample is sufficient. That the former factor is probably more productive of error in straw polls than the latter, has been demonstrated in this section. Sponsors and interpreters of these unofficial tests, alike, therefore, may well concentrate their primary attention upon the quality of the straw ballots gathered, rather than upon the quantity.

Change of Sentiment over Time

The final factor which may operate to cause inaccuracy in straw-vote returns is change of sentiment with the passage of time. Any measurement is valid only so long as the substance measured retains its original form, and straw polls are no exception to this rule. If a test of voting intention is made two months before the date of the election, and people change their minds meanwhile, the resultant forecast must be inaccurate.[14] There can be no evasion of this principle. Straw-vote returns are valid only if people do not change their minds after the ballots have been gathered, or, to put it more exactly, only if the desertions from one candidate are counterbalanced by desertions from the other, which is the same thing as saying that there has been no net change in voting sentiment.

Unfortunately, it is not possible at the present time to evaluate this factor of straw-vote error, because, despite the assertions of sponsors and interpreters of these unofficial polls, who have cited straw figures to prove drift of public sentiment during political campaigns, there are no trustworthy data on the subject. Before change of sentiment over time can be accurately gauged, two or more comparable measurements taken at separate points in time, are necessary. One of these measurements might be based on straw-poll returns, the other on official election totals. In this case, the spread between the two, which has here been called "error in prediction," would constitute a measure of change of voting intention. Before this divergence between straw and official returns could be properly charged to change in public sentiment, however, it would be necessary to show that no other factors such as those named previously under the heading of bias, were responsible for the distortion; or, to put it another way, it would be necessary to prove that the straw returns were a perfect measurement of voting intention at the time the ballots were gathered. This quality cannot be demonstrated for the polls which have been dealt with in the present volume, and the assumption that the plurality error shown by these returns represents a measurement of change in voting intention between the dates of the straw and official canvass, must accordingly be rejected.

An easier approach to the problem, it would seem, would be to make the two or more necessary preëlection measurements by means of straw polls exclusively, the several polls being taken by identical methods at successive points in time. It could then be assumed that similar biases were operating in each poll, and that the spread between them, after due allowance had been made for chance error

---

[14]Some political observers hold that the favor of many people is controlled by a desire to vote for the winning side. To the extent that a straw poll influenced this "band-wagon" vote, it would, of course, be the cause of its own error.

in sampling, constituted a measure of change in mass voting intention. But neither under this interpretation do the straw returns cited in the preceding pages throw any light on the problem. Some straw polls may have been taken in the past which meet the qualifications for measurement of the fluctuation of sentiment during a campaign, but the author is not aware of any such enterprises upon which the data are now available.

With most polls, the canvassing begins from one to three months before the date of the election and continues until a given territory is covered. Week to week reports on these undertakings are readily obtainable, but these reports are more likely to reflect the movements of canvassing crews, than change of public sentiment in response to the electioneering appeals of the candidates. There are, it is true, examples of a first canvass supplemented by a follow-up poll over the same territory, but these data are not to be relied upon as indicating change in sentiment, because the second canvass was likely to be sketchy and therefore of doubtful value for comparative purposes. In some instances, it has been found that straw ballots have been collected for a week or ten days, then published over a period of time to simulate continued canvassing. Also, as pointed out in an earlier connection, some editors believe it legitimate to manipulate day-to-day returns to make a contest exciting and thus heighten reader interest. For these reasons, the author has regarded all polls cited here as having been taken at one point in time, and therefore not amenable to analysis for change of voting intention. To take any other point of view, the author feels, would be to tempt irresponsible conclusions that would serve to cloud, rather than to clarify, thinking on this problem.

An example of the type of pitfall encountered in interpreting successive straw-vote returns as indicative of drift in preëlection sentiment, is afforded by the reports from the 1928 presidential poll of the *Wisconsin News*. The figures for August 21 and August 30 from this newspaper are given in Table 18.

TABLE 18

Two Reports from the 1928 Wisconsin-News Poll

	Total Vote	Hoover Vote	Percent	Smith Vote	Percent
Aug. 21.......	12,353	5,273	43	7,080	57
Aug. 30.......	7,669	4,241	55	3,428	45

On the face of these returns, political sentiment in Wisconsin is shown to have swung violently from Smith to Hoover during the latter part of August, the Republican candidate polling but 43 percent of the total straw vote up to August 21, then jumping to 55 percent during the next nine days. Actually these figures merely reflect the movements of the canvassers. The *Wisconsin News* polled Milwaukee first, 61 percent of the vote reported on August 21 having been gathered in the city which Budweiser was said to have made famous. Since this was an antiprohibition community, a strong sentiment was manifested for Al Smith. When the canvass was extended out through the state, where Hoover votes were more in evidence, the proportion of straw ballots marked for the Republican candidate climbed rapidly. Change of sentiment, therefore, was not reflected by these successive straw-vote reports, but only shift in the field of the canvass.[15]

The *Literary-Digest* polls throw no light on preëlection shift of voting intention, for, contrary to many interpreters who have seen significance in succeeding weekly reports, the *Digest* returns must be regarded as having been gathered at one point in time. In the 1928 presidential poll, for example, all ballot cards distributed were mailed between September 4 and October 1. For the smaller states, the ballots were mailed in one working day; other states of larger population required up to four days to complete the mailing job. By reading the post-office cancellation marks on the back of each ballot card, the approximate date each person voted can be ascertained.

[15]Most straw-poll returns are reported cumulatively, *i.e.*, the figures from the first week's canvass are added to those from the second week, etc. For a single poll taken as of one point in time, without attempt to measure drift in sentiment, this is correct procedure, since returns from east, west, north, and south must be added together to get a total for a given territory. But where the attempt is to measure change of sentiment during a campaign, which necessitates two or more comparable polls taken at successive points in time, cumulation should not be employed, since enlarging totals give successive returns less weight than they deserve. Interpreters generally have overlooked this fact. Suppose, for example, the *Gazette* conducts two perfect straw polls one month apart in Lake County. The first poll gives Jones 60 and Brown 40 votes per 100. By the time the second test is made, however, a great change of sentiment has taken place and the final poll gives Jones 40 percent, and Brown 60 percent of the total vote cast, exactly reversing their earlier position. Taken alone, the last poll is a perfect prediction and the spread between the first and second polls is a true measure of change in voting intention. Cumulated, however, the final poll would forecast a fifty-fifty split between Jones and Brown $\frac{40+60}{2}=50$ which would involve a 20 percent plurality error (zero plurality predicted; actual Brown plurality 20 votes per 100 cast; error 20 votes per 100 cast) and would also show a change in voting intention of but 10 votes per 100, whereas there was actually a shift of 20 votes per 100. Cumulation of returns, therefore, is correct only when assembling state totals for a single canvass taken as of one point in time. It is incorrect to interpret cumulated figures for change of sentiment over time.

POLLS ON CANDIDATES

Experiments of this nature on seven states, Iowa, Kansas, Louisiana, Oregon, South Carolina, Virginia, and Wisconsin, show that 71 percent of the participants mailed their ballot cards within a week after receiving them. The second week brought another 21 percent, while the third and successive weeks saw the remaining 8 percent dribble in. The figures describing these returns are shown in Table 19.

TABLE 19

Combined Daily Return of Ballots from Seven States in 1928 Literary-Digest Presidential Poll

Week	Time of voting* Day	Total ballots mailed from seven states	Percentage of grand total ballots mailed from seven states
First	1	9,889	4.6
	2	21,283	9.9
	3	23,851	11.1
	4	31,060	14.4
	5	28,654	13.3
	6	22,145	10.3
	7	16,001	7.4
Total first week		152,883	71.0
Second	8	13,230	6.1
	9	8,398	3.9
	10	4,441	2.1
	11	6,658	3.1
	12	4,576	2.1
	13	4,548	2.1
	14	3,507	1.6
Total second week		45,358	21.0
Total third and successive weeks	15 on	16,915	8.0
Grand total		215,156	100.0

*Measured from date ballots were distributed.

The vote in the 1928 *Literary-Digest* poll thus was cast principally in the first week after the participants had received their ballots, and was practically complete by the end of the second week. The *Digest* returns, therefore, give but a single measurement of preëlection sentiment and not a succession of indices, such as is necessary for an analysis of shift of voting intention during a campaign. Day-to-day reports, of course, could have been compiled by sorting the ballot cards according to the date of cancellation, as in the case of the seven states noted above, but these data could not be used for tests of change of sentiment because, though each day's returns might be adequate in size, they might not constitute a representative sample, nor be comparable with other daily figures because of such selective factors as procrastination, distance from post offices, etc., which influence the declining phases of the returns curve.

The question of change in voting intention previous to an election is an extremely important one, since in major campaigns, such as those for the presidency, millions of dollars and untold quantities of energy are spent by the principal parties in attempting to draw supporters from the opposing camp, or in resisting raids from the enemy. It would be desirable to check up on the results of this activity. Is this vast expenditure of money actually changing votes? Do the citizens respond to the propaganda fed to them during a campaign? What is the concrete result, in terms of votes, of a given party stratagem or a series of political maneuvers? Are campaigns won and lost before they start, or do they hang in the balance until election day?

On these questions two broad and divergent opinions are currently held. The one is that shifts of voting intention are customary features of a political campaign. According to this view, a large proportion of the voters make up their minds only after they have heard the political case presented to them by newspaper editors, campaign orators, and precinct workers. As this army of doubtful voters falls into line, or steps out of line, trends are set up or shifts occur that often decide the election. The *Chicago Record-Herald*, in describing preëlection movement in the presidential campaign of 1912, put it this way:

> There is a tremendous part of the voting population that will not decide how it will vote until the day of the election approaches closer. They are on the fence. If they get off the fence today the chances are that they will climb back tomorrow and perhaps the next day get off again on the other side.[16]

To men of this opinion, preëlection drifts, ground swells and last-minute switches are very real campaign phenomena, and must be carefully evaluated before substantial appreciation of voting intention can be gained.

[16]Sept. 22, 1912.

The second broad opinion is that voting intention is changed very little during a campaign. Most people, this view holds, make up their minds early in accordance with their party membership or on the basis of a "peeve" that has been growing upon them for months, and are little affected by campaign propaganda. Drifts, swings, undercurrents, last-minute switches, according to this view are largely figments of imagination, born of an impelling desire for victory or faulty observation. Campaigns change very few votes. Their chief function is to stir up party enthusiasm, and get predetermined convictions registered at the ballot box. Only in a very closely contested election, say men of this opinion, can electioneering win enough converts to throw the voting balance toward one party and away from the other.

If by means of straw polls precise measurements of public sentiment were made at stated intervals during a campaign, these divergent points of view could be resolved. The evidence of shift in preelection sentiment would then rest upon data objectively gathered, and not upon impressionistic observation and guesswork. With straw-poll appraisals, the results of electioneering effort could be studied in somewhat the same fashion as a business executive now ponders over his sales curve. As straw-voting technique becomes better known, students of politics will undoubtedly use this tool to make carefully controlled measurements of voting intention during political campaigns and thus throw a very significant light on an aspect of political campaigns that has yet been little explored.

Interpretation by Weighting

From the discussion of the many influences that may operate to distort straw-vote measurements of preëlection sentiment, it is apparent that skill is necessary in the handling of the straw-poll device. Like any other good tool, in this respect, results from its use are largely dependent on the proficiency of the craftsman. The wide range of error shown in a previous section for the straw polls of the past two decades is, to a large extent, no doubt, a reflection of the varying skill with which the individual canvasses were managed. The successful gauging of voting intention by means of the straw poll requires two kinds of competence: first, skillful collection of unofficial ballots in order that a representative sample of popular sentiment may be secured; and, second, interpretive insight whereby the quality of the straw returns may be judged. In the next five sections, these two classes of polling skill will occupy our attention. Putting the cart before the horse, the possibilities of interpretation will be examined first. At the outset, three manipulative techniques for distilling the truth from straw-vote figures, inaccurate on their face, will be discussed, and following this, straw-vote experience in general will be considered for salient practical points which may be of use to interpreters of future polls. In a succeeding section, skill in the collection of ballots will be considered, and certain maxims of good polling procedure, born of past experience, will be indicated. The present chapter will then be concluded with two final sections discussing the usefulness and the possible harm of straw polls.

The first interpretive technique for "correcting" straw-poll returns, with which we shall here deal, is called "weighting." This is a manipulation designed to counteract bias in a sample due to disproportionate group representation. For purposes of illustration, a poll with geographical bias can be hypothecated. The *Gazette*, located in Metropolitan, the largest town in the state, sponsors a straw vote to test popular sentiment with reference to the campaign for governor. Metropolitan customarily casts one-third of the total vote in the state, and is strongly Democratic. The remaining two thirds of the vote in the commonwealth comes from down-state where the Republican party is dominant. Since the *Gazette's* interests lie principally in Metropolitan, and since it costs money to send canvassers on the road, the newspaper collects half its votes in the queen city and the other half down-state, with returns as given in Table 20.

TABLE 20

HYPOTHETICAL RETURNS FROM THE *GAZETTE* STRAW POLL

	Jones (Dem.)		Brown (Rep.)		Total straw vote	
	Number	Percent	Number	Percent	Number	Percent
Metropolitan......	23,325	72	9,071	28	32,396	100
Down-state.......	11,663	36	20,733	64	32,396	100
Total state........	34,988	54	29,804	46	64,792	100

Thus in Metropolitan the straw returns give 72 percent of the total city vote to Jones, the Democratic candidate. Down-state, however, Jones polls but 36 percent of the straw votes. On their face, the unofficial totals for the state foreshadow victory for the Democratic candidate, with 54 percent of all the votes cast. But this would be an erroneous conclusion to draw from the *Gazette* poll, because half the straw votes were gathered in Democratic Metropolitan, whereas this city customarily casts but one third of the official vote on election day. Assuming for the purpose of the illustration that the straw sample for each part of the state is representative, a true prediction can be obtained from the *Gazette* figures only if the Metropolitan and down-state returns are weighted in accordance with the customary vote these sections officially cast. This may be done as follows: It is expected that 900,000 votes will be cast in the state, 300,000 in Metropolitan and 600,000 down-state. According to the straw poll, Jones will receive 72 percent of the ballots from Metropolitan or 216,000, and 36 percent of the down-state support, or 216,000 more, making a total of 432,000 votes for Jones, or 48 percent of the 900,000 total expected to be cast throughout the state.

Here, then, interpretation produces an accurate prediction from figures inaccurate on their face. Unweighted, the *Gazette* poll erroneously foreshadowed Jones' election with 54 percent of the state vote; weighted, the poll forecast Jones' defeat with but 48 percent of the people in the state supporting his candidacy.

The same principle of weighting, of course, can be used to correct disproportionate representation of groups other than geographical, provided the straw returns are tabulated separately by classes, *i.e.*, male and female, urban and rural, etc., and provided that satisfactory weights can be assigned to each class. Geographical weights are comparatively easy to fix, because past voting statistics are available, and given territories usually contribute about the same proportion of the total vote from one election to another. With sex composition of the effective electorate, the ratio is customarily fixed at 60 percent male and 40 percent female, though these figures may vary for specific localities and for separate elections. Weights fixed in the light of local circumstances are, of course, preferable to generalized values. In the fixing of weights, verifiable data should always be appealed to, for if these values are left to guesswork, the supposed correction may increase, rather than decrease, the predictive error of the straw returns.

Interpretation of straw polls by weighting is most important, of course, where disproportionate group representation in the sample is marked and where the favored class holds radically different political views from the neglected one. In the example cited above, those two factors purposely were made extreme for the sake of the illustration. Such excessive bias will not often be encountered in actual practice. Where it is not present, weighted and unweighted predictions will give practically the same results. It is understood, of course, that the manipulation of weighting does not correct bad sampling within classes, but only disproportionate selection between classes.

Interpretation on Theory of Recurrent Bias

The second interpretive technique that we wish to discuss here is that of adjusting original straw vote returns on the basis of "recurrent bias." Where straw polls are taken year after year by the same method and the various factors working for inaccuracy repeatedly give about the same error in prediction, this possibility of correcting current forecasts in the light of past experience arises. The essential condition for the application of this technique is a recurrent pattern of error.

Ballot-in-the-paper polls, reaching the same reading clientele year after year, may present the broad outlines of such a pattern, but the vagaries of this method of straw polling are such as to make correction on the theory of recurrent bias a highly speculative matter. In personal-canvass polls, repeated similarities in error seldom occur, because, though the polling procedure may be generally the same in successive undertakings, it is never identical, the random movements of the solicitors tending to bring them into contact with a new set of people in each canvass and thus effecting a complete reshuffling of participants. The personal-canvass polls of the *Columbus Dispatch* and *Cincinnati Enquirer*, taken biennially over a period of two decades, for example, have never revealed a recurrent pattern of bias, the predictive error now favoring one party and then another. Only in a mail poll, using the same type of addressing lists from year to year, is there a possibility of interpretive correction of current returns in the light of previous error.

In the 1924 and 1928 *Literary-Digest* polls of the tel-auto population, the Republican vote, as has been pointed out,[17] was consistently larger, proportionately, than that received in the official count. When the pluralities foreshadowed by the 1928 *Digest* poll were adjusted by the amount of plurality error of the 1924 poll, the average 1928 plurality error by state was reduced one-half, from 12 to 6 votes per 100 cast. This gives rise to the suggestion that if in 1932 the *Literary Digest* conducts another presidential poll,

---
[17]See pp. 72-73.

using telephone and automobile names for its mailing list, and if the struggle for votes in that year is largely bipartisan as it was in 1928, the straw returns can be corrected to advantage by adjusting the indicated pluralities in the light of the plurality error shown in the 1928 poll. Since the Hoover vote was overestimated in every state, this correction would call for the deflation of the Republican straw vote in 1932 in every state. For example, if the 1928 plurality error for a given state were 4 votes per 100, and the 1932 straw vote foreshadowed a Republican plurality of 12 votes per 100, then the corrected prediction would be 12-4=8 votes per 100, the indicated Republican margin. If, on the other hand, the straw vote showed a Democratic plurality of 12 votes per 100, deflation of Republican strength would require that the previous plurality error be added to the plurality indicated by the straw vote, and the prediction would be 12+4=16 votes per 100, the corrected Democratic plurality forecast.

The soundness of this interpretive correction, of course, rests on the assumption that the party struggle in 1932 will be comparable with that of 1928, and that the sampling flaws of the 1932 poll will be similar to those of the straw vote taken four years previously. The distortive factors affecting the accuracy of a 1932 poll, particularly those of selection in coöperation and change of sentiment over time, may operate differently than they did in 1928, but it has previously been argued that the principal cause of *Literary-Digest* error is the party bias in the mailing list, and, since this bias tends to be stable so long as the same mailing lists are used, it is highly probable that a 1932 *Digest* canvass of the tel-auto population, corrected in the light of the demonstrated error of the 1928 poll, will give a better prediction than the uncorrected returns alone. In applying this corrective technique, the interpreter should be thoroughly aware of the assumption upon which the methodology is based, namely that the sampling distortions of the current straw vote are the same as those of the previous poll. If there is reason to believe that the sampling flaws in the later poll are greatly dissimilar to those in the earlier one, the present correction technique is inapplicable.

Interpretation in Light of Indicated Past Preferences

In many straw polls, in addition to the question on present preference, or "How do you intend to vote this year?" a second question is asked on past preference, or "How did you vote in the last (comparable) election?" The answers to this second inquiry offer special interpretive possibilities which we wish to explore in this section.

In the first place, information on the past preferences of straw voters makes possible the computation of a corroboratory forecast. In questionnaire practice it is often the custom to cover a single point with two queries differently phrased. If the replies show consistency, the investigator has the more reason, within the limits of his sample, to place faith in his results. In straw-vote practice, similarly, if predictions from past-preference information give the same results as forecasts from present-preference data, the plausibility of the straw-vote measurement is enhanced.

Depending on how the straw-vote data are tabulated, there are two methods for computing predictions on the basis of past preferences. If the unofficial returns are arranged to show only the proportion of the total vote given to each party in the present and previous campaign, then the difference between party proportions thus shown must be calculated and this straw index of "net shift" must be added or subtracted, as the case may be, from the comparable party proportions of the total official vote of the previous election. In Table 21 this method is illustrated with an example in which the total vote for both straw and official polls is given as 100.

In this example, the comparison of the past and the present preferences of the straw voters shows a net gain of 5 votes for the X party, a net gain of 3 votes for the Y party, and a net loss of 8 votes for the Z party, from the previous election. When these gains and losses are applied to the official vote of the previous election, a prediction results which is identical with that based on figures of present voting intention. The illustration, however, is an ideal one, which assumes that the straw sample of both past and present voting preferences is perfect. As a matter of fact, this is seldom true, the division of the total vote between the several candidates usually showing some variation between the straw and official returns. In some cases this may lead to absurd forecasts, as in the example in Table 22, where the past-preference straw vote shows 5 less X votes, and 5 more Z adherents, than the official returns of the previous election:

TABLE 21
Straw-Vote Prediction from Past Preferences Computed by Method of Net Shift

Party	How the straw voters say they voted in the previous election	How the straw voters say they will vote in the present election	Indicated party gain or loss	How the voters officially voted in the previous election	Prediction for present election on basis of net shift
X	40	45	+5	40	45
Y	50	53	+3	50	53
Z	10	2	—8	10	2
	100	100*	0	100	100

*In practice, fewer past than present preferences are always revealed in a straw vote, because many participants are new voters or former "stay-at-homes," or if they did vote in the previous election, fail to indicate that fact on the straw ballot. In the 1924 and 1928 presidential polls of the *Literary Digest*, 19 and 16 percent of the participants, respectively, left the past-preference column blank. Straw-vote predictions on the basis of shift in party allegiance use only the ballots that reveal both a past and a present preference. If the present voting intentions of this group were widely different from those of the group that failed to express a past preference, predictions on the basis of shift might be prejudiced. As a matter of fact, however, the present choice of the two groups varies but little. In 1928, 64 percent of the *Literary-Digest* straw ballots that revealed a 1924 preference, were marked for Hoover; of the ballots returned with no past preference indicated, 59 percent were voted for the Republican candidate. Since the present preferences of both groups are much the same, and since, in any case, the number of ballots carrying no past preference is small, the ballots indicating shift in sentiment from the previous election provide a valid basis for prediction.

TABLE 22
Straw-Vote Prediction from Imperfect Sample Computed by Net-Shift Method

Party	How the straw voters say they voted in the previous election	How the straw voters say they will vote in the present election	Indicated party gain or loss	How the voters officially voted in the previous election	Predictions for present election on basis of net shift
X	40	45	+5	45	50
Y	50	53	+3	50	53
Z	10	2	—8	5	— 3
	100	100	0	100	100

Here the net shift from the Z party from the previous to the present election is shown by the straw poll to be 8 votes. Since the candidate of the Z party polled but 5 votes in the previous election, the prediction for the present nominee of this party is minus 3 votes, which is, of course, an absurd result. In a case of this kind it is obvious that a flaw exists, in the straw sample of the past or present preferences, or in both.

When the past-preference straw returns are tabulated to show party-to-party movement of voters, *i.e.*, how the Republican, Democratic, and minor party votes in the previous election will distribute themselves in the present election, a second method of computation is used. The straw past preferences for each party are first percentaged out to the parties which are to receive the present vote, then the official returns of the previous election are distributed according to these indices of party-to-party shift, as in the example given in Table 23.

TABLE 23
STRAW-VOTE PREDICTION FROM PAST PREFERENCES COMPUTED BY METHOD OF PARTY-TO-PARTY SHIFT

Party	How the voters officially voted in the previous election	How the straw voters say they voted in the previous election	How the straw voters say they will vote in the present election		Party-to party shift (Percentage)
X............	40	40	X	30	75
			Y	10	25
			Z	0	0
				40	100
Y............	50	50	X	14	28
			Y	36	72
			Z	0	0
				50	100
Z............	10	10	X	1	10
			Y	7	70
			Z	2	20
	100	100		10	100

Forecast for X party: 45 votes per 100 cast as follows:

75 percent of previous X vote = 30 (.75 × 40)
28 percent of previous Y vote = 14 (.28 × 50)
10 percent of previous Z vote = 1 (.10 × 10)
─────
45

POLLS ON CANDIDATES

Forecast for Y party: 53 votes per 100 cast as follows:

25 percent of previous X vote = 10 (.25 × 40)
72 percent of previous Y vote = 36 (.72 × 50)
70 percent of previous Z vote = 7 (.70 × 10)
———
53

Forecast for Z party: 2 votes per 100 cast as follows:

20 percent of previous Z vote = 2 (.20 × 10)

Theoretically the party-to-party method of computing shift predictions has an advantage over the net shift method, in that the former is less influenced by party bias in the sample. Consider the situation where 30 percent of the former X voters have shifted their allegiance to the Y party, and where this movement is perfectly reflected by a straw poll as in Table 24.

TABLE 24
Straw and Official Election Returns Which Show a 30-Percent Alienation of X Voters to the Y Party

Party	How the voters officially voted in the previous election	How the voters officially voted in the present election	How the straw voters say they voted in the previous election	How the straw voters say they will vote in the present election
X	70	49*	70	49
Y	30	51	30	51
	100	100	100	100

*49 = 70 − (.30 × 70).

Under these circumstances, predictions by the net shift and party-to-party methods, which we need not work out here in detail, will give perfect and identical results.

But now suppose that the straw vote sample reflects shift of allegiance perfectly, but is biased 10 votes for the Y party in the past preferences. In these circumstances, the net-shift forecast would show a predictive error, for each candidate of 3 votes per 100 cast, whereas the party-to-party method would give a perfect prediction as in Table 25.

TABLE 25

Straw-Vote Prediction from Imperfect Sample Computed
by Net-Shift and Party-to-Party Methods

Net-Shift Method

Party	How the straw voters say they voted in the previous election	How the straw voters say they will vote in the present election	Party gain or loss	How the voters officially voted in the previous election	Net-shift prediction	How the voters officially voted in present election	diction Error in prediction
X	60	42	−18	70	52	49	+3
Y	40	58	+18	30	48	51	−3
	100	100	0	100	100	100	0

Party-to-Party Shift Method

Party	How the voters officially voted in the previous election	How the straw voters say they voted in the previous election	How the straw voters say they will vote in the present election		Party-to-party shift (Percentage)
X	70	60	X 42		70
			Y 18		30
			60		100
Y	30	40	X 0		0
			Y 40		100
	100	100	40		100

Forecast for X party: 49 votes per 100 cast as follows:

    70 percent of previous X vote = 49 (.70 × 70)
    (Official X party vote in present election = 49; error none)

Forecast for Y party: 51 votes per 100 cast as follows:

    30 percent of previous X vote = 21 (.30 × 70)
    100 percent of previous Y vote = 30 (1.00 × 30)
                                               51
    (Official Y party vote in present election = 51; error none)

The party-to-party method of computation, therefore, has a distinct advantage over the net-shift method where the past-preference sample favors one party unduly.

POLLS ON CANDIDATES 123

Turning now to the second interpretive possibility of past-preference data, it has been suggested that these data may give a clue to the party bias of the straw-vote sample. In the illustration immediately preceding, for example, the past preferences showed 10 more votes for the Y group than that party officially received in the previous election. Under the present interpretation, this figure would be regarded as an index of party bias and the current preferences would be corrected by 10 votes, as in Table 26.

TABLE 26
PRESENT STRAW-VOTE PREFERENCES CORRECTED BY PARTY BIAS OF PAST STRAW PREFERENCES

Party	How the straw voters say they voted in the previous election	How the officially voted in the previous election	Bias	How the straw voters say they will vote in the present election	Corrected prediction in the light of bias	How the voters officially voted in the present election	Error-corrected prediction	Error-uncorrected prediction
X....	60	70	—10	42	52	49	+3	—7
Y.....	40	30	+10	58	48	51	—3	+7
	100	100	0	100	100	100	0	0

By this correction, the original error of the predictions based on present preferences is reduced from 7 to 3 votes per 100 cast. It should be observed that in correcting a straw-vote prediction by this method, the assumption is made that the party bias of past and present preferences is the same. This is not necessarily true, the effect of bolting tending to change the party bias of the sample. In the above illustration, the past-preference bias favored the Y party by 10 votes, but in the present preferences this bias was but 7 votes. The assumption of identical party bias, therefore, was in error 3 votes, which accounts for the identical error of the corrected prediction.

It would be desirable to test the theory of corroboratory predictions and that of correcting present-preference forecasts in the light of party bias of past preferences on actual straw vote data, but, unfortunately, this cannot be done with thoroughness, because of the inadequate reporting of past-preference figures by the leading straw-vote sponsors. The *Cincinnati Enquirer,* for example, has asked for past-preference information in practically all its straw polls, but has printed figures only on the movement of voters from the Democratic to the Republican parties and vice versa. In the absence of figures on shift between major and minor, and no shift, *i.e.* party regularity, these data are valueless for the present type of analysis. The *New York Herald* and collaborators similarly gathered information on past preferences, but failed to print much of the data on the movement between the major and minor parties.

In 1928, both the *Literary Digest* and the *Hearst Newspapers* printed past-preference returns for Coolidge and Davis, but forgot to mention the votes for La Follette. On the part of the *Literary Digest*, the error was due to the make-up of the ballot. In the space set aside for the voting of past preferences were printed three boxes, one marked "Republican," another labeled, "Democrat," and a third reserved for miscellany with the directions: "If you voted any other party, write name of party." Although 17 percent of the total popular vote went to La Follette in 1924, practically no one took the trouble to declare the fact by writing in the Wisconsin Senator's name on the 1928 *Literary-Digest* ballot. Analysis of the past-preference figures furnished by this poll, therefore, is of no avail because the distribution of the La Follette vote between the 1928 presidential aspirants is not indicated. This experience of the *Literary Digest* should serve to emphasize the practical necessity of printing on the straw ballot the name of every candidate or party involved in a straw poll.

Some of the polls of the *Columbus Dispatch* and the earlier undertakings of the *Literary Digest* furnish data upon which the desired tests can be made. For these polls, the predictive error resultant under the several interpretations here discussed is given in Table 27.

From Table 27, it appears that predictions based on uncorrected present straw-vote preferences (col. 1), and those computed from past preferences by the method of party-to-party shift (col. 2), are largely corroborative. If anything, the latter predictions are a shade the better, presumably for the reason that the party-to-party shift method of computation minimizes party bias in the sample. The forecasts from past preferences by the method of net shift (col. 3) are shown to be less accurate than those computed by the method of party-to-party shift (col. 2), and, with the exception of the *Literary-Digest* poll of six states in 1920, somewhat less accurate than the predictions from the present preferences corrected. Interpretive corrections of present preferences in the light of party bias of past preferences (col. 4), served no useful purpose in the five *Columbus Dispatch* polls, the predictive error being increased, rather than decreased, as a result of the manipulation. Because of the large La Follette vote in 1924, and the lack of a similar party vote in 1920, the method cannot be applied to all states in the 1924 *Literary-Digest* poll. When tested on those states in which the official La Follette vote was negligible, however, the correction again served only to increase the predictive error. In the 1920 *Literary-Digest* poll alone, did this manipulation reduce the inaccuracy of the forecast. No test can be made on the 1916 *Digest* poll, because in this year there was no Progressive vote comparable to that in 1912.

TABLE 27

Error in Predicting the Proportion of the Total Vote Received by the Winning Candidate by Four Methods of Computation

	1	2	3	4
	Present preferences, uncorrected	Past-preferences, party-to-party shift	Past preferences, net shift	Present preferences, corrected by party bias revealed by past preferences
Five *Columbus Dispatch* presidential and gubernatorial polls, 1920 to 1928—Average by polls.............	3.8	3.4	8.5	6.1
1924 *Literary-Digest* presidential poll—Average by states	6.1	4.8	6.8	*
1924 *Literary-Digest* presidential poll for the 20 states in which the La Follette vote was smallest—Average by states.................	6.9	5.3	7.0	8.2
Literary-Digest presidential poll of 6 states, 1920—Average by states...............	10.0	†	2.0	2.0
Literary-Digest presidential poll of 5 states, 1916—Average by states...............	9.9	8.1	11.6	*

*Method not applicable because of third party vote.
†Party-to-party data not available.

The analysis of past-preference returns is admittedly a complicated task, the more so because the data upon which experimental work can be carried on are largely inadequate. As a consequence, further consideration of this aspect of straw polls must await future experience and research.

Interpretation—General Considerations

In the interpretation of straw polls, scientific skepticism is always necessary. No poll should be accepted at face value. Trust can be placed in straw returns only after the interpreter has assured himself that the ballots have been collected in such a manner as to be representative of the whole body of voters. For skillful interpretation of straw figures, the political predictor needs to know what distortive influences to look for in straw-vote samples, and what allowances to make for these once they are discovered. In this section, interpretive criteria, born of the polling experience set forth in preceding pages, will be outlined for the benefit of predictors who may desire to use straw-poll returns as the basis of their forecasts.

In the study of the causes of straw-poll error, eight factors were named which might make predictions based on straw votes inaccurate. These eight factors may be employed as criteria of interpretation, the predictor testing the straw-poll returns on each of the eight counts. Following this outline, the questions that would be asked are:

(1) Is there any reason to believe that the sponsor manipulated his straw-vote figures for partisan or dramatic purposes? Practically no cases have been found where a poll was manipulated in the interests of a party or a candidate; some, however, have been discovered where day-to-day reports were juggled for the purpose of simulating a close race.

(2) Was there a chance for ballot-box stuffing? Is there any evidence of a major conspiracy against the poll, such as a sudden influx of votes all marked for the same candidate? Ballot-in-the-paper polling technique is more vulnerable in respect to stuffing and repeating than other methods of canvassing. Personal-canvass polls that establish semipermanent booths in public places are also to be viewed with suspicion. "Spot" personal canvasses, where the solicitor arrives unannounced, gathers his ballots systematically and leaves for other parts, are reasonably free from repeating. Mail

polls that allow small participation are difficult to stuff. The more cards sent out, the greater the possibility of duplication, of course. The character and experience of the sponsor must weigh heavily in evaluation of this factor as, indeed, it does with every other factor here considered. Good management can largely avoid stuffing of ballot boxes by reducing the opportunity to repeaters and by careful scrutiny of returns to detect fraudulent votes.

(3) Are the returns colored by geographical bias? Was the number of straw ballots drawn from each territory commensurate with the importance of that area in the official election totals? In the early stages of a poll, particularly, this factor of geographical bias must be guarded against, for in state polls, returns are often totaled for a state, whereas, in reality, they have come from restricted sections of that political unit. In the case of the 1928 *Wisconsin-News* poll, information that the early returns had been gathered largely in Milwaukee, a Smith stronghold, and not from Wisconsin as a whole, would have prevented a misinterpretation of the figures. Personal-canvass polls often neglect the rural vote, and it is usually desirable to inquire what provision a sponsor of this type of enterprise has made to cover this section of the electorate.

(4) Are the returns colored by class bias? Was the sampling procedure so arranged that it reached all groups, or was one group favored over another? If there is class bias in the sample, are the favored and neglected classes thought to hold dissimilar voting intentions? If there is class bias and also difference in political conviction between the classes involved, is there any way to overcome the distortion by weighting or by correction in the light of similar bias in previous polls? In a ballot-in-the-paper poll, reader clientele gives the clew to this type of bias. The 1928 *Pathfinder* presidential poll, a ballot-in-the-paper undertaking, for example, could at most be regarded only as a reflection of the farmer's point of view, since this magazine circulates primarily to country people. Personal-canvass polls with wide coverage are not likely to reflect class bias, though some may slight the inaccessible rural vote. Mail polls partake of the class bias of the mailing list upon which they are based. Names from a registry of voters or a city directory may involve little class bias. Mailing lists abstracted exclusively from ownership files, such as tax-assessment rolls, telephone directories, and automobile registers, are liable to be more colored, usually on the side of wealth and conservatism.

(5) Were the straw returns influenced by selection in coöperation? In mail polls, particularly, this form of distortion must be watched. It is most likely to appear in a campaign where one party, or the adherents to one point of view, are extremely active in forwarding their cause. It can sometimes be detected by comparing coöperation (the percentage of ballots returned to the total mailed out) in the current enterprise, where party zeal and enthusiasm is excessive, with coöperation in a previous poll where this animation was absent. As a general rule, reformers coöperate more than defenders of the *status quo*, and men more than women. There is no evidence to indicate differences in willingness to coöperate between Republicans and Democrats, as such, or between rural and urban people.

(6) Is there reason to believe that the poll reached large groups of people of one political conviction, but who are not likely to participate in the election? This test might be especially applicable to polls in the southern states, where negroes might vote Republican in the unofficial test, but fail to register their voices in the legal election.

(7) Are the returns large enough in number to avoid the erratic results that might result from chance fluctuations in small samples? In the discussion of the subject of adequacy, it was pointed out that straw-vote error is caused more by the quality than by the quantity of ballots gathered. In states or large cities, samples of 10 to 30 per 1,000 official votes have been found to be adequate in size. For smaller units, the size of the sample may have to be increased before it can be trusted on the score of adequacy.

(8) Is there any reason to believe that sentiment shifted materially after the unofficial ballots were gathered? If so, the straw-vote returns are unreliable to the extent of the change. As urged in a previous discussion of the subject, successive straw-poll returns do not offer evidence of shift of sentiment, unless the ballots were gathered in the same territory by the same method as the preceding poll. In case this qualification is met, and the later poll shows results different from the earlier canvass, the figures from the two undertakings should not be cumulated, but the prediction should be based solely on the latest returns, or possibly on the trend indicated by the successive measurements provided there is reason to believe that the trend will persist until the day of the election.

In general, the interpreter can be most skeptical of ballot-in-the-paper polls, and most trustful of mail and personal canvasses. Also in his appraisals, he can give liberal weight to the character and experience of the institution which sponsors a poll. Casual sponsors, through lack of knowledge or serious interest, often produce very erroneous straw-vote forecasts. On the other hand, managements with many years of training and with reputations to maintain, achieve a high degree of predictive accuracy.

Polls under multiple sponsorship—where several papers collaborate in canvassing a state or the nation—present more opportunities for sampling flaws than undertakings under single management. Despite announcements about uniformity of procedure, each editor conducts his part of the canvass according to his own lights and interests, and almost invariably inconsistency in technique and predictive accuracy results. In polls of a single state, where county papers enter into collaboration, this may be especially true. Particularly is geographical bias likely to be present in an enterprise of this type, because some editors go out after big numbers, thereby giving their county an importance in the unofficial state poll that it does not possess in the legal election. Even in such a highly integrated undertaking as the Hearst presidential straw vote of 1928, there were some significant lapses from uniform polling procedure. In most states, the *Hearst Newspapers* used a mail technique, supplemented by a personal canvass in the larger cities; but in Colorado, where the returns were collected by the independently-owned *Denver Post*, ballot-in-the paper methodology was employed. Throughout the nation, the Hearst poll was remarkably accurate, averaging but 5 percent plurality error per state. In Colorado, however, the plurality error ran to 41 percent. Polls under multiple sponsorship, therefore, cannot receive blanket interpretation, but must be appraised in the light of the polling procedure employed by each collaborator.

When straw-vote returns indicate a close race between two candidates, caution must be exercised in predicting the winner. If the variations due to the crudeness of the straw-poll measurements are sufficient to turn the balance, then designation of the winner is purely gratuitous and a matter of guesswork. In such circumstances, the only sound interpretation is to acknowledge the closeness of the contest and to declare the outcome in doubt. The precise area of uncertainty for straw polls cannot be generalized, for some enterprises are less accurate than others, and, moreover, there is always the factor of change of sentiment to be taken into account. The best approximation of the allowance to be made for crudeness in the straw-poll measuring device can be sought in the past performance of the sponsoring institution or the predictive record of polls similar to the one under consideration.

If a straw poll satisfactorily meets the tests here suggested, the interpreter can place faith in the trustworthiness of the returns. In the past, extremely accurate prediction has resulted from straw polls, and there is no reason why this performance may not be duplicated and even improved upon in the future.

The Sponsor and Sound Sampling Practice

The best single guarantee of the reliability of straw poll returns is good management. Susceptible though the sampling process is to distortive influences, the straw vote can be made to yield authentic measurements of voting intention if it is handled correctly. Of what does good management consist? In this section, past polling experience will be reviewed from the standpoint of the sponsor, as distinguished from that of the interpreter, and sound sampling practice will be indicated.

The general aim of a straw poll is to collect a limited number of voting preferences in such a manner that all shades of political opinion are represented in the sample in direct proportion to their importance in the electorate. This can be achieved by either a mail or a personal canvass, or by a judicious combination of the two. The *Columbus Dispatch*, for example, uses a personal-canvass technique in the cities, and reaches the more or less inaccessible rural voter by a mail poll. In 1928, the *Hearst Newspapers* gathered ballots by mail primarily, but in many large cities, where dwellers in foreign or slum areas might not be as responsive to mail solicitation, a personal canvass was employed. Ballot-in-the-paper technique is less desirable than either a mail or a personal canvass, and in serious attempts to measure preëlection sentiment, should be avoided.

If the poll is taken by means of postal cards, the sampling list is of prime importance. A list of registered voters should be the first choice, because, more than any other, it reaches the people who will cast the official vote. Next best is a list that has been drawn from mixed sources, city directories, telephone, automobile, tax-assessment names, which are commonly purchaseable from addressograph companies. With such a varied list, the possibilities are good that a fairly representative group of citizens will be reached.

Lists made up exclusively from one source, such as telephone directories, tax-assessment rolls, or automobile ownership, are least liable to effect complete coverage of the whole electorate. Before a list is accepted, the sponsor, so far as possible, should satisfy himself that it contains names from all classes in the population, rural and urban, factory and white-collar, male and female. Once a representative mailing list is secured, adequate quotas for election divisions, based on turnout at previous elections, can be set, and cards can be sent to names, selected at random—every tenth or every twenty-fifth name, say—until enough returns have been received to fill these quotas.

If the poll is of the personal-canvass variety, quotas for certain areas—wards, if the poll is confined to a city, and counties, if the poll is state-wide—can be laid down on the basis of votes cast in previous comparable elections. Within these areas, class quotas can be designated for the guidance of the canvassers. From census statistics and from personal acquaintance of the sponsor with the area to be sampled, a certain proportion of votes can be ordered from the rural and urban districts; or, in the cities, from factory and office workers. Usually personal-canvass polls contact the voter on the street corner or at his place of employment. Probably more accurate results would be obtained were citizens approached in the districts where they vote, the canvass being centered on the home and guided along strictly geographical lines, as in a party poll. This would require late afternoon and evening canvassing, however, and would involve much more labor, since it is easier to gather one hundred ballots at the factory gate than to collect them from as many separate homes. In the 1928 *Hearst Newspapers* poll, a random house-to-house canvass was made in a number of cities.

In the selection of canvassing points and in fixing quotas for the various classes of citizens to be contacted, newspapermen are often guided by their intuition, rather than by more objective techniques. If the straw returns give one candidate more votes than the sponsor thinks he should be receiving, for example, the canvass is sometimes ordered into opposition territory to even matters up a bit. This, of course, is bad practice. Once the plan is outlined, with quotas set up, it should be adhered to. If the returns from a given territory seem fantastic and unreasonable, then a repoll should be made. Forecasts thus arrived at will prove to be more accurate than predictions based on subjective considerations. It is true, of course, that a tremendous amount of practical sense must enter into the management of any straw poll, but "hunch" should not be allowed to control the report, for anyone, by choosing his sampling ground, can make a poll say anything he wishes it to say. The great advantage of straw-poll measurements is their objectivity; by their use the predictor is enabled to lift his appraisals of preëlection sentiment clear of the swirl of emotion that might otherwise unsteady his judgment during a political campaign. But objectivity is gained only when sampling rules have been adhered to, and certainly the collection of ballots by the "hunch" method is a clear violation of these precepts.

Fraud and ballot-box stuffing are an ever-present threat to straw-poll accuracy, and sponsors must always be on guard against these influences. In a mail poll, it is a wise precaution to mark the ballot cards in such a manner that spurious duplications can be recognized and rejected. Also a record of mailing should be kept in order that abnormalities in returns can be readily detected. The experience of the *Buffalo Courier-Express*, in its mayoralty poll of 1929, is illuminating in this regard. When the editors of this paper discovered cards being returned from wards which had not been sampled, the inference was plain that a conspiracy was afoot. The conspirators having failed to discover the identification mark on the legitimate cards, it was a simple matter for the *Courier-Express* to sort the spurious from the genuine straw votes and throw the former into the wastebasket.

Another method quite widely employed for detecting fraud in mail polls is to scrutinize incoming cards for likeness in handwriting and cancellation marks. When a number of ballots are received which bear identical handwriting, all canceled at the same post office, on the same day, and at the same hour, the evidence is sufficient that the poll is being stuffed. Such duplications can be readily cast aside and excluded from the count. While repeaters that arrive in the same mail are comparatively easy to weed out, by this method the defense is ineffective against duplication that dribbles in from day to day, since it is highly impractical to rescan cards for the purpose of comparing handwriting. In most cases, however, day-to-day duplication is the work of amateurs, and unless undertaken on a systematic scale does not seriously endanger the integrity of a poll. When ballot cards are sparingly distributed by the sponsors, it is difficult for perpetrators of fraud to gather enough legitimate ballots to influence materially the unofficial returns. The greater the number of cards mailed out, of course, the more susceptible is the poll to this form of tampering.

Personal-canvass polls can minimize repeating by "spot" soliciting, the agent appearing on the scene without previous announcement, gathering his ballots before duplicators have a chance to cast several votes and leaving promptly for other parts. Personal solicitation for preferences in crowds should be avoided so far as possible and, similarly, ballots should not be collected from semipermanent booths where passers-by may vote as often as they choose. Ballot boxes should never be left unattended, nor should ballots be deposited in quantities in merchandise shops for patrons to vote.

The quality of the soliciting personnel is of great importance in a personal canvass, for the accuracy of a straw vote can be destroyed as easily from within an organization as from without. The collection of voting preferences is hard, monotonous work, and the temptation to an irresponsible agent to pad his results is great. Many newspapers do not employ temporary assistance for their straw-vote canvass, but delegate this task only to trusted men on their permanent staff.

In a mail poll, wherever possible, provision should be made for the detection of the bias of selection in coöperation. The sponsor cannot be sure that his straw-vote sample is representative of the whole electorate, simply because he mailed ballots to all classes of voters; he must know, as well, if the various classes were equally coöperative in expressing their political preferences. The keying or numbering of cards for this purpose is objectionable, since it identifies the individual straw voter and tends to arouse his suspicions. A better method would be to mail special ballots to test groups of known characteristics. The proportion of cards returned by these control groups would then indicate variations in coöperativeness between classes.

The number of ballots that should be gathered depends upon the size of the electorate being polled. In states and large cities 10 to 30 straw to every 1,000 official votes has been found to be sufficient. For smaller electorates it may be necessary to increase the size of the sample. The general rule is to collect as representative a sample as possible, increasing the number of preferences gathered to the point where added choices do not significantly alter the returns.

The well-managed straw poll will signify in advance whether or not an attempt will be made to measure change of sentiment during a campaign. If it is desired to show the fluctuations of voting intention during the period of electioneering, arrangements will be made to conduct two or more separate and comparable polls in each territory covered. Such polls, for example, might run for two or three weeks at a time, and might be spaced one month apart. These details, however, are altogether dependent upon the circumstances that surround each individual enterprise. If it is not desired to measure change of sentiment during a campaign, but one canvass will be provided for. In this case, the gathering of the ballots may require two weeks or two months, the canvass proceeding until all sections of a given territory are covered. The assumption is made that sentiment does not change during the time the ballots are being collected.

In polls of the multiple-sponsorship type, a uniform method of canvassing, with needed local variations, should be agreed upon at the outset, and an attempt should be made to adhere to the plan. If the poll involves coöperation of two or more papers within a given election unit, say a county or a state, quotas for each collaborator should be fixed in conformity with the importance of his territory in the official election. By this means, the straw vote for a county or state will be correctly weighted and the poll will not require special interpretation to draw out its true significance.

The form which the straw ballot should take is largely an individual matter with each sponsor. In a personal-canvass poll, it is often a small square of paper with only appropriate boxes printed after each candidate's name to receive the voter's x. In ballot-in-the-paper and mail polls, the ballot always contains directions for marking, and usually it gives assurances that the voting is secret. Sometimes the voter is requested to write in the name of his state or county to assist in tabulation by special geographical units. The handwriting thus set down is also useful in detecting duplication. Some sponsors of ballot-in-the-paper polls ask for the name and address of the straw voter as an evidence of good faith, but this is not a successful practice, because few people will vote under that condition. One point that should be universally observed in making up a ballot is that the name of each candidate involved in the poll should be printed. This holds for past, as well as for present, choices. In 1928 several important sponsors who sought information concerning shift of voting allegiance, failed to print La Follette's name on their straw ballots. This oversight rendered all the past-preference tabulations worthless, because the current disposition of the large La Follette vote of four years previous was unknown.

In publishing straw-vote returns, there is no special form for the presentation of figures on current voting preferences, but if the sponsor is also printing data on shift from previous party allegiance, he should show party-to-party movement, and not simply the party division of the total past preferences. This can be accomplished with the following plan of tabulation.

State or county	Hoover—Republican					Smith—Democrat					So on for each candidate
	Current vote	How the same voters voted in				Current vote	How the same voters voted in				
		Rep.	Dem.	Minor	No vote		Rep.	Dem.	Minor	No vote	
Ala......											
Ariz......											

If the vote for single minor candidates is small, and it is felt that space is not available to print all the figures in detail, the current straw vote for each minor candidate can be shown, but the past vote can be totaled for all minor candidates as follows:

Minor						
Current vote			How the same voters voted in			
Thomas	Foster	Varney	Rep.	Dem.	Minor	No vote

The correct tabulation of past-preference returns is important, for, unless the complete data are printed, the figures are of no value for predictive purposes.

If the poll is taken by mail, the number of blank ballots distributed should be reported by suitable political units. In a nation-wide enterprise, this unit may be the state; in a state poll, the county; and in a city canvass, the ward. From these data, interpreters can compute the extent of coöperation by geographical unit and examine these indices for traces of the bias of selection in coöperation.

The general rule for publicizing straw-vote returns should be to print all details in such manner as to allow every man to interpret the figures according to his own lights. This will require, at the outset, a thorough and detailed description of the plan to be followed by the canvass, type of polling technique to be used, description of mailing list or source from which votes are to be personally solicited, and such other information as will enable a reader to make his own appraisal of the straw returns. As the canvass proceeds, alterations in polling technique should receive ample publicity. In day-to-day reports, the source of the returns should be indicated, in order that the reader may view them in the light of their geographical significance. No manipulation of figures will be tolerated by good management, the returns being printed as they are received.

The Utility of the Straw Poll

The utility of the straw poll lies in the fact that it offers a relatively inexpensive technique whereby popular sentiment on candidates or issues can be appraised without resorting to inclusive canvasses, on the one hand, or guess-work and impression on the other. Its use should enable both the practical and the theoretical worker in the field of politics to make his knowledge of the political preferences of the people more exact.

The legislator, for example, when confused on the division of sentiment among his constituents on major governmental questions, might employ the straw poll to clear away his doubt. This use of the device would serve to bring government closer to the people. In a similar vein, legislative pressure groups might use the straw poll to gauge the progress of their reforms with the voters. In the light of such measurements, together with data of qualitative nature, propaganda operations could be carried on more intelligently and reform energies conserved for the fields where their expenditure would bring the greatest return.

For the organization politician, whose interests lie largely in the election of public officers and the emoluments of administrative power, the straw poll may serve to supplement his customary gauging techniques. In Chapter I it was shown how the politician measures preëlection sentiment by means of opinion reports that come up through the party organization, house-to-house canvasses by the precinct workers, independent counsels from leading citizens in various communities and special reports from hired scouts. The chief weakness of this gauging system, it was argued ,was the inability of partisans to dissociate the will to win from cool observation of political realities. In the heat of battle, when party generals are being supplied with reports which may contain more of wish than of fact, straw votes might be used as a check on the reliability of this information.[18] The straw canvass might also be employed in areas poor in party organization, yet worthy of electioneering attention; or again, it might, on occasion, provide a relatively inexpensive substitute for an inclusive precinct canvass. It is not to be supposed that the straw poll can supplant the precinct canvass, however, because the function of the former is limited to the gathering of quantitative data about voting intention, whereas the latter provides information, not alone on how a citizen intends to vote, but as to the reasons for his choice as well. The inclusive canvass, moreover, enables the precinct worker to convey the campaign arguments to the voter, and also it bolsters the morale of the party organization by shouldering it with responsibility and by giving it petty canvassing patronage to dispense.

For the newspaperman, the straw poll provides a tool which enables him to report objectively the status of voting sentiment before elections. By its use he can systematically contact the voters themselves, gathering his information at the original source without being compelled to rely on politicians for his data or upon his own impressions. The reports of voting intention thus derived provide an added newspaper feature, which has proved of great interest to the reading public.

Finally, for the student of politics, the straw poll may serve as a measure of sentiment whereby the workings of public opinion in response to electioneering may be better understood. As yet we do not have systematic information on the process by which voting sentiment crystallizes during a campaign. Some observers hold that campaigns are won or lost before they start, the chief function of electioneering being to get fixed political sympathies registered at the polls. Others take the view that preëlection sentiment is in a constant state of flux until the date of the balloting, the shifting circumstances of the campaign stimulating the voters to cross and recross party lines in making their decisions. Carefully managed straw polls, taken at different points in time before an election, will throw much light on this point. Especially significant will be those researches which concentrate on small areas and which seek intimate knowledge of the political forces at work during a campaign. A

[18]The author has discovered some instances where this has been done.

student of this question might choose a single county for such an endeavor. He could conduct two or more straw votes at intervals before the date of balloting, and thus determine the net change in sentiment that took place during the campaign; he could study the electioneering appeals made to the voters through the radio, press and political organizations; he could talk widely with voters to learn of their reactions; and finally he could interpret these data against the social and economic background of the voting population and their political behavior in previous elections. Such studies as these will add much to our knowledge of the democratic process at its most crucial point.

The Possible Harm of Straw Polls

The discussion of the utility of straw polls is not complete until, against the possible usefulness of this measuring technique, is placed its possible harm. Some observers of politics hold that straw votes constitute a menace to the electoral system, because of the influence they exert on popular psychology during a political campaign. There are, according to this view, a large number of voters who have no well-defined political convictions, and who swing with the tide, their chief desire being to vote with the winner. Straw polls indicate the probable victor, and thus unfairly deliver this "band-wagon" support to the majority party. Equally bad, it is held, is the influence of these unofficial tests on the morale of party workers. When a straw poll shows one party to have a clear advantage, the spirit of the indicated losers is said to be sapped, party workers become indifferent in their campaign labors, contributors draw tight their purse strings, and the minority voters, with the feeling of "what is the use," remain at home on election day. "A positive menace tending to destroy the effectiveness of the real ballot" is the way one editor, in a letter to the author, characterizes straw polls. "A candidacy that still had the breath of life in it," says the *Greensboro News* (N. C.), "could be killed by a declaration of results generally known and accepted weeks in advance of election day."[19]

While the bill of complaint against straw polls is usually drawn up in the name of the minority party, it sometimes cites disadvantages for the majority party as well. In the latter case the argument is that indicated victory for one candidate gives his supporters overconfidence, which sets in motion the same chain of

[19] Oct. 22, 1928.

consequences as that released by underconfidence; the party workers lay down their tools, the campaign contributors feel that there is no need to give more money, and the majority voters, believing that the battle is won, fail to seal the victory by attendance at the polls.

The severity of these evils, it is said, depend largely upon the conviction which straw-poll returns carry. So long as the people regard these preëlection tests as propaganda, as has often been the case in the past, the forecasts have little psychological effect. As the straw returns demonstrate their reliability, however, and as they come to be popularly regarded as pronouncements of the inevitable, it is held that their harm increases.[20]

The judgment passed on this indictment by political leaders, who are in the best position to know the effects of straw polls on campaigns, is divided. Some are quite positively convinced that the returns from these unofficial canvasses sway a large number of voters and wreck party morale; a few think that polls do good in that they stir up interest in voting, others appear to be largely indifferent, believing that the influence of straw returns on the voters is negligible. This division of opinion was voiced to the author in conversations with scores of political leaders after the campaign of 1928, and is also revealed in a special test conducted on the subject of straw-poll menace in the state of Ohio.

Ohio has had more experience with straw votes than any other state, for since 1908 two of the leading newspapers, the *Cincinnati Enquirer* and the *Columbus Dispatch*, have regularly conducted pre-election polls in gubernatorial and presidential campaigns. The returns from these tests have been exceptionally accurate, foreshadowing the division of the official vote in the state with an average plurality error of but 7 votes per 100 cast.[21] Large numbers of citizens have participated in these polls and the returns have always been given wide publicity; hence the people of the state have had full opportunity to learn in advance of the polling day the probable outcome of their elections. If the political leaders of any state are competent to speak on the campaign influence of straw polls, those in Ohio must be so qualified, for this commonwealth has

[20]This argument, of course, involves a contradiction, since the greater the influence of straw votes on political preferences or willingness to go to the polls, the more unreliable is the straw-poll forecast.

[21]See Table 9.

had consistent, highly accurate and widely publicized polls biennially for a period of more than two decades.

An able and impartial Ohio newspaperman was asked to select eleven outstanding authorities on state politics to whom the question of the possible menace of straw polls might be submitted. Of those designated, nine were active party heads, one was a political writer on a leading Ohio newspaper, and one was a director of a non-partisan organization for the furtherance of good government. Through correspondence the case was impartially laid before these men, and an answer was requested to the following query: "Have the straw polls of the *Columbus Dispatch* and *Cincinnati Enquirer* affected in any way the elections of the state?" The replies to this question are given here in paraphrase as follows:

Mr. A., head of an important administrative department of the state:

Straw polls have considerable effect on the outcome of elections because they influence the voters who like to go with the tide.

Mr. B., Chairman of the Republican County Committee of a large and influential county:

Regardless of how careful or how conscientious people might be who are taking a straw vote, unfairness is bound to creep in. There is no doubt in my mind that the returns of such a poll, published in the newspapers from day to day, have a great influence on the doubtful voter.

Mr. C., sometime Chairman, Republican State Committee:

Straw polls tend to defeat the purpose of popular elections because they throw the band-wagon vote to the majority candidate, thereby hurting the minority aspirant. If straw votes were abolished, a man over sensitive to mob psychology would have no way of determining the prevailing sentiment and would have to use his own judgment in casting his ballot.

Mr. D., attorney and a leader of the progressive faction in the Republican party:

It never occurred to me that the taking of straw votes by Ohio newspapers affected the result of an election. However, they may influence weak-spined individuals who desire to vote with the winner.

Mr. E., mayor of one of largest cities in Ohio:

I should say that the influence of straw polls in attracting the band-wagon vote is small.

Mr. F., prominent state senator:

The advantage of a favorable straw poll may win a little support for a party, but personally, I do not think it amounts to a great deal. I see nothing to fear.

Mr. G., able political writer for a leading newspaper:

Political campaigns are won or lost before they start chiefly because of economic factors and set prejudices of the voters. Drifts may develop during a campaign due to personal appeal of the candidates, organization work, use of money, character of publicity etc., but I do not remember seeing a drift go far enough to swing an election. Straw polls merely reflect these drifts, but have little influence because desire to be on the winning side plays little part. If anything polls do more good than harm because they arouse interest in politics.

Mr. H., Democratic leader in one of largest counties:

I would say that straw polls have not in any way affected the elections.

Mr. I., progressive Democrat occupying a judicial position in one of principal cities:

I do not think that straw votes have affected the outcome of elections much. A certain number of people may be influenced to vote with the winner, but this is offset by extra effort made by the indicated loser. Straw polls probably encourage rather than discourage interest in voting.

Mr. J., sometime Chairman, Democratic State Committee:

I doubt if straw polls have much effect upon the voters. They tend only to confirm what probably would have been recognized anyway.

Mr. K., director of a nonpartisan organization for the furtherance of good government:

I do not believe that straw votes are in any sense a menace to the electoral system. In my opinion voters are no more governed by the results of straw polls than they are by editorials and information which appears in the newspapers. A free exercise of the ballot does not mean that the voters shall be kept ignorant of the opinions of other men. The more opinions and information a citizen can obtain, the more likely he is to cast an intelligent vote.

The views of none of these men were known in advance of their interrogation, the sole criterion for participation in the test being that of intimate acquaintance with the politics of the state where straw-poll evils have had the greatest opportunity to crop out. This canvass serves to illuminate the present attitude of political leaders toward straw votes.

The position of straw-poll sponsors on the possible menace of their undertakings is fraught with no misgivings. It is succinctly characterized by the reaction of a middle western editor, who, when asked by the author if his straw poll had not hurt the minority candidate, hammered on his desk and replied with vigor: "I am running a newspaper." According to this editor, his first concern as a newspaperman was not in helping a candidate, but in printing the news. How the people intended to vote was news of the greatest importance, and if he could get this story more accurately by means of a straw poll, that procedure was wholly legitimate. The truth, he declared, is always liable to hurt someone. A sufficient guarantee that he would be fair in his straw canvass and attempt to tell the truth, he said, was contained in the continual threat of loss of reader confidence, should he be derelict in his duty as a newspaperman.

Up to now, most opponents of straw polls have contented themselves with denunciation of what they regard as the evils of these preëlection tests. A few, however, have called for reform. Two methods have been generally proposed for curbing such canvasses. The first is to prohibit by law; the second is to educate the citizens not to participate in straw votes.

An anti-straw-poll law would, of course, put a speedy end to the practice of straw voting, but it is doubtful if such a proposal could overcome the potential opposition to its enactment. In the first place, the politicians would probably not favor it, for, as pointed out in Chapter I, they themselves canvass the preferences of voters in order to learn the status of voting sentiment. Moreover, political leaders continually give out forecasts, supposedly based on these unofficial polls, but practically always colored, for the purpose of bolstering up party morale or bidding for the "band-wagon" vote. If legal restrictions on straw voting were made, it would be extremely difficult to draw the line between the polling practices of the politicians and those of the newspapermen.

In the second place, the journalistic profession would probably oppose such a law. In the straw poll the newspapermen have a scientific tool for gathering the news of voting intention, and any attempt to prohibit the use of this reportorial device would doubtless be fought as an interference with the freedom of the press. If the status of preëlection sentiment may not be told, it would be argued, how long will it be until legal restrictions are made upon the printing of other types of political news? There is no cause for which a newspaperman will fight harder than for the right to print what he sees fit and, if an anti-straw-vote bill aroused this interest, as is reasonable to suppose, the journalistic profession would furnish a brand of opposition that would not be easily overcome. Because of the complications involved in curbing straw polls by law, it would seem that this type of reform holds for its proponents little promise of success.

The second method suggested for combating straw polls is to teach the citizens not to reveal their voting intentions in advance of election day. If this could be done, straw votes would quickly disappear, for the success of these preëlection tests quite obviously depends upon the willingness of the voters to express their preferences on candidates or issues.

Like the proposed legal curb, however, a general movement to arouse public opinion against straw polls would, it seems, be easier to invoke in theory than in practice. The politicians could hardly join in such a movement, for if they educate the people to be silent on their voting preferences they are closing their own avenues of information. Press support would be denied to a large extent, because newspapers themselves sponsor preëlection canvasses. Nor would the natural assertiveness of the human kind be easily overcome. In the 1928 presidential poll of the *Pathfinder*, 13,000 letters were received which volunteered information that was not requested.[22] The *Literary Digest*, in every nation-wide poll it has undertaken, has received thousands of requests for ballots from people who were not included on the mailing list.[23] An educational movement might cause some people to refuse participation in a straw poll, but this might serve only to reduce the number of ballots voted, without in the least affecting the accuracy of the returns.

If the educational campaign is undertaken by partisan groups, however, this method for curbing straw votes holds more promise of success, since straw polls accurately reflect the voting intentions of the electorate only if all points of view are fairly represented in the balloting. If the supporters of one candidate or one side of an issue refuse to express a preference, the straw returns are automatically distorted and their reliability is destroyed. In the next chapter it will be shown how refusal of the drys to coöperate in the prohibition poll sponsored by Mr. Pierre S. du Pont in the state of Delaware, made the returns from that undertaking wholly worthless as a measurement of public sentiment on the liquor question. It

---

[22]Letter from George O. Gillingham, Assistant Editor, The *Pathfinder*.

[23]*Literary Digest*, March 15, 1930.

will also be shown that nonparticipation of dry voters in the nation-wide prohibition polls of the *Literary Digest* render these measurements of uncertain value. Possibly the boycott of straw polls by partisan groups, therefore, offers the best solution for the question of public control of these unofficial canvasses. A curb of this sort imposes no arbitrary prohibition such as that implied in a legal enactment, but allows people to deal freely with polls as they choose.

Chapter VI
STRAW POLLS ON ISSUES

While straw polls have been used for the most part in gauging popular sentiment toward candidates standing for governmental office, they have also been employed as unofficial referenda to determine the position of the voters on important public questions. Technically, polls on issues involve the same sampling problems as polls on candidates, but the former present a body of experience which may well be dealt with separately. This will be undertaken in the present chapter. At the outset a number of straw polls involving public questions will be described, and then attention will be concentrated on the three prohibition polls of the *Literary Digest*, and their report on the division of wet and dry sentiment in the United States.

Polls on Public Questions

One of the earliest polls on issues, of which the author has knowledge, is the unofficial referendum of the *Chicago Journal* in 1907 on a city-traction ordinance which was then being hotly debated preparatory to the official vote. The ordinance provided that the city be empowered to take over the local traction lines, then under private ownership, rehabilitate and improve them, and provide municipal operation. Before the measure could be carried, a 60 percent affirmative vote was required. The *Journal's* poll indicated that the ordinance would fail of adoption, with only 59 percent of the people voting "yes." As matters came to pass, but 55 percent of the citizens were officially reported as favoring the measure, hence the *Journal's* prediction revealed a plurality error of 8 votes in 100 cast.[1]

In 1917, when the United States government was on the verge of declaring war on Germany, a very interesting as well as dramatic poll was conducted by Congressman Ernest Lundeen of the Fifth Congressional District of Minnesota on the question of American entry into the world conflict. Lundeen had debated fiercely in the House of Representatives against this country's participation in the War, and had held that if the people were allowed to make the

[1] *Chicago Journal*, March 18 to March 29, 1907.

choice, there would be no resort to arms. To prove that what he said was true, Lundeen mailed to all of the 54,000 registered voters in his district a ballot card with the declaration: "I believe that the people should be consulted before Congress declares war." The question was then put: "Shall the United States declare war on Germany?" The Minnesota Congressman reported that 8,800 replies to his questionnaire had been received, and that of this number 8,000, or practically 90 percent of his constituents, had voted against war.[2]

The type of question to which polls on issues have been applied is quite varied. In July, 1922, in connection with its prohibition poll, the *Literary Digest* sounded popular sentiment on the granting of a bonus to World War veterans, and in February, 1924, this magazine conducted a nation-wide referendum on the plan which Secretary of the Treasury Mellon had proposed for the reduction of taxes. Of late, prohibition has been the overwhelming topic of public interest and this moot subject has inspired a great many straw polls.

The *Chicago Journal* conducted a straw test in the city of Chicago before each of the official Illinois referenda on prohibition in 1922 and 1926. The earlier poll was a very curious one. The question at issue was that of modifying state and national laws to permit the manufacture and sale of beer. Ten months before the date of the election, the *Journal* commenced its poll and continued to gather ballots throughout the whole of this period. The resultant forecast proved exceptionally good. The straw totals indicated that 82 percent of the citizens of Cook County would be aligned on the wet side of the issue;[3] officially, 80 percent of the people voted for beer. This was a plurality error of 4 percent. In 1926, however, when Illinois was voting on the question of allowing individual states to define the alcoholic content of intoxicating liquor, the *Journal* was not so successful. On this occasion the newspaper's poll, which was hastily taken, indicated a wet vote of 83 percent[4] of the total cast, whereas officially it turned out to be but 60 percent. This is a plurality error of 46 percent.

An illuminating illustration of how, under certain conditions, a straw poll may fail utterly to reflect public sentiment is contained in the attempt of Mr. Pierre S. du Pont to determine the prohibition stand of the people in Delaware in 1930. Mr. du Pont, a member of

[2]*Cong. Record*, Vol. 55, Part 1, p. 366, April 5, 1917.
[3]*Chicago Journal*, Nov. 4, 1922.   [4]*Chicago Journal*, Nov. 1, 1926.

Delaware's leading family and an outspoken antagonist to national prohibition, secured from the state income tax office the names of all state residents over twenty-one years of age, and mailed to each person a questionnaire containing six questions. Two of these, for example, were:

> Do you think that change in existing prohibition laws is needed?
>
> If you favor a change in our laws but do not want the old saloon back, would you vote for a change that permitted sale of spirits, wine and beer, through properly conducted and government supervised places of sale?

Shortly after the questionnaire went forward, dry organizations such as the Woman's Christian Temperance Union, the Methodist Preachers' Association, and the Anti-Saloon League of Delaware, printed advertisements in the local papers urging drys not to participate in the straw vote undertaking sponsored by the state's leading antiprohibitionist. Apparently these appeals had effect, for, though 40 percent of the questionnaires were returned, practically no drys participated, the vote on each of the six queries showing approximately 97 percent of the participants against prohibition. Recognizing the absurdity of this figure, Mr. du Pont did not set forth his returns as a measurement of prohibition sentiment in Delaware, but submitted them to the state legislature as a petition for dry law reform.

The Literary-Digest Prohibition Polls

Of all the straw polls on issues, the most outstanding, of course, are the three national prohibition referenda taken by the *Literary Digest* in 1922, 1930 and 1932. In 1922, 8,000,000 ballot cards were mailed to owners of telephones throughout the United States. Special polls of factory workers and women were also taken in this year, but we shall here concern ourselves only with the principal undertaking. Each person was asked to choose one of three alternatives. These were:

> 1. Do you favor the continuance and strict enforcement of the Eighteenth Amendment and Volstead Law? (or)
> 2. Do you favor a modification of the Volstead Law to permit light wines and beers? (or)
> 3. Do you favor repeal of the Prohibition Amendment?

Approximately 800,000 people in the United States voted their preference. Combining the vote for light wines and beer with that for repeal, the figures showed that wet sentiment was then uppermost in 46 states.[5]

In 1930 the same questions were asked of 20,000,000 automobile and telephone owners in the nation, and the enormous number of 5,000,000 votes was received in return. Again combining the modification and repeal vote, this poll revealed wet majorities in 43 of the 48 states.

In 1932 the question concerning modification was dropped and the tel-auto public was asked to choose between enforcement and repeal alone. The returns from this referendum placed every state except Kansas and North Carolina in the repeal column.

Because of the inclusion of the modification category in the 1922 and 1930 polls, the meaning of these earlier returns has been variously interpreted, but the 1932 referendum raised squarely the issue of enforcement versus repeal, and the results show without equivocation that a majority of the people in every state save two are in favor of the latter alternative. If these returns accurately reflect the wishes of the electorate, the fight for repeal of the Eighteenth Amendment, so far, as public sentiment is concerned, is already won, for in February 1932, not only were the necessary 36 states in line for repeal, but the verdict was virtually unanimous. This is a grave conclusion, however, which cannot safely be drawn until the reliability of the *Literary Digest* prohibition referenda is determined. Let us subject the three polls to a critical examination, such as suggested in Chapter V.[6] In the course of this analysis, an interpretation of the 1922 and 1930 modification vote can also be sought. The 1930 and 1932 polls can be dealt with jointly, since the returns from both referenda were drawn from the tel-auto population and involve similar sampling problems.

[5]The proportion of the total vote cast for modification and repeal (combined) in the polls of 1922 and 1930, and for repeal in 1932 is given by states in Table 30. For the original data on the three prohibition referenda, see the *Literary Digest*, July 8 to September 9, 1922; March 8 to June 7, 1930; and February 13 to May 14, 1932.

[6]See pp. 126-30. The *Literary Digest* sought to assure its readers on this point of reliability by arguing that its presidential polls had been proved accurate by comparison with subsequent official election returns, that the same sampling technique had been employed in its prohibition poll, and that, therefore, the returns from the latter poll were likewise reliable (Feb. 27, 1932). This argument, however, is not valid, because the sampling factors that influenced the presidential poll may not have been operative in the prohibition referendum. Sound interpretive practice requires that every straw poll be separately examined for possible sampling distortions.

Reliability of 1930 and 1932 Literary-Digest Polls

The first and second interpretive tests for distortion of the sample, suggested in Chapter V, were for manipulation of returns by the sponsor and duplication and fraud in the gathering of the straw ballots. All responsible critics have agreed that the character of the *Literary-Digest* management is such as to be wholly above manipulation of its poll figures, but on the second point the charge was persistently made in 1930 and 1932 that many people received more than one card from the magazine, and voted each ballot. Much of this criticism is based on a misunderstanding of the polling program of the periodical. In both years the *Digest* conducted a poll of professional people in addition to the principal referendum. As owners of a telephone or an automobile, doctors, lawyers, educators, and preachers received one ballot card and, as members of a specified profession, received another, but the second card was plainly marked in order that it might be counted apart from the main poll. From this circumstance arose the appearance of duplication in voting, whereas in reality there was none. The *Literary Digest*, as has been pointed out, takes elaborate precautions to safeguard its polls from fraud, and it can be said with assurance that irregularities of this nature were at a minimum consistent with the size of the undertaking. Distortion of the sample from this source, therefore, can be ruled out without further consideration.

The third test was for geographical bias. The renowned Socialist writer, Upton Sinclair,[7] and other critics, declared that the *Literary-Digest* returns were greatly biased in favor of the wets because city people, who tend to be wet, were canvassed in greater proportions than country folk, who are aligned more with the drys. In Chapter IV it was experimentally shown that in the 1928 presidential poll, in which a tel-auto mailing list was employed like that of 1932, the straw vote from the rural districts was slightly less, in proportion to the total vote cast in the official election, than in the urban areas. This difference in representation, however, was so small that it could have had little distortive effect on the sample. When the distribution of ballot cards to urban and rural states in 1932 is considered, the number of ballots mailed to the states in which half or more of the population is rural (1930 census), equaled 53 percent of the effective electorate, as judged by the presidential

[7] *New Republic*, Aug. 13, 1930.

vote cast in 1928.[8] The comparable figure for the states in which more than half of the population is urban, was also 53 percent. It is fair to conclude, therefore, that for all practical purposes the rural voters were given as much opportunity to participate in the 1930 and 1932 prohibition polls as the urban voters.

Class bias was the subject of the fourth interpretive test. The *Literary-Digest* mailing list, as has been pointed out, reaches only those who own automobiles and telephones. Many factory workers and members of the laboring class generally are unable to meet this economic qualification, and hence were excluded from participation in the prohibition referenda. Since the working classes are believed to be more wet than the population at large, the *Digest* returns probably carry a dry bias on this account. Other than affirming that such bias does exist in the prohibition returns, little else can be said, because we do not know what proportion of wage earners are excluded from the tel-auto population, nor do we know how far the included and excluded classes differ on the wet and dry question. The contention, on the face of it, appears to be sound, and we must accordingly recognize the existence of this factor as operating to favor the cause of the drys.

A second class bias charged against the *Literary Digest* sample is that of sex discrimination. It is contended that the *Digest* poll reached a greater proportion of men than women, and that, since the women vote drier than the men, the returns are biased in favor of the wets. This contention appears to be sound. It has been shown that in about 90 percent of the cases the ownership of telephones and automobiles is listed in the name of the male member of the household, and it has also been demonstrated that a greater proportion of the men than the women vote their straw ballot; hence the *Literary-Digest* sample is more than 90 percent the expression of the masculine point of view. That the women favor prohibition more than the men is also demonstrable. In 1922, in addition to its principal prohibition poll, as has been pointed out, the *Literary Digest* took a separate vote among the women. In the main undertaking, which was more than nine-tenths male, 39 percent of the vote was cast for enforcement, whereas in the exclusively female

---

[8]The ten states of the Solid South are excluded from this computation, because the total vote cast in their general elections is relatively small, thereby making the number of *Literary-Digest* cards mailed appear proportionately large. Since all these states save Florida are 50 percent or more rural, their inclusion would make it appear that rural states as a class are better represented in the *Digest* poll than they are in fact.

poll, 45 percent took the dry side. In 1932 a special tabulation of the *Digest* returns by sexes for the city of Portland, Maine, showed 24 percent of the men and 38 percent of the women for enforcement[9]. The 1930 prohibition poll of the Scripps-Howard newspapers returned 7 percent of the male and 17 percent of the female vote in the enforcement category,[10] and that of the *Virginia* (Minnesota) *Enterprise* in the same year revealed 21 percent of the men and 34 percent of the women for enforcement.[11] Thus a sex bias favoring the wets is present in the *Literary-Digest* returns, since it has been demonstrated that the women vote drier than the men and that they were not represented in the straw returns in proportion to their influence in the electorate.

The fifth test was for selection in coöperation. Many critics charged that bias of this nature was present in the *Literary-Digest* returns, because the leaders of dry organizations generally counseled their following not to participate in the referendum. The perfect test for this form of bias, of course, would be to send ballot cards to a limited number of known wets and drys, and then observe the proportion of cards returned by each partisan group. Up to now, however, no straw-poll sponsor has collected these essential data; hence information on the operation of selection in coöperation must be sought by indirect means.

That refusal of drys to mark and return straw ballots had some distortive effect on the 1930 and 1932 *Literary-Digest* prohibition polls is suggested by the following experiment. For each poll the 48 states were ranked according to degree of wetness.[12] These rankings were then divided for summary purposes into four groups of twelve states each, representing four stages of wetness. The percentage of coöperation, *i.e.*, the number of people who returned ballot cards out of every 100 who received them, was then set down for each state for the 1928 presidential poll, in which the factor of wet selection in coöperation was presumably not operative, and for the 1930 and 1932 prohibition referenda in which this form of distortion was said to be present. The coöperation for each group of twelve states was then averaged, with the results as shown in Table 28.

[9]*Literary Digest*, April 9, 1932.
[10]*New York Telegram*, April 24, 1930.
[11]*Virginia Enterprise*, May 1, 1930.
[12]Modification and repeal combined in 1930; repeal in 1932.

TABLE 28

Coöperation* by Groups of Twelve States, Ranked According to Wetness, for the 1928 Presidential and 1930 and 1932 Prohibition Polls of the Literary Digest

State groups by 1930 wet ranking (1)	Coöp- eration 1928 (2)	Coöp- eration 1930 (3)	Increase in coöp- eration 1930 over 1928 (4)	State groups by 1932 wet ranking (5)	Coöp- eration 1928 (6)	Coöp- eration 1932 (7)	Increase in coöp- eration, 1932 over 1928 (8)
I†	14	26	12	I†	14	22	8
II	14	26	12	II	14	23	9
III	13	23	10	III	13	21	8
IV‡	12	17	5	IV‡	13	18	5

*Defined as the number of people who voted their straw ballot out of every 100 who received a ballot.
†Includes 12 states with greatest wet vote.
‡Includes 12 states with least wet vote.

It will be observed from this table that in the 1928 presidential poll when the wet and dry issue was not primarily at stake (Columns 2 and 6), there was little variation in coöperation between the four groups of states, but that in the 1930 and 1932 straw referenda, when the prohibition question was placed in the balance, (Columns 3 and 7) this variation became more pronounced, the states with the largest wet vote tending to return a greater proportion of their cards than the states with the smallest wet vote. Or, putting it in other terms, with coöperation in the 1928 poll as the norm, the increase in coöperation in 1930 and 1932 tended to be largest in the states which cast the greatest wet vote.

This conclusion squares with other evidence on the same point. We have already seen how the drys refused to coöperate in the du Pont poll of Delaware. In a letter to the author, a newspaper editor, who sponsored a straw vote to verify the 1932 *Literary-Digest* figures, observes that his poll is of importance "in that it illustrates how loath the drys are to participate in tests of this sort." We know that dry leaders have counseled their followers not to mark straw ballots, and, probably of greater significance, we know that the state of mind of wets and drys is such as to produce selection in coöperation in a straw vote. The drys are complacent. They have the constitutional victory of prohibition, and they are not easily stirred from their inertia to refight the liquor battle. The wets, on the other hand, are fired with the zeal of reform; they are indignant; they want to do something about the prohibition amendment, and straw polls serve as a convenient vehicle for the expression of their dissatisfaction. Wet selection in coöperation is the result.

The remaining points suggested in Chapter V for critical evaluation of a straw poll may be passed over quickly. No data are available on the possible distortion resultant from "participation—nonparticipation." The factor of "change of sentiment over time" is largely irrelevant here, because there is no subsequent official referendum with which the straw returns can be compared. As for the number of ballots collected by the *Literary Digest*, the mounting totals reported from week to week showed practically no change in the division of votes between the wets and the drys; hence it can be concluded that the polls were adequate in size.

What, now, can be said of the reliability of the 1930 and 1932 *Literary-Digest* prohibition returns? Distortion due to fraud was ruled out. Representation of urban and rural voters in the sample was shown to be fair. A bias favoring the drys was found in the fact that many laboring people of wet inclination were excluded from participation in the referendum. Two biasing influences, inadequate representation of women, and the greater willingness of wets than of drys to vote the straw ballot, were discovered that favored the wets. It would be desirable to weigh the precise effect of each of these biases on the reliability of the *Digest* sample, but the data are not available for this analytical refinement. The fact, however, that two biases favored the wets, particularly that of selection in coöperation, whereas but one bias favored the drys, suggests that the *Literary-Digest* returns overstate the size of the wet vote.

Other Appraisals of Prohibition Sentiment

This conclusion is strengthened when the *Literary-Digest* figures are compared with other appraisals of prohibition sentiment, the first of which result from official state referenda on various phases of the liquor question. Since 1919, when the Eighteenth Amendment was adopted, 31 such tests have been made in 19 states.[13] Approximately two thirds of these referenda have dealt with enactment or repeal of state-enforcement laws, the remainder raising the

[13] Detailed information on these referenda is given in Appendix B.

issues of light wines and beer, repeal of the Eighteenth Amendment, or state dispensation. If we look only at the latter half of this post-Amendment period, from 1926 to the present, we have official election figures on some angle of the prohibition question for ten states.

In voting on prohibition, it appears that people do not discriminate to any great extent between precise issues, but tend to vote more on their fundamental wet or dry convictions. In the 1930 Illinois referendum, for example, which involved three separate propositions, 67 percent of the voters favored repeal of the state prohibition law, 66 percent were for modifying the Volstead Act to allow states to define the alcoholic content of intoxicating liquor, and 66 percent stood for abolishing the Eighteenth Amendment. Here the vote on either state enforcement or light wines and beer would have provided a satisfactory index of sentiment for repeal of the Prohibition Amendment. If the 1926 Illinois referendum involving the right of states to define the alcoholic content of intoxicating liquors had been taken as the latest prohibition test in this state, the wet index would have stood at 60 percent, which is a fair approximation of the 66 percent figure recorded for repeal in 1930. To give but one more illustration, of several that might be cited, the Massachusetts electorate in 1928 voted 63 percent in favor of abolishing the Eighteenth Amendment; in 1930, 64 percent of the voters favored repeal of the state enforcement act. Presumably, therefore, the returns on state enforcement, light wines and beer, and repeal of the Federal Amendment, are largely interchangeable, the vote on one issue furnishing a reasonably good index of the division of the electorate on other angles of the liquor question. As a result, we have, for each of the ten states in which prohibition referenda have been taken since 1926, an official approximation of sentiment for repeal. Also we have the clew for a plausible interpretation of the 1922 and 1930 *Literary-Digest* returns. Apparently the people who voted for modification in these referenda would, for the most part, have chosen repeal in preference to continuance of the Eighteenth Amendment if these had been the only alternatives offered; hence the combined modification and repeal straw vote can, without great error, be regarded as an index of sentiment for repeal. This interpretation will be given the 1922 and 1930 *Literary-Digest* returns in the pages that follow and, similarly, the wet vote in the official state referenda will be regarded as a vote for repeal.

POLLS ON ISSUES

In Table 29, for the ten referendum states, the official figures on repeal sentiment are set alongside those derived from the *Literary-Digest* polls of 1930 and 1932.

TABLE 29

COMPARISON OF REPEAL SENTIMENT IN TEN STATES, AS SHOWN BY OFFICIAL REFERENDA, 1926-1930, AND THE LITERARY-DIGEST POLLS OF 1930 AND 1932

State	Year of Referendum	Percent of total vote cast for repeal			Official repeal votes for every 100 straw repeal votes	
		Official*	Literary Digest 1930	Literary Digest 1932†	Literary Digest 1930	Literary Digest 1932
(1)	(2)	(3)	(4)	(5)	(6)	(7)
R. I...........	1930	78†	78	84	100	93
Nev...........	1926	77†	82	85	94	91
N. Y..........	1926	75	81	85	92	88
Ill............	1926 and 1930	60and66†	75	81	88	81
Mass..........	1928 and 1930	63†and64	72	79	89	81
Wis...........	1926 and 1929	66 and 63	77	84	82	75
Mont.........	1926 and 1928	53 and 54	72	80	75	67
N. D..........	1928	48	70	76	68	63
Calif..........	1926	47	70	77	67	61
Colo..........	1926	41	57	61	72	67
				Mean Average	83	77

*Ranked in order of wetness as shown by the latest official vote. The 1926 referendum in Missouri is not shown because the wets in this state opposed the test as untimely; hence the returns are probably not a fair indication of wet strength.

†Pure repeal vote on direct issue of repeal vs. continuance of Eighteenth Amendment. See p. 167 for application.

From these figures it is observed that in each state in which a prohibition referendum has been held since 1926, save one, the *Literary-Digest* polls show more repeal sentiment than is revealed in the latest official referendum. It may be argued, of course, that this discrepancy is due to wet gains made after the official referenda were taken, but it is difficult to reconcile this explanation with other data bearing on the case. The independent appraisals of prohibition sentiment, shortly to be described do not lend support to this view, nor do the official referenda figures printed in Table 29. In Rhode Island, Illinois and Massachusetts the official vote was cast about ten months after the 1930 straw vote. The official and unofficial tests give the same results in the first state, but in the latter two the official repeal vote is considerably less than that reported by the straw poll, giving clear evidence that the straw returns overemphasized the wet vote. In the case of Nevada and New York the official and 1930 *Digest* figures can be reconciled by assuming wet gains of about the same amount as appear to be registered in Illinois between 1926 and 1930, but to reconcile the two measurements for Wisconsin, Montana, North Dakota, California and Colorado, it is necessary to assume an enormous growth of anti-prohibition sentiment, which is not reflected, at least, by the figures for the four states which held two referenda between 1926 and 1930.[14] The comparison between the latest official prohibition vote and the 1932 straw returns is less meaningful, of course, because the time interval separating the two measurements is longer, but even assuming wet gains for the whole interval at the rate indicated by the 1930-1932 straw polls, the official repeal vote in all but three of the ten referendum states would yet fall below that reported by the *Literary-Digest*. There is a strong probability, therefore, that the discrepancy between the *Literary-Digest* and official returns cannot be explained by gain in anti-prohibition sentiment alone, but represents as well exaggeration of the wet vote.

A second independent appraisal of prohibition sentiment is to be drawn from the stand of the members of the House of Representatives on the wet and dry issue. On March 14, 1932, the House voted on the question of bringing out from the Judiciary Committee the Beck-Linthicum resolution, which proposed that Congress pass on the matter of submitting to the states an amendment to the Constitution permitting state control of the liquor traffic. The immediate issue at stake was a parliamentary one, but the test was widely regarded as an indication of the division of the House on the prohibition question. The roll call[15] shows that, while the wets appear to have made some gains, the Representatives from 26 states voted wholly or predominantly dry, notwithstanding the

[14]Some observers may prefer to explain the apparent 1930 *Digest* overstatement of the repeal vote on the ground that many people who voted for light wines and beer in the straw poll would have chosen enforcement instead of repeal if these had been the only two alternatives offered, but the combined modification and repeal straw vote might be regarded as a vote for beer (instead of a vote for repeal as assumed by the author) and still it would exceed the official vote for beer.

[15]*New York Times*, March 15, 1932. A second test, held May 23, 1932, on the question of discharging the Ways and Means Committee from further consideration of the O'Connor-Hall beer-for-revenue bill, revealed practically the same wet and dry division in the House. The *New York Times*, May 24, 1932.

fact that their constituencies were reported to be wet by the 1932 *Literary-Digest* poll. It might be argued, of course, that these Congressmen do not reflect the prevailing point of view in their home districts, sentiment having changed since they were elected, but when comparison is made with the 1930 *Digest* returns, which were gathered eight months before the congressional election, it is found that dry Representatives were chosen from 23 states in which wet majorities were then reported by the straw poll. It is readily conceivable that some Congressmen might be elected who are out of harmony with the dominant wishes of their constituents, but it is highly improbable that half the states in the nation could be represented in the House by drys if the majority of the voters were of other persuasion on such an important question as prohibition. The vote on the Beck-Linthicum resolution, therefore, is strong evidence that the 1930 and 1932 *Literary-Digest* polls overemphasized sentiment for repeal.

The third independent appraisal of prohibition sentiment comes from members of the newspaper profession. Believing that it would be desirable to compare the *Literary-Digest* returns with opinion estimates of the extent of wet sentiment, the author in May, 1931, wrote a personal letter to the editors of all the more important daily newspapers in every state in the Union except Illinois, Massachusetts, Montana, Nevada, New York, Rhode Island and Wisconsin. These states were not included because data from official prohibition referenda were available. California, Colorado, Missouri, and North Dakota might have been passed over on the same grounds, but it was decided to include these states in the canvass because the referendum in each case had been held in 1926, and little extra labor was involved in securing the current judgment.

In each letter it was explained to the editor that the author was making an analysis of the *Literary-Digest* prohibition polls, and that he desired to check the straw figures for the editor's state by securing the unbiased judgment of the local newspapermen. The request was then made for a reply to the following question:

If the citizens of your state were asked today:
"Do you favor the repeal of the Eighteenth Amendment " out of a normal turnout of ....
How many would vote for repeal?   ....
How many would vote against repeal?....................
          Total   ....

The turnout figure for each state was set in accordance with the customary vote cast in several presidential elections previous to 1930, and was typewritten after the word "of" and again in the space marked "Total."

The response to this letter was highly gratifying. Out of 1,004 editors to whom letters were sent, 613 replied. Forty-six felt that they could not give a reliable estimate, or gave their answer in such form that it could not be used. One editor wrote that he had put the question to at least fifty people around town before answering, and many stated that they had conferred with their editorial staffs or special political writers before making a reply. Thirty-three editors qualified their estimates by saying that if the public had a guarantee that the saloon would not come back, or if some workable plan for liquor control could be substituted for the present system, a larger number of people than indicated would be in favor of repeal.

In summarizing the editors' appraisal of repeal sentiment, the individual estimates were translated into percentages and ranked for each state according to wetness, the editor giving the wettest opinion being ranked as number one, the next wettest number two, and so on. The estimate located at the half-way point in this ranking was designated as the single judgment most representative of the newspapermen's opinions.[16] These median estimates are given by states in Table 30.

The compilation shows that in each of the 41 states for which comparisons are available, the newspapermen's estimate of the extent of repeal sentiment is far below that reported by the *Literary Digest* in 1930 and 1932. The editors agree with the 1930 *Digest* poll that Arkansas, Kansas, North Carolina, Oklahoma and Tennessee retained dry majorities and that Connecticut, Louisiana, Maryland, New Jersey, New Mexico, and possibly Delaware and Ohio—the estimate in these two states was 50 percent for repeal— were preponderantly wet, but in the remaining 29 states, the 1930 *Literary-Digest* poll reported wet majorities, whereas the editors believed that these states were dry. As in the case of Congressmen, there are many circumstances that might cause newspaper editors to misjudge prohibition sentiment in their communities, but they, like public officers, must know something about the wishes

[16]The concentration of opinion was such that 72 percent of the estimates for all the states fell within a range of ten votes above and below the median estimate.

TABLE 30
REPEAL SENTIMENT BY STATES AS REPORTED BY THE LITERARY-DIGEST STRAW POLLS OF 1922, 1930, AND 1932 AND BY OPINION ESTIMATES OF THE EDITORS OF DAILY NEWSPAPERS

	Percent total vote for repeal			
	Literary Digest			Newspaper editors†
State	1922*	1930*	1932	
Alabama	55	52	55	35
Arizona	66	65	73	44
Arkansas	52	48	52	40
California	65	70	77	47
Colorado	54	57	61	39
Connecticut	69	82	84	65
Delaware	64	66	72	50
Florida	61	69	75	41
Georgia	57	60	64	35
Idaho	58	61	67	40
Illinois	64	75	81	
Indiana	53	61	68	45
Iowa	58	58	64	38
Kansas	42	42	50	29
Kentucky	62	66	67	38
Louisiana	76	77	82	55
Maine	59	60	69	40
Maryland	72	74	77	63
Massachusetts	63	72	79	
Michigan	56	73	78	45
Minnesota	59	70	76	46
Mississippi	54	52	56	35
Missouri	59	68	71	48
Montana	69	72	80	
Nebraska	55	58	63	39
Nevada	75	82	88	
New Hampshire	62	63	69	40
New Jersey	70	81	85	64
New Mexico	58	66	75	56
New York	72	81	85	
North Carolina	53	49	50	35
North Dakota	65	70	76	47
Ohio	56	68	72	50
Oklahoma	50	49	54	39
Oregon	58	63	70	40
Pennsylvania	63	72	75	44
Rhode Island	70	78	84	
South Carolina	56	58	60	36
South Dakota	55	61	68	40
Tennessee	53	50	51	38
Texas	53	56	60	40
Utah	65	64	69	37
Vermont	62	63	70	44
Virginia	66	65	63	45
Washington	54	67	76	46
West Virginia	56	62	65	40
Wisconsin	67	77	84	
Wyoming	66	71	78	46

*Modification and repeal vote combined.
†Median estimate. See p. 158. Seven states not canvassed.

of the people or they could not hold their jobs. Their judgment runs contrary to the 1930 *Literary-Digest* returns in more than half the states in the nation.

Reliability of 1930 and 1932 Literary-Digest Polls Recapitulated

The whole discussion of the reliability of the 1930 and 1932 *Literary-Digest* prohibition polls may be conveniently summarized in the form of a chart. In Diagram II, the 48 states are ranked on the horizontal axis according to repeal sentiment revealed in the 1932 straw vote. On the vertical axis is placed a scale representing the proportion of the total vote estimated for repeal by the several methods of appraisal. The unbroken line at the top of the diagram pictures the percent of the total vote cast for repeal by states as reported by the *Literary-Digest* poll of 1932. The dotted line immediately below shows repeal sentiment (modification and repeal combined) by states as registered in the magazine's referendum of 1930. Examination of the sampling distortions that might have influenced the straw returns in both years, it will be recalled, showed that one bias, nonparticipation of laboring people, operated to favor the drys, and that two biases, inadequate representation of women and selection in coöperation, colored the returns to the advantage of the wets. The preponderance of wet biases over dry, it was thought, caused the *Literary-Digest* figures to overemphasize the vote for repeal. This is reflected on the chart by undue elevation of the 1930 and 1932 *Digest* repeal lines.

This conclusion was corroborated by other evidence. The x marks on Diagram II stand for the repeal vote in the official referenda in 10 states, taken between 1926 and 1930. In every case, save Rhode Island in 1930, it will be noted, these authoritative indices fall below the wet marks recorded by the *Literary-Digest* polls. That in the majority of these states wet sentiment could have increased from the levels indicated by the official tests to those reported by the straw polls during the time interval separating these measurements, was thought improbable, since this explanation assumes extremely large wet gains that are suggested neither by the official vote in the states in which two referenda have been taken since 1926, nor by the 1930-1932 straw returns.

The dots in Diagram II represent the repeal estimates made by the editors of daily newspapers in May, 1931. In every

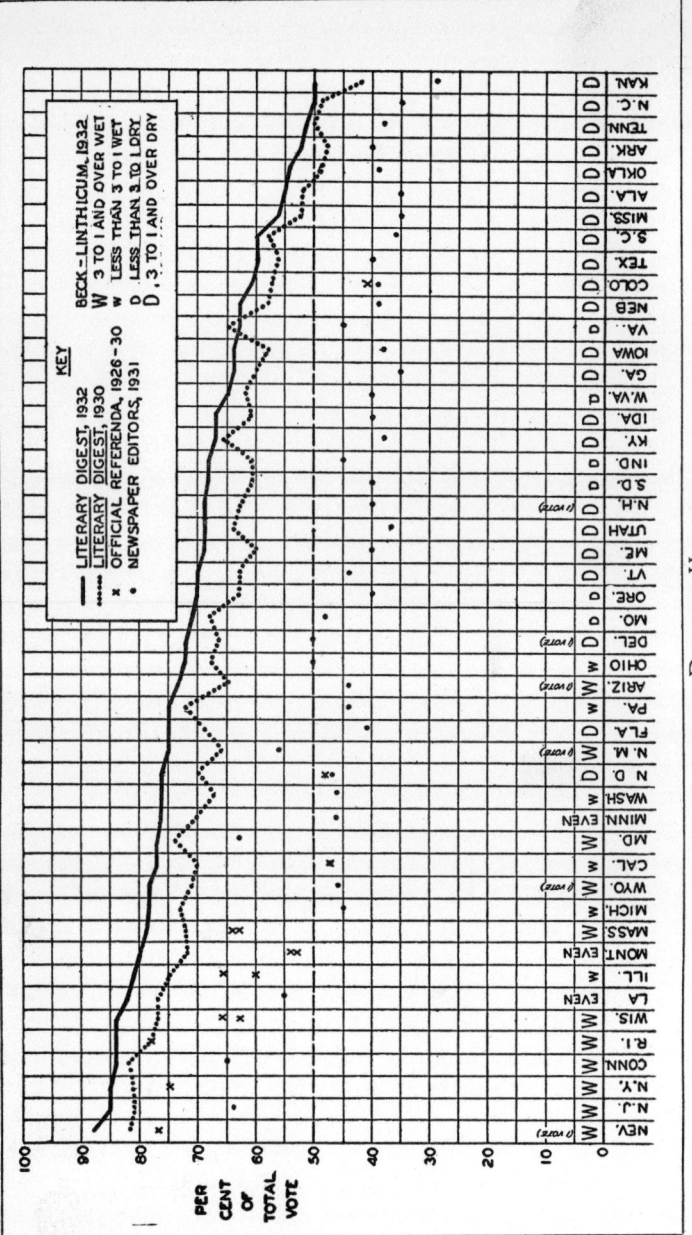

DIAGRAM II

Recent Appraisals of Sentiment for Repeal Compared

Literary-Digest polls, 1930 and 1932; official referenda in ten states, 1926–1930; estimates by editors of daily newspapers, 1931; Beck-Linthicum vote, 1932. States ranked by wetness on basis of 1932 *Literary-Digest* returns.

state, it will be observed, the editors report less repeal sentiment than is recorded by the *Literary Digest*. Agreement as to which side of the prohibition dispute commands the majority vote is to be seen in a few states at each end of the repeal scale, but, in the opinion of the editors, 29 states which show pronounced wet majorities in the 1930 straw poll should, as late as May, 1931, be listed as dry.

Finally, the characters at the bottom of Diagram II stand for the vote in the House of Representatives on the Beck-Linthicum resolution on March 14, 1932. Those states whose Representatives stood 3 to 1, or more, against the resolution, are marked "D"; where the division was less than 3 to 1 in opposition, the state is distinguished by "d." States whose Representatives voted 3 to 1 or more in favor of the resolution are indicated by "W," and where the division was less than 3 to 1 in the affirmative, by "w." Where the Representatives from a state divided evenly on the question, that state is marked "Even." When but one Representative voted from a state, this fact is noted. It will be observed on the diagram that the W's and w's concentrate on the left-hand side, where the wet states are located by the *Literary Digest* and other appraisals, and that the D's and d's appear on the right-hand side in general conformity with the other measurements. But the *Literary-Digest* polls, it is seen, reported wet majorities in 23 states in 1930 and 26 states in 1932 which were represented in the House by dry delegations.

If the *Literary Digest* had sampled the prohibition wishes of the voting population at random and without bias, the straw returns might be accepted as reliable measurements of sentiment for repeal, opinion estimates to the contrary notwithstanding, but the magazine's referenda do not measure up to this standard, since it has been shown that a preponderance of biases operated to color the returns in favor of the wets, and since this view has been corroborated by appraisals of other types. It must be concluded, therefore, that the 1930 and 1932 *Literary-Digest* prohibition returns, are, at face value, unreliable in that they overstate the vote for repeal.[17]

[17] In both 1930 and 1932 a number of daily newspapers over the country sponsored independent prohibition polls for the purpose of verifying the *Literary -Digest* returns. The comparisons for 1932 were as follows:

Reliability of 1922 Literary-Digest Poll

The reliability of the 1922 poll can be determined more briefly. In that year, as has been pointed out, the *Literary-Digest* mailing list did not include owners of automobiles, but was based on telephone directories alone.[18] The possible distortions in the returns from manipulation and fraud and from the size of the sample can be ruled out for reasons cited in connection with the analysis of the 1930 and 1932 polls. As for favoritism in the distribution of the ballots between urban and rural areas, there probably was some urban bias in the returns, for the magazine itself has released figures showing that its telephone list reaches but one person in 24 in communities with fewer than 2,500 inhabitants and one person in 8 in cities of 2,500 and over.[19]

On the score of class bias, there are no data to show what proportion of laboring men and factory workers own telephones, but, as with the more recent polls, it must be assumed that these people were largely excluded from participation in the referendum. That the women's vote was not adequately represented in the poll is

Paper	Area Covered	Percent of Total Straw Vote Cast for Repeal	
		Independent sponsors	Literary Digest
Des Moines Register and Tribune	Iowa	57	64
Fredericksburg Free Lance-Star	Fredericksburg, Va.	70	72
Burlington Daily Enterprise	Burlington, N. J.	57	74
Burlington Daily Enterprise	Florence, N. J.	81	73
Richmond News	Richmond, Va.	91	81
Wichita Beacon	Wichita, Kansas	57	60
South Bend News-Times	South Bend, Ind.	73	77
South Bend News-Times	Mishawaka, Ind.	69	76

Whatever the degree of conformity in return here shown between these check-up polls and that of the *Literary Digest* for local areas, great importance cannot be attached to the verifications, because, with possibly one exception, the independent polls may not be free from the sampling flaws that biased the *Digest* referendum. The *Des Moines Register and Tribune* poll was a combination of mail, ballot-in-the-paper and personal canvass, the latter technique accounting for about one-fifth of the ballots. The *Fredericksburg Free Lance-Star* gathered its returns by mail from qualified voters. The *Burlington Daily Enterprise*, the *Richmond News*, and the *Witchita Beacon* employed the ballot-in-the-paper technique. In each of these the door was left open for the bias of selection in coöperation, and in the ballot-in-the-paper polls, repeating may have further contributed to the distortion of the sample.

The *South Bend News-Times* poll was an inclusive house-to-house canvass in which selection in coöperation was presumably reduced to the minimum. A sex bias favoring the drys may have colored the returns to some extent, since the ballots were largely cast by housewives. If allowance be made for this bias, the *Times* poll for South Bend and Mishawaka shows practically the same percentage of the electorate for repeal as that of the *Literary Digest*, thus affording corroboration for the latter. It is unfortunate that dependable check-up measurements have not been made in a number of cities and states throughout the nation for, as will be pointed out later, these data would provide a basis for the correct interpretation of the 1932 *Literary-Digest* poll.

[18] See p. 147.   [19] See p. 86.

evidenced by the magazine's declaration that its telephone mailing list is 90 percent male and only 10 percent female.[20] The effective electorate, it will be recalled, numbers about 4 women to 6 men.

The results from the test for selection in coöperation, such as employed in the analysis of the 1930 and 1932 polls, are given in Table 31. The figures show that coöperation for all groups of states in both the 1924 presidential poll, in which prohibition was not a moot issue, and the 1922 referendum, which dealt exclusively with the wet and dry question, was practically the same, the states that revealed the largest wet vote returning about the same proportion of the straw ballots mailed to them as the states showing the smallest wet vote. Apparently in 1922 the opposition to the Eighteenth Amendment was neither so pronounced nor so articulate as it is now; hence there was less desire on the part of wets to give expression to their dissatisfaction by voting a straw ballot.

TABLE 31
Coöperation by Groups of Twelve States, Ranked According to Wetness,*
for the 1924 Presidential and 1922 Prohibition Polls of the
Literary Digest

State groups by 1922 wet ranking	Coöperation, 1924	Coöperation, 1922	Difference, coöperation, 1922, compared with 1924
I†...	16	14	—2
II...	15	12	—3
III...	15	11	—4
IV‡...	15	12	—3

*Modification and Repeal Combined.
†Includes 12 states with greatest wet vote.
‡Includes 12 states with least wet vote.

Examination of the sampling technique employed by the *Literary Digest* in 1922, then, shows that one bias—exclusion of people of small means—favored the drys in the returns, and that two biases —inadequate representation of women and rural voters—favored the wets. This circumstance suggests that the 1922 *Digest* straw poll, like the two referenda of more recent date, exaggerated the extent of the sentiment for repeal.

Corroboration for this conclusion is to be found in a comparison of the *Literary-Digest* returns with the vote in official state prohibition referenda held between the years 1919 and 1924. Sixteen such tests in ten states are available. Two-thirds of these referenda

[20] See p. 91.

dealt with the question of state enforcement; in the remaining one-third the issue raised was that of light wines and beer. These tests, like those held between 1926 and 1930, may be regarded as furnishing reasonably accurate indices on repeal sentiment.

In Table 32 and Diagram III, the 1922 *Literary-Digest* and official repeal figures (1919-1924) are compared. It will be observed that in every state save one, the straw poll reported a larger percent of the electorate in favor of repeal than that recorded in the official referendum. It is true, of course, that about two-thirds of the official tests antedated the straw poll from two to three years, but the vote for repeal in thirteen official referenda in 1922 and thereafter, including eight tests made between 1926 and 1928, falls below the early *Digest* wet mark; hence the only conclusion to be drawn is that the 1922 straw poll, like those of 1930 and 1932, overstated the vote for repeal.[21]

TABLE 32

Comparison of Repeal Sentiment in Ten States as Shown by Official Referenda, 1919-1924, and the Literary-Digest Poll of 1922

State	Year of referendum	Repeal votes for every 100 cast		Official repeal votes for every 100 repeal votes Literary Digest 1922
		Official	Literary Digest 1922	
Ky.	1919	49	62	79
Mich.	1919	38	56	68
Ohio.	1919	50	56	89
Texas.	1919	47	53	89
Cal.	1920	54	65	83
Mass.	1920	50	63	79
Mo.	1920	47	59	80
Ohio.	1920	42	56	75
S. D.	1920	54	55	98
Wis.	1920	32	67	48
Cal.	1922	48	65	74
Ill.	1922	67	64	105
Mass.	1922	57	63	90
Ohio.	1922	44	56	78
S. D.	1922	40	55	73
Mass.	1924	49	63	78

[21] It may be objected that the apparent *Literary-Digest* overstatement of repeal sentiment in 1922 is due, not to faulty sampling as here supposed, but to the arbitrary lumping of the returns for modification and repeal, there being many voters who would favor light wines and beer but not repeal. This argument is not tenable, however, for the combined *Digest* modification and repeal returns, viewed as a vote for beer, still exceeds—with one exception—the beer vote in those states which held referenda on the question of modification between 1919 and 1924.

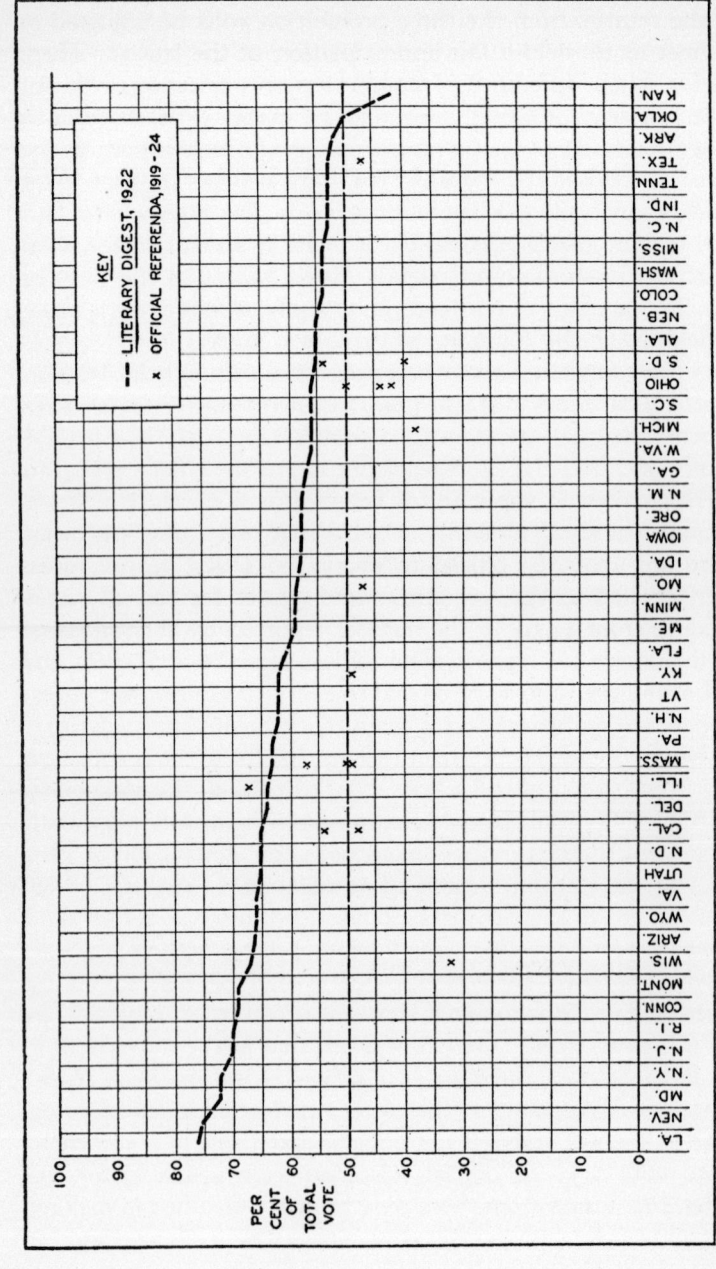

DIAGRAM III

Repeal Vote, *Literary-Digest* Poll, 1922, and Official Referenda in Ten States, 1919-1924, Compared
States ranked by wetness on basis of 1922 *Literary-Digest* returns.

Interpretive Correction of the Literary-Digest Polls

Can the returns from the three prohibition polls be adjusted in such manner as to yield a fair approximation of the truth? There is room for much difference of opinion on this question. No interpretive headway, it would seem, can be made by attempting to weigh the precise effect that each of the several biases had on the reliability of the sample, because the data are not available for this type of analysis. Of more promise is the attempt to find authentic measurements of repeal sentiment in several states, then to correct the *Literary-Digest* returns for all states in the light of these control figures. Even this type of analysis, however, is beset with difficulties as the following example will show.

It has been suggested that the returns from the official tests in the ten referenda states (1926 to 1930) be regarded as true measures of sentiment for repeal, comparable in point of time with the *Literary-Digest* polls, and that the average proportion of the official repeal to *Digest* repeal votes in these states be used as a correction factor (See Columns 6 and 7, Table 29). For the 1930 poll, this would mean that there are about 83 official to every 100 *Digest* repeal votes, and when applied to the wet straw vote figures for the 48 states would reduce from 43 to 34 the number reported by the magazine to have majorities for repeal. The same technique applied to the 1932 poll, using the ratio of 77 official to every 100 *Digest* wet votes, would reduce the number of states in the repeal column from 46 to 33. This method, however, is open to criticisms that make the conclusions resultant from it of doubtful value. For one thing, the variability of proportions of official to straw repeal votes in the 10 referendum states upon which the correction factor is based, is sufficient to give this index a substantial degree of unreliability. Again, if wet sentiment has grown since the latest official test in the 10 referendum states, the correction factor would minimize the vote for repeal. Finally, the proposed correction index is derived almost wholly from experience in the states that show the greatest repeal vote. In Table 29 (Columns 6 and 7) it will be noted that as the states decline on the scale of wetness, the number of official repeal to *Digest* repeal votes grows less. Apparently, therefore, a correction index based on experience in the wet states is not equally applicable in states more inclined to vote dry. If official referenda were available for the drier states and if data from these were properly included in making up a correction ratio, the number of states shown by the 1930 and 1932 polls to have majorities for repeal might be reduced.[22]

The problem of adjusting the *Literary-Digest* prohibition returns would be greatly simplified if reliable measurements of repeal voting strength, comparable in point of time with those of the magazine, were available for a dozen states of all shades of wetness (or dryness). These control indices could then be plotted against the *Literary-Digest* ranking of states and fitted with an appropriate curve, the most probable proportion of the vote for repeal for each of the 48 states being read from this curve. For the earlier *Literary-Digest* polls, of course, the time has passed for making the necessary control measurements for the application of this corrective technique, but some analytical headway might yet be made with the 1932 returns. The control indices might be derived either from official referenda—a number of states will vote on prohibition issues in November, 1932—or from straw votes. If the measurements were made by the latter means, the bias of selection in coöperation, which has consistently challenged the validity of unofficial prohibition referenda, could probably be overcome by use of the personal canvass technique. Until some scientifically defensible discounting of the *Literary-Digest* referenda is made, the returns are likely to continue to prove misleading to students of the prohibition question.

GROWTH OF SENTIMENT FOR REPEAL

Leaving now the question of the reliability of the *Literary-Digest* prohibition polls, do not the returns from the three referenda indicate an increase in sentiment for repeal during the past decade? In Diagram IV the proportion of the total straw vote cast for repeal in each state is plotted for the three polls on the basis of the 1932 wet ranking. From this diagram it will be observed that the 1930 repeal level generally exceeds that of 1922 and that the 1932 line has, in most states, been pushed beyond that of 1930. The fan like spread of the three lines suggests that the greatest wet gains have been made in the states where the supporters of repeal have been the most numerous.

These conclusions appear to be reasonable. The determined

[22] Dr. Walter F. Willcox of Cornell University, who was the first to make a thoroughgoing critical analysis of the 1922 and 1930 *Literary-Digest* prohibition polls, interpreted these referenda to mean that in 1922 a majority of the people in 16 states were ready to vote for repeal and that by 1930 sentiment for repeal was uppermost in 37 states. Dr. Willcox' paper can be found in the *Journal of the American Statistical Association*, Sept., 1931.

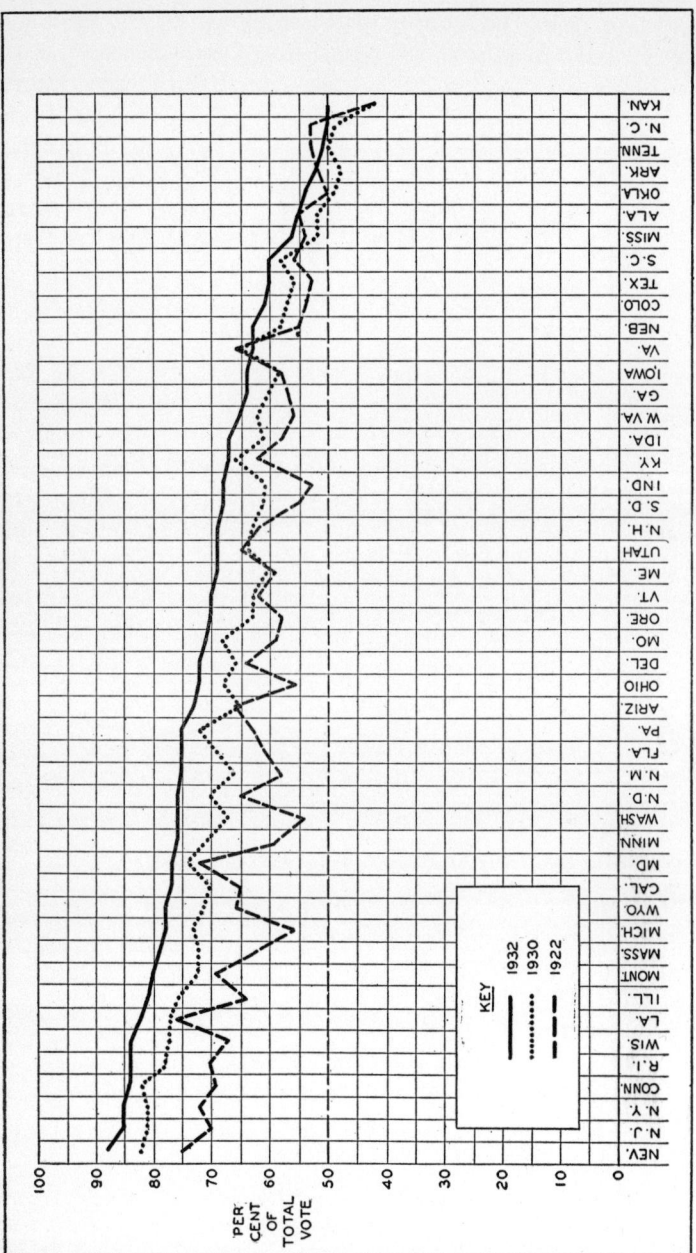

DIAGRAM IV

Growth of Anti-Prohibition Sentiment as Reflected by a Comparison of the Vote Cast for Repeal in the *Literary-Digest* Polls of 1932, 1930, and 1922

States ranked by wetness on basis of 1932 *Literary-Digest* returns.

activities of repeal organizations, the increasing concern evidenced by drys, the tenor of newspaper editorials, the willingness of politicians to run for office on wet platforms, the returns from official prohibition referenda and from the *Literary-Digest* straw polls, all imply a growing opposition to Federal prohibition. It is reasonable to suppose, too, that the wet gains have been greatest in states where repeal voters are most numerous, for prohibition has been least successful in these states, and the demand for reform has been more insistent.

Whether we can go beyond these general conclusions, however, and say that the spread between the three *Literary-Digest* repeal lines is a precise measurement of wet gains during the past decade is an open question. If none of the polls had been affected by sampling biases, or if these distortions had remained constant, the measurement of change in sentiment toward repeal might be regarded as reasonably authentic. But sampling flaws have been found in each poll, and we have no way of knowing if their net influence on the three referenda was the same. From the tests for selection in coöperation it appears that this form of distortion may have been more operative in the 1930 and 1932 polls than in the poll of 1922. If this is true, some of the spread between the earlier and later repeal lines may be due to increased willingness of the wets to mark a straw ballot, rather than conversion of drys to the side of repeal. Without doubt the three *Literary-Digest* polls do reflect growth of repeal sentiment, but the degree of precision with which this change is measured is uncertain.

Reliability of Straw Referenda in General

In discussing the utility of straw polls in Chapter V it was suggested that this device might be used to measure sentiment on broad public issues. In the present chapter the outstanding examples of such usage have been examined, and it has been found that the resulting measurements are unreliable. Must not the original statement be retracted, then, and the conclusion be drawn that straw polls on issues serve only to cloud, rather than to clear, our appreciation of the stand of the electorate on public questions? The answer to this query lies in discrimination between straw polls. Correctly managed, straw polls should yield reliable results; incorrectly managed, these tests give rise to erroneous reports.

With the du Pont poll in Delaware, the difficulty lay in the fact that the drys would not participate in the referendum. As pointed out in Chapter V, this can be an inexorable limitation of straw-poll technique, but in the Delaware undertaking this distortive factor was no doubt accentuated by the partisan sponsorship of the poll and by the use of the mail technique in the gathering of the ballots. If the referendum had been sponsored by a neutral agency, and if the preferences of the voters had been solicited by means of a personal canvass, the straw poll would probably have yielded more faithful results. With all straw polls, and with those on prohibition in particular, care must be exercised to control the factor of selection in coöperation.

With the *Literary-Digest* prohibition polls, the underlying difficulty is that business needs do not wholly meet the sampling requirements for scientific measurement of wet and dry sentiment. The *Digest* distributes ballots only to owners of telephones and automobiles because these people are potential subscribers to the magazine. While the tel-auto group comprises a sizable part of the electorate, it is unrepresentative of the whole body of voters to the extent that it excludes electors in the lower economic brackets and women. Moreover, the business necessity of achieving wide distribution of subscription offers, called for a mail canvass, where, from a scientific point of view, personal solicitation would have been of more avail in overcoming the indifference of the drys. The cost of gathering straw preferences by the latter method is no more than by the former, since about 100 ballots must normally be distributed by mail for every 15 or 20 returned.

Experience with the straw poll on issues, described in the foregoing pages, then, does not show that this device is necessarily unreliable as a referendum technique, but that it requires careful management, and that it may not be capable of meeting the business needs of its sponsor, and at the same time, the requirements for scientific measurement of public sentiment.

Chapter VII
PAST ELECTIONS AND PREDICTION[1]

The key word for all sound political prediction is objectivity. Major political campaigns—at least those which are contested—are veritable maelstroms where excitement is rampant and where emotions rise to fever pitch. In the heat of the struggle for votes, when red fire illuminates the streets and mobs are cheering for their candidate, it is extremely difficult to maintain a sober appreciation of election realities. In times such as these rumors become readily credible, opinions take on the authority of fact and partisan enthusiasm subtlely distorts the picture of a candidate's true vote-getting ability. To preserve a clear view of realities throughout this turbulence, it is necessary to rely heavily on predictive techniques that eliminate, so far as possible, subjective biases. Systematic contact with the voters, either in the form of inclusive canvasses, such as the politicians use, or in the form of selective sampling, as in a straw vote, have been pointed to as one means for gaining objectivity in gauging the voting intention of the electorate. A second means is the acquirement of historical perspective through study of the past party alignments of the voters.[2]

Party Continuity and the Stability of the Partisan Vote

The significance of such studies for political prediction is enhanced by two characteristics of American politics. In the first place party organizations have been few in number and largely continuous. The Democratic party, one of the two major contenders today, dates its beginnings back almost to the birth of the nation. The Republican party, the second principal contender, made its first appearance in 1854. The present Democratic-Republican dichotomy, therefore, has been in existence for three quarters of a century,

[1] This chapter is frankly tentative. A large amount of research has been required for the present volume and neither time nor resources have been available for exploring this section of the field in other than a preliminary way. In subsequent work, the author hopes to consider at greater length the use of past-election data in political prediction.

[2] We are thinking here in terms of general as distinguished from primary elections. In the primaries the contest is between factional groups which are less formal than party groups and which are continually arising and disappearing, leaving little in the way of precedent to guide current forecasts. With this type of election, therefore, we are not concerned in the present chapter.

during which period it has largely dominated elections. If we look at the 19 presidential elections from 1856 to 1928, we find that in 14 instances the combined vote for the Democratic and Republican candidates in the nation represented 94 percent or more of the total vote cast, the remaining proportions being polled with more or less consistency by the candidates of minor parties.[3] In 5 elections, third parties appeared to contest the supremacy of the older political groups, but these parties were short-lived and their electoral support was quickly reabsorbed into the customary alignments. The importance of the Democratic-Republican dichotomy varies with states, of course, and with the type of election, but these two party organizations have been uppermost in the nation's political life for the better part of a century, and have left a long record of election precedents which is of material importance to the political predictor.

The forecasting significance of studies of past elections is secondly enhanced by the stability of the party division of the vote from one election to another. The nature of partisanship makes for this characteristic. In voting, men do not act so much as judges who have impartially weighed the merits of a case, but more as confirmed supporters of a given point of view. With varying degrees of loyalty, they "belong" to one side or the other in the election dispute. A not inconsiderable number[4] are active in organization work, contributing funds and labor to the cause and enjoying the political prerogatives that come from such participation. Among these party loyalty is unswerving. The rank and file are at least predisposed to regularity. Perhaps they have acquired their political allegiance in childhood, and have carried this attachment over into maturity. Periodically they avow group identity in order to participate in the caucus or primary, and this tie is further strengthened with each adherence to the party ticket in the general election. The man who calls himself a Republican is likely to vote Republican, and, more often than not, he who is a Democrat will cleave to the symbol of Democracy. Party alignments of the voters, as a result, exhibit a tendency toward stability.

[3]Examination of the vote for representative to the United States Congress shows that in 25 out of the 30 elections held during the period from 1870 to 1928, the two major parties together polled 93 percent or more of the total vote cast in the nation.

[4]Merriam and Gosnell in their volume, *The American Party System* (rev. ed., p. 70), estimate that, normally, about 700,000 party workers are active in national campaigns, and that in times of excitement and enthusiasm this figure may be doubled. The vote of family members and near relatives which these workers control would, of course, add greatly to the total.

In Diagram V are distributed the variations by state of the proportion of the total vote cast for the Republican presidential candidates for successive regular elections for the periods 1872 to 1900 and 1900 to 1928.[5] From this graph it will be observed that the number of instances where the Republican proportion of the total vote cast varied but little from one election to another, are the most numerous, the number of cases declining as the size of the variations increase. This, of course, is the configuration to be expected from the influence of partisanship on voting preferences. If the changes in the Democratic proportion of the total vote had been plotted instead of the Republican, the histograms would be almost identical, since, barring the influence of minor contenders, the loss of adherents by one party is reflected in the other party's gain. The distribution for the period from 1900 to 1928 shows greater flatness than that for the period from 1872 to 1900, which means, of course, that party lines held more firmly in elections before the turn of the century than after this date, but both distributions clearly reveal a tendency for small variations to predominate. In contests for state and local offices, party alignments are probably more flexible than in presidential elections, since in the former the voters are closer to the men and issues at stake and are less swayed by partisan loyalties; but in these elections, as in others, party organization is bound to resist disaffection and thereby stabilize the party division of the vote.

As a political ponderable, then, partisanship plays an important part in determining the outcome of elections. It organizes men around party symbols and exacts a kind of loyalty that predisposes them to regularity in voting. To a Republican, Republican campaign arguments carry the most weight; to a Democrat, merit reposes in the Democratic case. An election outcome, therefore, depends not alone on the issues of a campaign, but also on

[5]For example, in Indiana the Republican proportion of the total vote cast for all candidates in two successive presidential elections was: 1916, 47 percent; 1920, 55 percent; difference, 8 percent (in terms of total vote cast). This 8 percent variation is distributed in the 5.5 to 8.5 class represented by the corresponding vertical bar in the 1900-1928 histogram in Diagram V. An election was regarded as regular where discontinuous third parties (Greenback, Peoples, Union Labor, Progressive, Farmer-Labor, as distinguished from the more continuous minor parties such as Socialist, Socialist-Labor, Prohibition) polled 5 percent or less of the votes. To increase the number of cases, the elections before and after the appearance of a third party were considered successive, as, for example, 1908-1916. The choice of periods is arbitrary. By extending the survey back only to 1872 the political unsettlement incident to the Civil War is largely eliminated. The division of the periods at the year 1900 assigns an equal number of elections to each histogram and practically an equal number of cases.

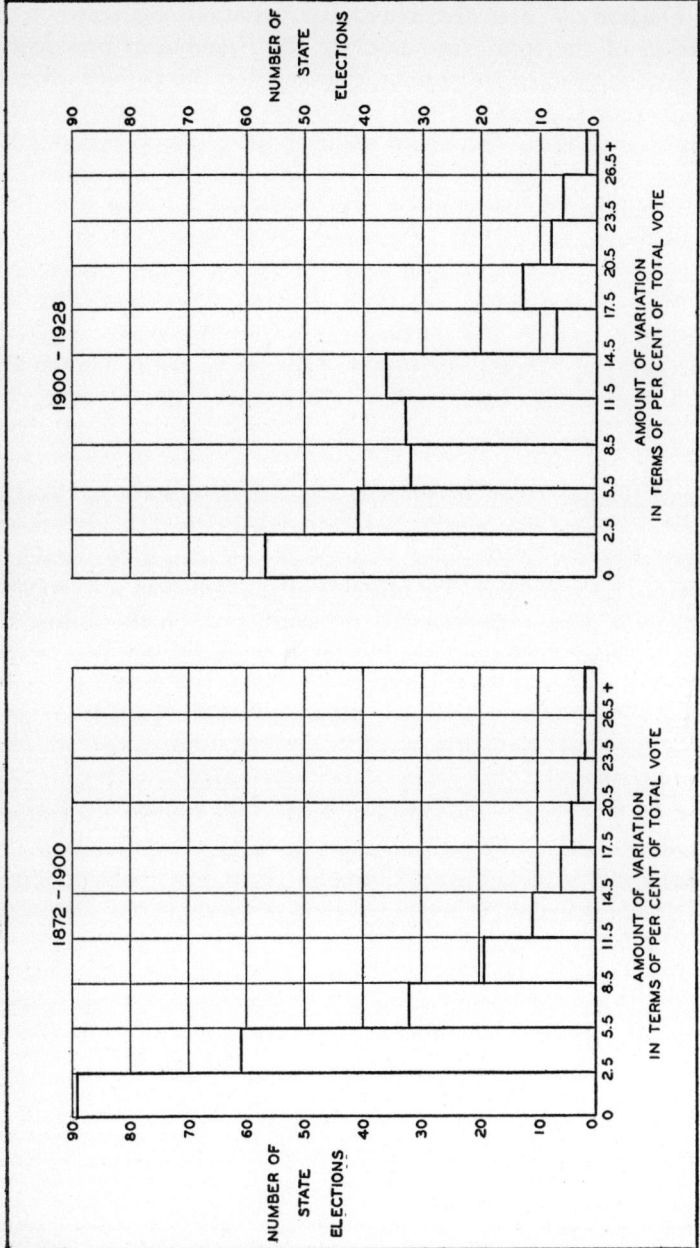

DIAGRAM V
Stability of Party Alignments

Distributions of variations by state of the Republican percentage of the total vote cast for president in successive regular elections for the periods 1872-1900 and 1900-1928. (See page 174.)

the prevalence of the party point of view. If one party has customarily polled six votes to its opponent's four, this two-vote plurality constitutes a barrier which prejudices the minority's chance for victory and enhances that of the majority. This fact makes for the predictability of elections.

Charting the Past Party Vote

In utilizing past-election data for forecasting purposes, the predictor needs to know, first, the statistical position of past party alignments and, second, so far as possible the factors that controlled the division of the vote. The most satisfactory way to visualize the statistics of party alignments is by means of charts. Through graphic presentation the observer is enabled to grasp a synthesis of detail at one glance, and also to see relationships which would not be apparent from examination of election figures alone. The preparation of political charts must first occupy our attention.

The returns from past elections for the construction of charts may be obtained from several sources. Many states issue annual statistical reports in the form of a state *Manual, Blue Book*, or *Register*.[6] In most cases county data is printed, and in some instances compilations by precincts are given. The authenticity of these data is guaranteed by the official or semiofficial nature of the publications. Unfortunately not every state has recognized the desirability of publicizing social data in this manner; hence for many states election figures must be sought from other sources. These are sometimes to be found in printed reports by the secretary of state or in official compilations by election canvassing boards. Where printed tabulations are not available, figures may oftentimes be obtained from original election documents on file in state archives, though fire and bad record-keeping have left significant gaps even in these sources.

When official election data cannot be obtained, the compilations printed in *The World Almanac* and the *Chicago Daily News Almanac* are of great service.[7] In these publications can usually be found

---

[6]No attempt is made here to give more specific references, since a complete and authoritative bibliography of election statistics would in itself constitute a sizable study. It is unfortunate that detailed official election statistics are not periodically gathered by some central agency and printed in a single work of reference. A compendium of this kind would save much duplication of labor on the part of individual students, and would greatly forward research on American political life.

[7]The *World Almanac*, now published by the *New York World-Telegram*, is available from 1868 to date. The *Chicago Daily News Almanac* covers the period 1885 to date. For the period 1838 to 1914, the (New York) *Tribune Almanac*, known as the *Whig Almanac* previous to 1856, is also a serviceable reference work.

the vote for president, United States senator, representative to Congress, and governor. Data by county units are available in many instances. The popular nature of the almanacs and the haste incident to their preparation sometimes allow error to creep into their tabulations, but by and large the almanac rendering of election figures is faithful, and data gathered from these references can be used by serious students with confidence.

Following the collection of past voting statistics, it is necessary to reduce them to percentages before they can be charted. This merely requires the computation of the proportion of the total vote received by each party, or, in other words, the number of ballots polled by each party out of every one hundred votes cast. When stated in these terms, party strength for any number of elections may be compared. In practical politics the outcome of past elections is usually described in terms of the actual number of votes received by each party, or the margin of votes (plurality) separating the winning party and the runner-up. In so far as the total turnout of voters varies between elections, however, this practice leads to faulty reasoning. As pointed out in the discussion of Maine as a political barometer, a plurality of 480 votes in a turnout of 8,000 (6 percent plurality) is a better showing than a margin of 1,000 in a turnout of 25,000 (4 percent plurality) though the former appears to be the smaller if the total number of votes cast in the two elections is not known.[8] For analyses involving comparisons of party strength from election to election, therefore, the raw figures should always be reduced to percentage form.

When reduced to percentages, the past voting data can be charted as in Diagram VI, showing party alignment for presidential electors

---

[8] See pp. 39-40. The discussion of the vote-getting ability of Alfred E. Smith provides a further illustration of the desirability of conceptualizing party strength by a percentage figure, rather than by the actual number of votes cast. In 1928 Governor Smith received 15,000,000 votes, by far the largest number ever polled by a Democratic candidate for president. As a result, Smith is popularly hailed as the greatest vote getter in the history of the Democratic party. The mere attraction of votes, however, is not the essence of the matter. To win an election, a candidate must not alone draw popular support, but draw more than his nearest opponent. Smith, it is true, received an astoundingly large number of ballots, but he also stimulated a great number of people to align themselves with the opposition. The same political forces that were at work to increase the Democratic vote were likewise operative in swelling the Republican vote. Smith's effective political strength, therefore, cannot be gauged by the actual number of ballots marked for him, but only by a percentage figure indexing the proportion that this vote bears to the total vote cast for all candidates. When viewed in this light Smith polled 40.7 percent of the total vote cast in 1928, which is a smaller proportion than that recorded for any Democratic presidential candidate since the Civil War, save for Parker in 1904 (37.6 percent), Cox in 1920 (34.6 percent), and Davis in 1924 (28.9 percent).

178   PAST ELECTIONS

in the state of New Jersey from 1888 to 1928.[9]   The figures used in this diagram are given in Table 33.   The horizontal scale on the chart gives the dates of the several elections.   On the vertical scale, running from zero to one hundred, is measured the percentage of the total vote polled by each party.   The party percentages of the total vote are plotted for each election and these points are connected by straight lines.[10]   The top line represents the voting strength of the majority party, the second line that of the runner-up. The space between the two lines represents the winner's plurality,

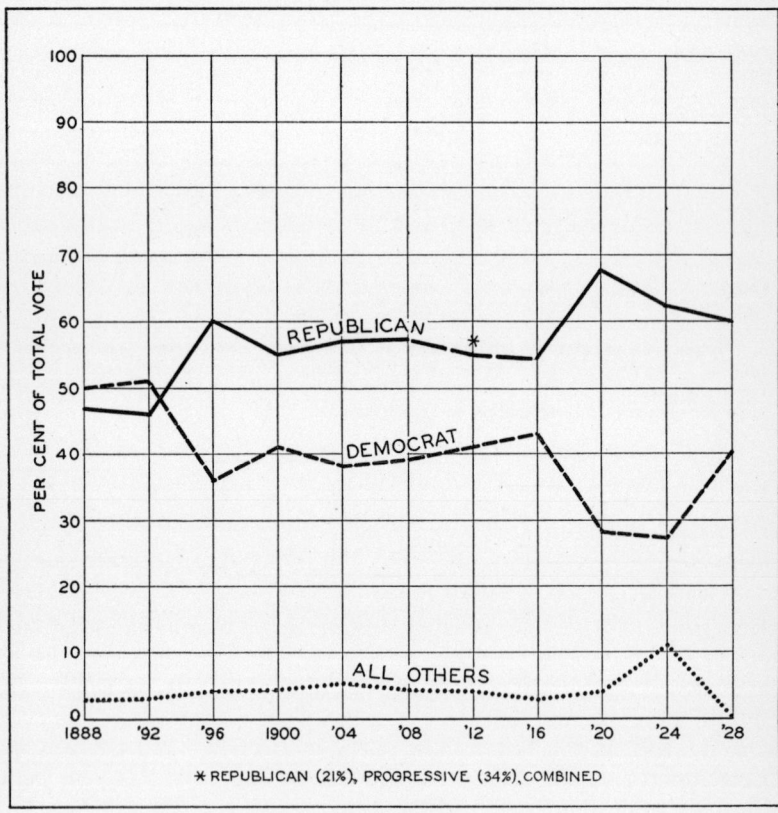

DIAGRAM VI
Vote for Presidential Electors by Parties in New Jersey, 1888-1928

[9]The selection of this period is an arbitrary one, the past-election data being charted back to 1888 in order to show the shift in party control of the state which occurred in 1896.

[10]Change of sentiment between elections probably does not proceed in a linear manner, but this is the most convenient assumption to make in graphing past voting alignments, and emphasizes the continuity of party adherence.

expressed as a percentage of the total vote cast. This space might well be called the "plurality gap." As this gap widens, the election contest becomes one-sided; as it narrows, the struggle for votes between the majority party and the runner-up becomes more intense.

TABLE 33

PRESIDENTIAL ELECTION RETURNS (IN TERMS OF PERCENTAGE OF THE TOTAL VOTE CAST) FOR THE STATE OF NEW JERSEY, 1888 to 1928

Year	Rep.	Dem.	All Other	Plurality	Plurality Shift †
1928	60	40	..	R. 20	15
1924	62	27	11	R. 35	5
1920	68	28	4	R. 40	29
1916	54	43	3	R. 11	3
1912	55*	41	4	R. 14*	4
1908	57	39	4	R. 18	1
1904	57	38	5	R. 19	5
1900	55	41	4	R. 14	10
1896	60	36	4	R. 24	29
1892	46	51	3	D. 5	2
1888	47	50	3	D. 3	

*Republican (21 percent) and Progressive (34 percent) vote combined for purposes of analysis. The Democratic candidate, Woodrow Wilson, actually won New Jersey in 1912 with a plurality of 7 votes per 100 cast over Theodore Roosevelt, the Progressive candidate.

†See pp. 180-81 for explanation and application.

The third plotted line stands for the second runner-up. In this chart but three party categories have been employed: Republican (straight line), Democrat (broken line), and all others (dotted line), the latter heading including the minor and third-party vote. The strength of every minor party, of course, can be charted separately, but New Jersey election history has been written largely in terms of the Republican and Democratic parties, and the detailed plotting of the all-other vote would serve only to complicate the graph.

The split in the Republican party in 1912, it will be noted, has been ignored on the chart, the Republican figure for this year being derived from the combined vote for Roosevelt and Taft. This reconstruction simplifies the picture of Republican and Democratic strength—which is after all the subject of principal interest—and does no great violence to the facts, since the Roosevelt vote was drawn almost wholly from Republican sources. The line from 1908 to 1916 is broken, to indicate this manipulation.

From the chart the reader will observe that the Democrats held a small plurality of 3 percent (3 votes per 100) over the Republicans in New Jersey in 1888. In 1892 the Democratic lead was increased to 5 votes per 100. Four years later, in the memorable sound money campaign, the Republicans reversed this lead, and thereafter maintained a plurality margin of from 10 to 20 percent until 1920, when this advantage was increased to 40 percent. Since 1920 the Republican plurality gap has been closing, dropping to 35 percent in 1924 and contracting to 20 percent in 1928.

Use of Charts in Prediction

This chart reveals to the predictor at a glance the statistical background of his problem. He sees in the last recorded position of the party alignments the base lines from which current possibilities must be measured. He notes the historical juxtaposition of these alignments and observes the degree of flexibility which they exhibit. From these materials alone, provided, of course, that the contest be fought out along traditional party lines, he can compute rough probabilities of the current outcome, reasoning somewhat in the following manner:

The last recorded plurality gap in New Jersey was open 20 points in favor of the Republicans, that is to say, in 1928 the Republican candidate for president polled 20 votes more per 100 cast in this state than the Democratic nominee. To win New Jersey in 1932, the Democrats must close this gap and open it in their own favor, which calls for a minimum plurality shift (defined as the difference between the pluralities of any two successive comparable elections) of 20 points on the chart or, in other words, the net alienation of about one-sixth of the 1928 Republican vote.[11]

In the light of past presidential election returns in New Jersey,

---

[11]Plurality shift might also be caused by the bolting of major party voters to the all-other group or by variations in the size of the stay-at-home vote. The theoretical possibilities are as follows: Say that in New Jersey the 1928 division of the total presidential vote between Republican, Democratic and all other parties were as 6, 3 and 1, respectively, with the Republicans holding a plurality of 3 votes; then the alienation of 1 Republican voter to the Democrats in 1932 would cause a plurality shift of 2 points, since the party division of the vote would then be 5, 4, 1, with the G. O. P. maintaining a plurality of 1. If the Republican voter bolts to the all-other party or remains at home, the plurality shift would be 1 point, the division of the vote in the first situation being 5, 3, 2, and in the second, 5, 3, 1, the Republican party holding a plurality of 2 votes in either case. If one Republican bolted to the Democratic party, and one Democrat bolted to the Republican party, or if an equal interchange were made by any other permutation, plurality shift would be zero. It follows from this that the direction of bolting and the ability of a party to draw its supporters to the polls is of importance to the political predictor.

this appears to be a very large task. The chart shows plurality shift for ten elections from 1888 to 1928. In seven instances—1892, 1900, 1904, 1908, 1912 as reconstructed,[12] 1916 and 1924—the plurality shift ranged from 1 to 10 points. In another case, that of 1928, the shift was 15 points. Only in the elections of 1896 and 1920, do we find shift of sufficient magnitude—29 points in both years—to close the 1928 Republican plurality gap.

On the basis of the bare statistics of past party alignments, therefore, the odds appear to weigh heavily against a Democratic victory in New Jersey. The Republicans have long held the advantage in this state, the last recorded plurality gap is wide, and the voting lines show great inflexibility. It is conceivable, of course, that forces operative in 1932 may be of such character and strength as to close the 1928 Republican plurality gap and open it in favor of the Democrats, but in the light of past-election statistics, this would be an unusual occurrence. At least before forecasting a reversal of this kind at the polls, the predictor would need well authenticated evidence that an exceptional political upheaval was actually taking place. If the Democrats do win New Jersey, their power to attract votes is likely to be well spent by the time they have overcome the customary Republican margin; hence predictions of sweeping Democratic pluralities in this state may be viewed with skepticism.

Every state, of course, presents a different problem. In Tennessee, a small 1928 Republican plurality gap preceded by three reversals, then a long series of highly stable Democratic pluralities, suggests the possibility of a 1932 victory for either party with the weight of partisan advantage accruing to the Democrats. In Nevada, marked flexibility of voting lines and a tendency to interweave indicates weakness in the party tie and a chance for victory by either party. In Texas, a wide and relatively inflexible Democratic plurality gap, terminated by a sudden reversal in 1928 to give the Republicans a small advantage, implies possible doubtfulness in

---

[12] It may be argued, of course, that the reconstruction of the 1912 figures minimizes plurality shift in this year, since many progressive Republicans probably would have voted for Wilson in preference to Taft if their insurgency had not been formally organized by the Progressive party. While there is no doubt some merit to this point, it is not to be supposed that all supporters of Roosevelt would have voted for Wilson, for it was one thing to bolt to the camp of a former Republican president, and quite another thing to go over to that of the ancient political enemy. Apparently Republican regularity was again well established by 1916, since this party's proportion of the total vote in that year was practically the same as it had been since 1896.

1932 with a strong partisan pull toward the Democracy. In Pennsylvania, persistent Republican pluralities of large dimensions suggest an intrenched partisanship which nothing short of a political revolution would overcome. As pointed out in the discussion of New Jersey, and as will be emphasized again on a following page, the predictor must always allow for the operation of current forces that influence the party division of the vote, but examination of charted past voting statistics, as here suggested, reveals where the weight of partisanship lies and constitutes an important first step toward the attainment of a historical perspective which will enable the election forecaster to retain a sense of proportion throughout the turbulence of a political campaign.

Some predictors may wish to make more definite forecasts on the basis of the statistics of past elections, attempting to find correlations between the party division of the vote and economic and other variables, or endeavoring to recognize trends for the purpose of extrapolating party voting lines to future elections. While the practical worth of the former type of analysis in election forecasting is open to considerable skepticism,[13] the latter approach may have some value. If, for example, the very simple forecasting formula, "the plurality in the current election will be identical with that in the preceding election," were applied to the presidential contests in New Jersey from 1888 to 1928, the average (median) plurality error would be 5 votes per 100 cast for the ten predictions.[14] The same rule, applied to all the states for the periods from 1872 to 1900, and 1900 to 1928, yields an average (median) plurality error of 12 and 16 votes, respectively, for every 100 cast per state.[15] The reader will recall that the average plurality error for both the 1924 and the 1928 presidential polls of the *Literary Digest* was 12 votes for every 100 cast per state.

Need for Qualitative Data

The predictor who would make the fullest use of past election data, however, cannot stop with an examination of voting statistics alone. He would want to know also as much as possible about

[13] Stuart Rice, in studying the fluctuations of the vote for Republican assembly candidates in New Jersey, found a relationship of $r = -.247$ between cycles of the party vote and those of certain business indices. *Quantitative Methods in Politics*, pp. 280-293.

[14] See Table 33, column marked "Plurality Shift."

[15] Applied to successive regular elections as defined on p. 174.

the factors that influenced the party division of the vote. Heretofore partisanship has been viewed as one important factor controlling the outcome of elections. Other factors might be singled out in such categories as the following:

Major agitations: such as hard money, the League of Nations, prohibition, etc., causing alienation of voters from one party to another. Organized schisms.

Satisfaction or dissatisfaction with the majority conduct of government: administrative successes, official scandals, failure to live up to campaign pledges, prosperity and depression.

Type of candidates: qualities of leadership, religion, nativity.

Organization factors: factional strife, endowment, ability to draw supporters to the polls.

Group endorsements cutting across party lines.

Concurrent elections: relationship between national, state and local elections.

Equipped with knowledge of past elections of this type, the predictor is better prepared to evaluate current election situations. He can single out the factors that are operative in the present campaign, and, weighing these against his background of precedent, sense the direction in which the voting lines are likely to move. From this type of analysis, he might even formulate an idea of the reasonable degree of movement to be expected, but for this information he would ordinarily rely more heavily on systematic measurements such as straw polls. Opinion, of course, must necessarily play an important part in these analytical forecasts, but there is a degree of objectivity to be gained by the critical use of this method which is at least superior to prediction by guess.

A Twofold Approach to Political Prediction

As presented in this volume, there are two approaches to political prediction. One is by analysis of past party alignments and appraisal of current election situations in the light of this experience. The other is by systematic canvass of the preferences of the voters. The former approach brings to bear on current forecasts the sobering influence of past election performance, but its application depends upon the validity of precedent and requires the use of opinion judgments which limit its objectivity. The latter approach is more arduous to apply, but it will work in unprecedented situations and it is highly objective. Of the two methods, the systematic canvass must be regarded as the more dependable, but it is to the predictor's advantage to employ both techniques in order to verify his conclusions from every possible angle. Given careful application of the gauging techniques here described, the outcome of elections can be predicted within reasonable limits of accuracy.

APPENDICES

Appendix A

ELECTORAL COLLEGE PREDICTIONS USED IN CHAPTER II TO TEST FORECASTING ABILITY OF NEWSPAPERMEN

1928

Walker S. Buel	*Cleveland Plain Dealer*......................	Nov.	4
Thomas Carens	*Boston Herald*.............................	Oct.	28
Raymond Clapper	*Albany Evening News*.......................	Nov.	5
Edw. B. Clark	*Chicago Evening Post*.......................	Nov.	3
Ludwell Denny	*Youngstown Telegram*.......................	Nov.	5
George S. Earle	*Buffalo Evening Times*.......................	Nov.	2
Editorial Staff	*Chicago Daily News*.........................	Nov.	2
Carter Field	*Philadelphia Inquirer*........................	Nov.	5
Edwin W. Gableman	*Cincinnati Enquirer*.........................	Nov.	4
Clinton W. Gilbert	*Syracuse Herald*............................	Nov.	4
Arthur Sears Henning	*Chicago Tribune*............................	Nov.	4
James P. Hornaday	*Indianapolis News*..........................	Nov.	3
C. W. Howard	*Canton Sunday Repository*...................	Nov.	4
Theodore A. Huntley	*Pittsburgh Post-Gazette*.......................	Nov.	3
W. M. Kiplinger	*Kiplinger Washington Letter*.................	Oct.	29
George H. Manning	*New Brunswick Home News*................	Nov.	3
Lorenzo Martin	*Louisville Times*............................	Nov.	5
Charles Michelson	*New York World*...........................	Nov.	4
Carl D. Ruth	*Cleveland News*............................	Nov.	4
Robert Smith	*Philadelphia Public Ledger*...................	Nov.	4
Leroy T. Vernon	*Chicago Daily News*........................	Nov.	3

1924

George Akerson	*Minneapolis Tribune*........................	Nov.	1
Robert B. Armstrong	*Los Angeles Times*..........................	Nov.	2
Carter Field	*Cincinnati Enquirer*.........................	Nov.	3
C. W. Gilbert	*New York Evening Post*......................	Nov.	1
George Harvey	*Cincinnati Enquirer*.........................	Nov.	4
Arthur Sears Henning	*Chicago Tribune*............................	Nov.	2
James P. Hornaday	*Indianapolis News*..........................	Nov.	1
G. Gould Lincoln	*Washington Star*...........................	Nov.	2
Joint Forecast George N. McCain, Robt. Barry, Louis Seibold and Thos. F. Healey	*Philadelphia Public Ledger*...................	Nov.	2
Charles Michelson	*New York World*...........................	Nov.	1
James Morgan	*Boston Globe*..............................	Nov.	3
Robert L. Norton	*Boston Post*................................	Nov.	3
Mark Sullivan	*New York Tribune*..........................	Nov.	2

APPENDIX A

Leroy T. Vernon	*Chicago Daily News*..........................	Nov. 1
Frederick Wm. Wile	*Philadelphia North American*................	Oct. 30
No name	*New York Evening Post*......................	Nov. 1
No name	*Philadelphia Inquirer*.......................	Nov. 2
No name	*Pittsburgh Gazette-Times*...................	Nov. 4

1920

George F. Authier	*Minneapolis Tribune*........................	Nov. 1
Richard J. Beamish	*Philadelphia Inquirer*.......................	Oct. 31
C. C. Brainferd	*Brooklyn Daily Eagle*.......................	Oct. 31
Carter Field	*New York Tribune*...........................	Oct. 31
Arthur Sears Henning	*San Antonio Express*........................	Oct. 31
James A. Hollomon	*Atlanta Constitution*........................	Oct. 31
David Lawrence	*Atlanta Journal*.............................	Oct. 29
Henry P. Robbins	*St. Louis Times*.............................	Oct. 27
John Snure	*Washington Times*...........................	Oct. 30
Mark Sullivan	*New York Evening Post*......................	Oct. 30
Wm. R. Tokes	*Wilmington News*............................	Oct. 28
No name	*Philadelphia Public Ledger*..................	Oct. 31

1916

John Corrigan, Jr.	*Atlanta Constitution*........................	Nov. 5
Summer Curtis	*Washington Post*............................	Nov. 5
Arthur M. Evans	*Chicago Herald*.............................	Nov. 5
Stevenson H. Evans	*New York Tribune*...........................	Nov. 5
Arthur Sears Henning	*Los Angeles Times*..........................	Nov. 5
James P. Hornaday	*Indianapolis News*..........................	Nov. 4
David Lawrence	*New York Times*.............................	Nov. 5
Frank W. Leach	*Philadelphia North American*................	Nov. 5
Angus McSween	*Philadelphia North American*................	Nov. 5
No name	*Brooklyn Daily Eagle*.......................	Nov. 5
" "	*Denver Rocky Mountain News*................	Nov. 5
" "	*New York Sun*...............................	Oct. 29
" "	*New York Tribune*...........................	Nov. 6
" "	*New York Times*.............................	Nov. 4
" "	*Philadelphia Public Ledger*..................	Nov. 6
" "	*San Francisco Examiner*.....................	Nov. 5

1912

Two forecasts by special correspondents unnamed	*Baltimore Sun*..............................	Nov. 3
No name	*Boston Sunday Globe*........................	Nov. 3
" "	*Chicago Record-Herald*, as reprinted in the *Boston Sunday Globe*......................	Nov. 3
" "	*Harper's Weekly*, as reprinted in the *Nashville Tennessean and American*.................	Nov. 2
" "	*New York Evening Post*......................	Nov. 2

No name	*New York Sun*, as reprinted in *Boston Post*...	Nov. 3
" "	*New York World*, as reprinted in the *Boston Sunday Globe*............................	Nov. 3
" "	*New York American*, as reprinted in the *San Francisco Examiner*.......................	Nov. 4
" "	*Washington Post*............................	Nov. 3

1908

Angus McSween	*Philadelphia North American*.................	Nov. 2
Jacob S. Rosenthal	*Baltimore Sun*..............................	Oct. 27
J. C. Welliner	*Washington Times*...........................	Nov. 2
Walter Wellman	*Chicago Record-Herald*......................	Nov. 3
No name	*Brooklyn Daily Eagle*........................	Nov. 1
" "	*Cincinnati Enquirer*..........................	Nov. 3
" "	*Jacksonville Times-Union*.....................	Nov. 2
" "	*Harper's Weekly*, as reprinted in the *San Antonio Express*............................	Nov. 2
" "	*Kansas City Star*............................	Nov. 2
" "	*Knoxville Journal and Tribune*................	Nov. 1
" "	*Memphis Commercial Appeal*.................	Nov. 1
" "	*New York Tribune*..........................	Nov. 1
" "	*New York Times*............................	Oct. 25

1904

James P. Hornaday	*Indianapolis News*...........................	Nov. 5
No name	*Baltimore Sun*..............................	Oct. 31
" "	*Boston Daily Globe*..........................	Nov. 8
" "	*Chicago Daily News*.........................	Nov. 7
" "	*Chicago Tribune*, as reprinted in *Philadelphia North American*...........................	Nov. 6
" "	*Denver Daily News*..........................	Nov. 7
" "	*New York Tribune*..........................	Oct. 30
" "	*New York World*, as reprinted in *Boston Sunday Post*..............................	Nov. 6
" "	*Philadelphia Inquirer*.........................	Nov. 7
" "	*Philadelphia North American*.................	Nov. 6
" "	*Philadelphia Public Ledger*....................	Nov. 7
" "	*San Antonio Express*.........................	Nov. 6
" "	*St. Paul Pioneer Press*.......................	Nov. 6

Appendix B

STATE PROHIBITION REFERENDA, 1919-1930[1]

California

Nov. 2. 1930. Referendum on Harris Act, a proposed state code to enforce the Eighteenth Amendment to the United States Constitution:

For........................	400,475	46.2 percent
Against....................	465,537	53.8 percent

Nov. 7, 1922. Referendum on the Wright Act, a state code to enforce the Eighteenth Amendment to the United States Constitution:

For........................	445,076	52.0 percent
Against....................	411,133	48.0 percent

Nov. 2. 1926. Initiated measure to repeal the Wright Act, a state code to enforce the Eighteenth Amendment to the United States Constitution:

For........................	502,258	47.0 percent
Against....................	565,875	53.0 percent

Colorado

Nov. 2, 1926. Initiated Amendment to the state Constitution to enable the legislature to provide for the manufacture, importation and sale of intoxicating liquors by and through the state, for personal or domestic use; such amendment to be inoperative as long as in conflict with the laws of the United States:

For........................	107,749	41.1 percent
Against....................	154,672	58.9 percent

Illinois

Nov. 7, 1922. Referendum initiated by petition submitting the following question: "Shall the existing State and Federal prohibitory laws be modified so as to permit the manufacture, sale, and transportation of beer (containing less than four percent by volume of alcohol) and light wines and beer for home consumption?"

For........................	1,065,242	67.5 percent
Against....................	512,111	32.5 percent

Nov. 2, 1926. Referendum initiated by petition submitting the following question: "Should the Congress of the United States modify the Eighteenth Amendment to the Constitution of the United States so that the same shall not prohibit the manufacture, sale, transportation, importation, or exportation of beverages which are not in fact intoxicating, as determined in accordance with the laws of the respective States?"

For........................	840,631	60.2 percent
Against....................	556,592	39.8 percent

[1]Except where otherwise noted, these data are taken from Laura Lindley's *State Wide Referenda in the United States on the Liquor Question*, The American Issue Publishing Company, Westerville, Ohio.

APPENDIX B

Nov. 4, 1930.[2] "Shall the Eighteenth Amendment to the Constitution of the United States, which among other things prohibits the manufacture, sale, or transportation of intoxicating liquors for beverage purposes within the United States, be repealed?"

> For.................... 1,054,432   65.6 percent
> Against................   551,741   34.4 percent

Nov. 4, 1930.[2] "Shall the Congress of the United States modify the National Prohibition Act to enforce the Eighteenth Amendment to the Constitution of the United States (commonly known as the Volstead Act) so that the same shall not prohibit the manufacture, sale or transportation of beverages which are not in fact intoxicating, as determined in accordance with the laws of the respective states?"

> For....................   968,652   65.6 percent
> Against................   506,973   34.4 percent

Nov. 4, 1930.[2] "Shall the Illinois Prohibition Act be repealed?"

> For.................... 1,060,004   66.9 percent
> Against................   523,130   33.1 percent

KENTUCKY

Nov. 4, 1919. Prohibition Amendment to the State Constitution:

> For....................   208,755   51.3 percent
> Against................   198,038   48.7 percent

MASSACHUSETTS

Nov. 2, 1920. An Act to regulate the manufacture and sale of beer, cider, and light wines:

> For....................   442,215   50.5 percent
> Against................   432,951   49.5 percent

Nov. 7, 1922. An Act to carry into effect, so far as the Commonwealth of Massachusetts is concerned, the Eighteenth Amendment to the Constitution of the United States:

> For....................   323,964   43.1 percent
> Against................   427,840   56.9 percent

Nov. 4, 1924. An Act to prohibit the manufacture, transportation importation, or exportation of intoxicating liquors as defined by law, or certain nonintoxicating beverages, unless there shall have been obtained the permit required by the law of the United States:

> For....................   454,656   50.5 percent
> Against................   446,473   49.5 percent

Nov. 6, 1928. A question of public policy: "Shall the Senator from this district be instructed to vote for a resolution requesting Congress to take action for the repeal of the Eighteenth Amendment to the Constitution of the United States, known as the Prohibition Amendment?"

> For....................   707,352   62.6 percent
> Against................   422,475   37.4 percent

[2]*Blue Book of the State of Illinois*, 1931-1932, pp. 852-57.

Nov. 4, 1930.[3] Law proposed by initiative petition: "Shall the proposed law which amends the General Laws by striking out chapter 138, section 2A, which provides that, 'No person shall manufacture, transport by aircraft, water craft or vehicle, import or export spirituous or intoxicating liquor as defined by section three, or certain non-intoxicating beverages as defined by section one unless in each instance he shall have obtained the permit or other authority required therefor by the laws of the United States and the regulations made thereunder,' which law was disapproved in the House of Representatives by a vote of 110 in the affirmative and 123 in the negative and in the Senate by a vote of eleven in the affirmative and twenty-six in the negative, be approved?"

    For...................... 649,592   63.8 percent
    Against.................. 368,544   36.2 percent

Michigan

April 7, 1919. Amendment to the State Constitution to allow the manufacture and sale of vinous and malt liquors:
    For...................... 322,603   37.8 percent
    Against.................. 530,123   62.2 percent

Missouri

Nov. 2, 1920. State-wide Prohibition Law:
    For...................... 481,880   53.4 percent
    Against.................. 420,581   46.6 percent

Nov. 2, 1926. Repeal of State-wide Prohibition Law:
    For...................... 294,388   34.1 percent
    Against.................. 569,931   65.9 percent

Montana

Nov. 2, 1926. Initiated measure to repeal all State enforcement laws:
    For...................... 83,231   53.3 percent
    Against.................. 72,982   46.7 percent

Nov. 6, 1928. Initiated measure to reenact the enforcement laws:
    For...................... 68,431   45.9 percent
    Against.................. 80,619   54.1 percent

Nevada

Nov. 2, 1926.[4] Resolution calling on Congress to call a Constitutional Convention to amend the Eighteenth Amendment:
    For...................... 18,131   77.2 percent
    Against.................. 5,352   22.8 percent

New York

Nov. 2, 1926. Question submitted by the Legislature: "Should the Congress of the United States modify the Federal Act to enforce the Eighteenth Amendment to the Constitution of the United States so that the same shall not

[3]Secretary of the Commonwealth of Massachusetts, pamphlet giving 1930 election returns, p. 18.

[4]Letter from Secretary of State of Nevada.

prohibit the manufacture, sale, transportation, importation, or exportation of beverages which are not in fact intoxicating, as determined in accordance with the laws of the respective States?"

 For...................... 1,763,070   74.7 percent
 Against................... 598,484   25.3 percent

North Dakota

June 27, 1928. Repeal of State Prohibition Law (Initiated):
 For...................... 96,837   48.3 percent
 Against................... 103,696   51.7 percent

Ohio

Nov. 4, 1919. Initiated measure providing for the manufacture and sale of 2.75 percent liquor:
 For...................... 474,907   48.5 percent
 Against................... 504,688   51.5 percent

Nov. 4, 1919. Repeal of Prohibition Amendment to the State Constitution:
 For...................... 454,933   47.8 percent
 Against................... 496,786   52.2 percent

Nov. 4, 1919. Approval of State Prohibition Enforcement Act:
 For...................... 474,078   48.7 percent
 Against................... 500,312   51.3 percent

Nov. 4, 1919. Referendum on action of the Legislature in ratifying the Eighteenth Amendment:
 For...................... 499,971   50.0 percent
 Against................... 500,450   50.0 percent

Nov. 2, 1920. Approval of State Prohibition Enforcement Act:
 For...................... 1,062,470   57.9 percent
 Against................... 772,329   42.1 percent

Nov. 7, 1922. Amendment to State Constitution to legalize 2.75 percent beer (Initiated):
 For...................... 719,050   44.2 percent
 Against................... 908,522   55.8 percent

Rhode Island

Nov. 4, 1930.[5] Question submitted to the people by the legislature: "The Eighteenth Amendment to the Constitution of the United States shall it be retained?"
 For...................... 47,652   31.7 percent
 Against................... 171,960   78.3 percent

South Dakota

Nov. 2, 1920. Amendments to strengthen the Prohibition Enforcement Laws:
 For...................... 75,870   46.3 percent
 Against................... 87,986   53.7 percent

[5]*Rhode Island Acts and Resolves*, 1930, Chap. 1507, p. 63. Returns from: Rhode Island State Returning Board, *Official Count of the Ballots Cast at the Elections*, Nov. 4, 1930, p. 71.

Nov. 7, 1922. Repeal of the State Sheriff Law (State enforcement officer):
For........................ 64,221 40.5 percent
Against.................... 94,241 59.5 percent

Texas

May 24, 1919. Prohibition Amendment to the State Constitution:
For........................ 159,723 53.3 percent
Against.................... 140,099 46.7 percent

Wisconsin

Nov. 2, 1920. Ratification of the Mulberger Act for Prohibition:
For........................ 419,309 67.7 percent
Against.................... 199,876 32.3 percent

Nov. 2, 1926. Referendum on the following question: "Shall the Congress of the United States amend the Volstead Act so as to authorize the manufacture and sale of beer for beverage purposes, of an alcoholic percentage of 2.75 percent by weight, under government supervision, but with the provision that no beverage so purchased shall be drank on the premises where obtained?"
For........................ 349,443 66.3 percent
Against.................... 177,602 33.7 percent

April 2, 1929. Referendum on the following question: "Shall the State Prohibition Enforcement Act, generally known as the Severson Act, be repealed?"
For........................ 338,642 63.3 percent
Against.................... 196,402 36.7 percent

April 2, 1929. Referendum on the following question: "Shall the State Prohibition Enforcement Act, generally known as the Severson Act, be amended so the State shall not arrest or fine anyone for manufacture, sale, or possession of beer of not more than 2.75 percent alcohol by weight?"
For........................ 321,688 61.6 percent
Against.................... 200,545 38.4 percent

INDEX

INDEX

Adrian Telegram, 69
Akerson, George, 187
Alabama, 20, 22, 58
Altoona Tribune, 69
American Issue, 78
Anti-Saloon League of Delaware, 147
Arizona, 23
Arkansas, 58, 158
Armstrong, Robert B., 187
As goes Maine, *see* Maine, as political barometer
Associated Press, 1
Atlanta Georgian, 97
Atlantic News-Telegraph, 69
Authier, George F., 188

Baker, Newton D., 28
Baltimore Sun, 5, 11
Band-wagon vote, 1, 27, 78, 108, 138, 140, 142
Bangor Whig and Courier, 32
Barry, Robert, 187
Beamish, Richard J., 188
Beck-Linthicum resolution, 156, 157, 162
Betts, Curtis, 16
Blaine, James G., 33
Borah, William E., 27
Boston Globe, 48
Brainferd, C. C., 188
Brown, George Rothwell, 10
Bryan, William Jennings, 23
Buchanan, James, 38
Buel, Walker S., 19, 187
Buffalo Courier-Express, 69, 83-84, 132
Buffalo Evening Times, 53, 69
Burleson, Albert S., 28
Burlington Daily Enterprise, 163
Burton, Theodore, 27

California, 22, 50, 156, 157, 190
California Outlook, 69
Canton Daily News, 69

Carens, Thomas, 187
Charts, political: construction of, 176-180, use of, in election forecasting, 180-82
Chicago American, 48, 69
Chicago Daily News Almanac, 176
Chicago Examiner, 49
Chicago Herald and Examiner, 49, 69, 83
Chicago Journal, 48, 68, 73, 105, 107, 145, 146
Chicago Record-Herald, 48, 69, 71, 112
Chicago Tribune, 11, 49, 50, 53, 54, 68, 73, 80, 89, 96, 97, 105
Cincinnati Enquirer, 16, 48, 50, 52, 53, 68, 71, 73, 76, 80, 83, 104, 107, 116, 123, 139, 140
Cincinnati Times-Star, 69
Clapper, Raymond, 19, 187
Clark, Champ, 28, 33
Clark, Edward B., 19, 187
Cleveland News, 69
Cleveland News-Leader, 69
Cleveland Press, 69
Colby, Bainbridge, 28
College Humor, 50
Colorado, 71, 129, 156, 157, 190
Columbus Dispatch, 17, 48, 50, 52, 53, 54, 68, 73, 76, 83, 92, 97, 104, 107, 116, 124, 125, 130, 139, 140
Connally, Representative Tom, 80
Connecticut, 72, 158
Continuity of party alignments, 172-173
Coolidge, Calvin, 23, 27, 32, 64, 72, 73, 78, 93, 106, 124
Cooper, Myers, 80
Correlation: coefficients of, 42, 93, 106; of economic and political variables, 182; Maine, scatter diagram, 40-41
Corrigan, John, Jr., 188
Cox, Gov. James M., 10, 11, 15, 16, 177

Cromwell, Thomas B., 16
Curtis, Charles, 28
Curtis, Sumner, 19, 188

Daniels, Josephus, 28
Dansville Breeze, 69
Davis, John W., 11, 72, 73, 124, 177
Decatur County, typical of Illinois, 89
Delaware, 143, 146, 147, 158, 170-71
Democratic National Committee, 29
Democratic party: beginnings of, 172; predictions by leaders of, 8-13, 74, 76
Denny, Ludwell, 187
Denver Post, 71, 129
Denver Republican, 48
Des Moines Register and Tribune, 163
Des Moines Tribune, 69
Du Pont, Pierre S., 143, 146-47, 152, 170-71

Earle, George S., 187
Editor and Publisher, 14, 15, 23, 75, 76
Eighteenth Amendment, 147, 148, 153, 154, 157, 164
Elation: influence of, on predictions by politicians, 10-12; use of straw poll to counteract, 136-37
Election statistics, sources, 176-77
Electoral college forecasts: as criterion of straw-poll error, 58-61; by newspapermen, 18-24
Erie Dispatch-Herald, 53, 69
Error, plurality: defined, 6, 15, 57-65; of forecasts by newspapermen, 14-18, 24, by politicians, 5-9, 12-13, by straw polls, 65-74, 145, 146, by newspapermen, politicians and straw polls compared, 74-77; from past election statistics, 182
Error, single candidates, defined, 57-65
Evans, Arthur M., 19, 188
Evans, Stevenson H., 188

Fairbanks, Charles W., 27
Farmer-Labor party, 174
Farm Journal, 49, 50, 67, 70, 72, 75
Fernald, Bert M., 31, 34
Fess, Simeon D., 28

Field, Carter, 19, 187, 188
Florida, 15, 22, 23, 71, 150
Fond du Lac County, typical of Wisconsin, 89
Fort Madison Democrat, 69
Fort Wayne Sentinel, 69
Franklin, Fabian, 58, 60, 63, 64, 65
Fredericksburg Free Lance-Star, 163

Gableman, Edwin W., 187
Garfield, James R., 28
Gazette, hypothetical straw poll of, 60, 110, 114-15
Gibson, Charles Dana, 28
Gilbert, Clinton W., 19, 187
Gillingham, George O., 143
Gore, Thomas P., 28
Gosnell, Harold F., 1, 102, 173
Greenback party, 174
Greensboro News, 138
Gregory, Thomas W., 28

Harding, Warren G., 15, 22, 23, 28, 31, 32, 92
Harrison, Senator Pat, 78
Harrison, Gen. William Henry, 25, 26
Harvey, George, 187
Hays, Will H., 27, 31-32
Healey, Thos. F., 187
Hearst Newspapers, 49, 50, 52, 55, 67, 70, 71, 72, 74, 75, 76, 77, 86, 87, 92, 97, 104, 107, 124, 129, 130, 131
Henning, Arthur Sears, 11, 19, 187, 188
Hewitt, Oscar, 89
Hollomon, James A., 188
Homogeneous political areas, 88-89
Hoover, Herbert, 6, 7, 8, 15, 16, 20, 22, 23, 50, 58, 59, 61, 63, 64, 70, 72, 73, 76, 88, 92, 93, 94, 106, 110, 117, 119
Hormell, Orren Chalmer, 29
Hornaday, James P., 19, 187, 188, 189
Howard, C. W., 187
Hughes, Charles E., 11, 12, 22, 23, 27, 31, 49, 59
Huntley, C. W., 187

Illinois, 20, 49, 50, 54, 80, 89, 154, 155, 156, 157, 190

INDEX

Inclusive canvass, 4, 7, 98, 137, 172
Indiana, 26, 48, 49, 50, 174
Iowa, 23, 26, 86, 111
Iowa Magazine, 69

Jefferson, Thomas, 25
Jones, Norman L., 80

Kansas, 32, 59, 86, 111, 148, 158
Kent, Edward, 26
Kent, Frank, 5, 11
Kentucky, 16, 20, 23, 48, 58, 191
Kiplinger, W. M., 19, 187

La Follette, Robert M., 72, 73, 93, 124, 134-35
Lawrence, David, 188
Leach, Frank W., 188
League of Nations, 31, 32, 183
Lewis, J. Hamilton, 28
Lincoln, Abraham, 40
Lincoln, G. Gould, 19, 187
Lindley, Laura, 190
Literary-Digest straw polls: adequacy of sample in, 103-7, 153; business needs vs. sampling requirements in, 171; cancellation sorting of ballot cards of, 86-87, 110-11; change of sentiment over time in: in prohibition polls, 153, presidential polls not a measure of, 110-12; class bias in: economic, 91, 150, 153, 160, 163, 164, sex, 91-93, 150, 151, 160, 163, 164, party, 72-73, 93-96, 116-17; coöperation in, 97, 143; correction of: by bias of past preferences, 124-25, on theory of recurrent bias, 72-73, 116-17, prohibition polls, 167-68; cost of, 78; error of, plurality: defined, 58-65, described, 67, 68, 70, 72-73, 74, 75, 76, 77; geographical bias in, 86-88, 149-50, 153, 163, 164; mail method employed in, 55-57; manipulation in, 78, 80-81, 149, 153, 163; number of, 49-51, 146, 147-48; on prohibition, 147-71: compared with other appraisals of sentiment, 168-70, measures of change of sentiment on, 168-70; past preference vote in, interpretation of, 119, 124-25; promotional value of, 51, 55; public interest in, 51, 143; Republican overprediction in, 72-73, 93-96, 116-17; selection in coöperation in, 99, 100, 101, 144, 151-53, 160, 163, 164, 170; stuffing the ballot box in, 84, 85, 149, 153, 163

Lodge, Henry Cabot, 27
Log Cabin and Hard Cider campaign, 25
Long Island Daily Press, 69
Longworth, Nicholas, 27
Lord of Telephone Manor, The, 86
Los Angeles Times, 48
Louisiana, 86, 111, 158
Lundberg, George A., 89
Lundeen, Congressman Ernest, 145-46

McAdoo, William G., 28
McCain, George N., 187
Macon County, typical of Illinois, 89
McSween, Angus, 19, 188, 189
Maine, as political barometer, 89, 177; attempts to change date of state election, 33-35; formula of identical fluctuation, 42-43; formula of Republican norm, 38-42; history of, 25-26; literal formula, 37-38; monetary aid from national committees, 28-30; nonresident speakers, 27-30; relation of, to local campaign, 30-36; turnout predictions from, 43-44.
Malone, Dudley Field, 28
Manning, George H., 187
Marshall, Thomas R., 28
Martin, Lorenzo, 187
Maryland, 20, 23, 158
Massachusetts, 15, 23, 58, 85, 154, 155, 157, 191
Mellon plan, *Literary-Digest* poll on, 50, 146
Merriam, Charles E., 1, 102, 173
Methodist Preachers' Association, 147

Michelet, Simon, 102
Michelson, Charles, 19, 187
Michigan, 3, 86, 192
Milliken, Carl E., 31
Mills, Ogden, 28
Minnesota, 145, 151
Mississippi, 78
Missouri, 16, 20, 23, 77, 155, 157, 192
Montana, 23, 156, 157, 192
Morgan, James, 19, 187
Moses, George H., 28
Multnomah County, test for party bias in, in *Literary-Digest* poll, 93, 94

Nation, The, 50, 90
Nebraska, 23, 32
Neprash, Jerry Alvin, 89
Nevada, 20, 23, 156, 157, 181, 192
New Hampshire, November campaigns, nonresident speakers in, 28
New Jersey, 20, 49, 50, 87, 158, 178-82
New Mexico, 23, 158
Newspaper editors, estimates of repeal sentiment by, 157-60, 161-62
Newspapermen: accuracy of plurality predictions by, 14-18, 24; as sponsors of straw polls, 47-51; attitude of, on harm of straw polls, 138, 141-43; criticism of, of 1928 Hearst poll, 77; electoral-college forecasts by, 18-24; forecasts by, compared with those of politicians and straw votes, 74-77; utility of straw polls to, 137
New York, 47, 49, 50, 156, 157, 192
New York City, cancellation study in, 87
New York Daily News, 50, 53, 54, 56
New York Evening Telegram, 69
New York Globe, 69
New York Herald, 47-48, 67, 70, 71, 124
New York Herald Tribune, 25
New York Times, 25, 90
New York World, 15, 69
New York World-Telegram, 176
Norris, George W., 27
North Carolina, 15, 22, 23, 148, 158
North Dakota, 23, 156, 157, 193
Norton, Robert L., 187

O'Connor-Hall beer-for-revenue-bill, 156
October states as election barometers, 126
Ohio, 17, 26, 48, 49, 50, 70, 73, 76, 92, 97, 104, 139, 140, 158, 193
Oklahoma, 58, 158
Omaha Daily News, 69
Omaha World-Herald, 53, 69
Oregon, 16, 86, 111
Ossining Citizen-Sentinel, 69
Outagamie County, typical of Wisconsin, 89
Overacker, Louise, 29

Parker, Alton B., 11, 23, 28, 177
Parkhurst, Frederick H., 31
Partisanship, influence on voting, 173-176
Party alignments: continuity of, 172-173; stability of, 173-76, 180-82
Past election data, use of, in prediction, 172-84
Pathfinder, the, 49, 50, 52, 67, 70, 71, 72, 75, 127, 143
Pennsylvania, 3, 20, 26, 97, 182
Peoples party, 174
Pepper, George W., 28
Percentage, use of: in analysis of party vote, 39, 40, 177; in expressing plurality error, 6, 15, 58-65
Philadelphia, cancellation study in, 87
Philadelphia Press, 69;
Pierce, Franklin, 33
Pittsburgh Sun Telegraph, 69, 92, 97
Plurality error, *see* Error, plurality
Plurality gap, 179, 180
Plurality shift, 180, 181
Politicians: accuracy of plurality predictions by, 5-9; attitude of, on harm of straw polls, 139-44, elation complex of, 10-12; forecasts by, compared with those by newspapermen and straw votes, 74-77; techniques used by, 1-5, utility of straw polls to, 136-37
Pomerene, Atlee, 28

INDEX

Portland, Maine, special *Literary-Digest* prohibition poll in, 151
Portland Oregonian, 16
Portland, Oregon, test for party bias in, in *Literary-Digest* poll, 93, 94
Portland Press-Herald, 32
Progressive party, 174, 181
Prohibition; an issue in 1928 presidential campaign, 76; referenda on, official state, 153-55, 164-68, 190-94; straw polls on, 50, 86, 143-44, 145-71
Prohibition party, 174
Propaganda: predictions by politicians as, 1, 6, 142-44; straw polls regarded as, 78, 139; value of Maine September returns as, 29-35, 45

Qualitative data, need for, in analysis of past elections, 182-83

Redfield, William C., 28
Religion, an issue in 1928 presidential campaign, 13, 19, 95
Repeal of Eighteenth Amendment: growth of sentiment for, 168-69; polls on issue of, 145-71
Republican National Committee, 29, 31, 35
Republican overprediction in *Literary-Digest* polls, 58-64, 72-73, 93-96, 116-17
Republican party: beginnings of, 172; predictions by leaders of, 6-13, 74, 76
Rexall drug stores, 49, 67, 70, 71
Rhode Island, 15, 23, 58, 155, 157, 160, 193
Rice, Stuart, 89, 182
Richmond News, 163
Robbins, Henry, 188
Roosevelt, Franklin D., 28
Roosevelt, Theodore, 23, 27, 179
Rosenthal, Jacob S., 189
Ruth, "Babe," 62
Ruth, Carl D., 187

St. Louis Post-Dispatch, 16
St. Louis Republic, 48
St. Louis Times, 69, 83

Sait, Edward M., 5
Salt Lake City Tribune, 71
Schwab, Frank X., 83
Scripps Howard Newspapers, 151
Seibold, Louis, 187
Sentinel, hypothetical straw poll of, 60
Sheboygan Press, 69
Silent vote, 4, 8, 98
Sinclair, Upton, 149
Slogans in Maine campaigns, 31
Smith, Alfred E., 7, 8, 11, 15, 16, 20, 23, 37, 50, 58, 59, 63, 70, 72, 76, 90, 94, 110, 127, 177
Smith, Robert, 187
Snure, John, 188
Socialist party, 174
Socialist-Labor party, 174
Solid South, 15, 20, 102, 150
South Bend News-Times, 163
South Carolina, 64, 106, 111
South Dakota, 23, 193
Stability of party alignments, 173-76, 180-82
Stanley, A. Owsley, 17
Statistics, election, sources of, 176-77
Stay-at-home vote, 101-2, 119
Straw poll: accuracy of, *see* Straw poll: error, plurality; adequacy of sample in: as cause of error, 78, 103-107, 153, interpretation of, 128, test for, 104, 107, 133; ballots: form of, 83, 134-35, keying of, 98-99, 132, 133; ballot-in-the-paper method in, 52-53, 66, 71, 72, 75, 82, 85, 90, 96, 97, 98, 102, 116, 126, 127, 128, 129, 130, 134; bias in sample in: recurrent, 72-73, 93-96, 116-17 (*see also* Straw poll: class bias in, geographical bias in, participation-nonparticipation, bias of, in, selection in coöperation, bias of, in); buttons, campaign, personal canvass with, 53; cancellation sorting of ballot cards, in 86-87, 110-111; certified public accountants employed in, 79; change of sentiment over time in: as cause of error, 78, 107-13, 153, interpretive allowance for, 128, *Literary-Digest* prohi-

bition polls as measure of, 168-70, polls on candidates as measure of, 137-38, sponsor's need to plan for, 133, 134; class bias in: as cause of error, 77, 90-96, economic, 91, 150, 153, 160, 163, 164, party, 72-73, 93-96, 116-17, sex, 91-93, 150-51, 160, 163-64, interpretive allowance for, 115, 116, 127; coöperation in, 92, 96-98, 128, 135, 143 (*see also* Straw polls: selection in coöperation, bias of in); correction of: by bias of past preferences, 123-25, by weighting, 114-16, in *Literary-Digest* prohibition polls, 167-68, on theory of recurrent bias, 70, 72-73, 116-17; corroboratory forecasts from past preferences in, 118-25; cost of: *Literary-Digest*, 78, personal canvass, 171; crudeness of, as measure, allowance for, 60-61, 129-30; cumulation of returns in, 110; error, plurality: causes of, summary, 77-78 (*see also* Straw polls: adequacy of sample in, change of sentiment over time in, class bias in, goegraphical bias in, manipulation in, participation-nonparticipation, bias of in, selection in coöperation, bias of, in, stuffing the ballot box in), compared with that of newspapermen and politicians, 74-77, defined, 57-65, electoral-college placement as criterion of, 58-61, on candidates, 65-74, on issues, 145, 146; fraud in, *see* Straw poll: manipulation in, stuffing the ballot box in; geographical bias in: as cause of error, 77, 85-89, 149-50, 153, 163, 164, avoidance of, by sponsor, 131, 134, interpretive allowance for, 113-116, 127, polls under multiple sponsorship, 129; harm of, 138-44; history of, 47-51; honesty of, 77, 78-81, 149, 153, 163, 109, 126, 136; interpretation of: by recurrent bias, 116-117, by past preferences, 117-26, by weighting, 113-16; criteria for, 126-30; mail method of, 52, 55-57, 66, 73, 83, 86, 87, 91, 97, 98, 100, 102, 126, 127, 128, 129, 130, 131, 132, 133, 134, 135; manipulation in: as cause of error, 77, 78-81, 149, 153, 163, interpretive allowance for, 109, 126, sponsors will avoid, 136; Mellon plan, *Literary-Digest* poll on, 50, 146; miscellaneous, 69, 74; net shift prediction from past preferences in, 118-20, 124-25; on prohibition, 50, 86, 143-44, 145-71; on traction referendum by *Chicago Journal*, 145; on World War: American entry into, 145-46, bonus to veterans of, 50, 146; participation-nonparticipation, bias of, in: as cause of error, 78, 94, 101-103, 153, interpretive allowance for, 128; party-to-party shift prediction from past preferences in, 120-26, tabulation of returns for, 135; past preference returns in: ballot form for, 134-35, interpretation of, 117-26; personal-canvass method in, 52, 53, 66, 71, 72, 82, 83, 85-86, 89, 90-91, 96-97, 98, 100, 102, 116, 126, 127, 128, 129, 130, 131, 133, 168, 171; publicity for returns of, rules for, 135-36; recurrent bias in, 72-73, 93-96, 116-17; regarded as propaganda 78, 139; repeating in, 71, 77, 81-85, 126, 132-34, 149, 156, 163; selection in coöperation, bias of in: as cause of error, 78, 92, 96-101, 144, 151-53, 160, 163, 164, 170, control of, by sponsor, 98-99, 133, 168, interpretive allowance for, 128, 135; size of sample in, 78, 103-7, 128, 133, 153; sponsor of: attitude on harm of, 141-42, factor in interpretation, 127, 129, 130, intuition, use of, by, 54, 131-32, rules for good management, 130-36; spot canvassing in, 54, 83, 126, 133; stuffing the ballot box in: as cause of error, 71, 77, 81-85, 149, 153, 163, interpretive allowance for, 126, sponsor, protection against, 132-34; tabulation of returns in, 135; utility of, 51-52, 136-

138, 172; weighting of: as test for geographical bias in *Literary-Digest* poll, 87, 88, in interpretation of returns, 113-16, 127

Sullivan, Mark, 19, 42-44, 187, 188

Taft, William H., 23, 31, 179, 181
Taylor, Zachary, 38
Tennessee, 15, 20, 22, 23, 158, 181
Texas, 15, 22, 23, 80, 181, 194
Thompson, "Big Bill," 92
Tokes, Wm. R., 188
Trenton Sunday Times-Advertiser, 69

Underwood, Oscar, 28
Union Labor party, 174
Untermeyer, Samuel, 28
Utah, 71

Van Buren, Martin, 25
Vermont, 3, 20, 26
Vernon, Leroy T., 187, 188
Virginia, 15, 22, 23, 86, 87, 97, 100, 111
Virginia Enterprise, 151
Volstead Law, 147, 154

Washington, 23
Washington (D. C.) Herald, 97, 100

Washington (D. C.) Post, 10
Watson, James E., 28
Welliner, J. C., 189
Wellman, Walter, 19, 189
West Virginia, 48
Whig Almanac, 176
Whig party, 25, 26, 28
White, George, 92
Wichita Beacon, 163
Wile, Frederick William, 19, 188
Willcox, Walter F., 168
Willis, Frank B., 28
Wilson, Woodrow, 12, 15, 16, 22, 30, 38, 48, 49, 59, 181
Wisconsin, 86, 89, 110, 111, 127, 156, 157, 194
Wisconsin News, 109-10, 127
Woman's Christian Temperance Union, 147
Woods, William Seaver, 80
World Almanac, 76
World War: American entry into, straw poll on, 145-46; bonus to veterans of, straw poll on, 50, 146

Yamhill County, cancellation study in, 87
Yonkers Herald, 69
Youngstown Vindicator, 69

COLUMBIA UNIVERSITY PRESS
COLUMBIA UNIVERSITY
NEW YORK

FOREIGN AGENT
OXFORD UNIVERSITY PRESS
HUMPHREY MILFORD
AMEN HOUSE, LONDON, E. C.